Toni Morrison and the
Queer Pleasure of Ghosts

Toni Morrison and the Queer Pleasure of Ghosts

Juda Bennett

Cover image entitled "Wings Not Meant to Fly" by Jamea Richmond-Edwards, courtesy of artist (ink, acrylic, and mixed media collage on canvas), 2012. 36" × 36".

Published by State University of New York Press, Albany

For information, contact State University of New York Press, Albany, NY
www.sunypress.edu

Production by Diane Ganeles
Marketing by Fran Keneston

Library of Congress Cataloging-in-Publication Data

Bennett, Juda.
　Toni Morrison and the Queer Pleasure of Ghosts / Juda Bennett.
　　pages cm
　Includes bibliographical references and index.
　ISBN 978-1-4384-5355-2 (hardcover : alk. paper)
　ISBN 978-1-4384-5357-6 (ebook)
　1. Morrison, Toni—Criticism and interpretation. I. Title.

PS3563.O8749Z55 2014
813'.54—dc23   2013048556

10 9 8 7 6 5 4 3 2 1

For Johnny

But my ghosts were once people, and I cannot forget that.

—Jesmyn Ward, *Men We Reaped*

Contents

Acknowledgments

This project grew out of a presentation ("Hitting the Wrong Note") submitted to Yvonne Atkinson for the ALA Conference panel on "Toni Morrison and Aurality" in San Francisco in 2010. I am indebted to Atkinson and my many new friends at the Toni Morrison Society for making me feel welcomed into a dynamic, creative, and generous community. Inspired by this experience, I attended the Sixth Biennial Conference of the Toni Morrison Society in Paris, France, in November of 2010, presenting a paper on the queer narrator in *Love*. I am eternally grateful to the many society members who attended my panel and provided feedback. At this conference, I found it invaluable to meet and speak with Deborah McDowell, Justine Tally, Jan Furman, and others, but one scholar changed my life by stating very clearly, "Write that book!" For the greatest inspiration, wisdom, and wit, I am indebted to Stephanie Li.

The first draft of this book was written during a sabbatical, and I am indebted to the sabbatical committee at The College of New Jersey for seeing merit in this project, which was originally entitled *Queering the Ghost*. As the project evolved, Cassandra Jackson provided guidance, suggestions, and enthusiasm. I often left her office with a head full of ideas and a renewed passion for the project. Every scholar should be so fortunate as to have someone down the hall, on speed dial, and at lunch, and this project would not have been as rewarding—let alone finished—without her.

I am thankful to the outside reviewers for State University of New York Press for their insightful, careful, and generous readings of the manuscript. One reviewer was very kind to say that even a great manuscript could be made into a better book, and these reviewers have certainly offered guidance, sometimes very specific and sometimes quite expansive, that has definitely moved this book to a better place.

State University of New York Press has been a joy to work with, and I am especially thankful to Beth Bouloukos for her important role as support, guide, and advocate, and Rafael Chaiken for his role in shepherding the book to press.

I have been teaching the works of Toni Morrison for two decades, and I have been reading her for a much longer time. I first read *Song of Solomon* while living in a commune in Ithaca, New York. I remember opening the flap to my tipi in order to get more light because I wanted to read into the night. This study of Morrison really starts in a tipi. It starts with Toni Morrison in a tipi with me, her pages illuminated by moonlight, her presence a blur of black and white in the moonlight. There is a real person responsible for those words, and I am deeply thankful for the gifts she has given the world.

I am especially thankful to my partner, John Bennett, and our beautiful child, for reminding me that a productive life does not stop either at the front door of a house nor at the door of the office. The heart in this project belongs to you.

Chapter 1

∾

Introduction

Bringing back the dead (or saving the living from the shadow of death) is the ultimate queer act.

—Sharon P. Holland, *Raising the Dead: Readings of Death and (Black) Subjectivity*

I am very happy to hear that my books haunt.

—Toni Morrison, in Nellie McKay, *Conversations with Toni Morrison*

In delivering her acceptance speech to the Nobel committee in 1993, Toni Morrison invoked the ghosts of past recipients: "I entered this hall pleasantly haunted by those who have entered it before me." Ten years later, Morrison explains what she meant by this statement: "I think of ghosts and haunting as just being alert. If you are really alert, then you see the life that exists beyond the life that is on top. It's not spooky, necessarily. It might be. But it doesn't have to be. It's something I relish, rather than run from" (Morrison, "Toni Morrison's 'Good Ghosts' "). I begin this book imagining Morrison's many memorable ghosts—L from *Love*, Circe from *Song of Solomon*, and Dorcas from *Jazz* (to name just a few)—haunted by Beloved. What they tell us about Morrison's most famous specter is rather simple but surprisingly important. She has captivated readers, so much so that all other ghosts in the Morrison canon have had to fight for their due. Beloved, they remind us, is just one of many specters and not even the first one to be fully realized in the Morrison canon. Why must she eclipse the others, and what do we learn from listening to the others, asking all of them to speak in chorus?

Toni Morrison and the Queer Pleasure of Ghosts queers one of the most fertile and beloved topics in Toni Morrison scholarship, the ghost. Moving beyond, but not ignoring, Morrison's representation of ghosts as the forgotten or occluded past, the book uncovers how Morrison imagines the spectral sphere as always already queer, a provocation and challenge to heteronormativity—with the ghost sometimes an active participant in disruptions of compulsory heterosexuality, sometimes a figure embodying closet desires, and sometimes a disembodied emanation that counterpoints homophobia. In the introduction to *In a Queer Time and Place*, Judith Halberstam argues that "[f]or the purposes of [her] book, 'queer' refers to nonnormative logics and organizations of community, sexual identity, embodiment, and activity in space and time" (6). It is interesting to note that such an important queer theorist as late as 2005 must define the term as if it were still a new concept in the field, but such are the implicit demands of such a flexible term. It is this flexibility that is both its strength and weakness. In 2011, an anthology of queer theorists (a virtual who's who in the field), debated the meanings, future, and even limitations of the term in *After Sex? On Writing since Queer Theory*, edited by Jonathan Goldberg and others. In this study I have tried both to capitalize on the term's flexibility while also holding close to Halberstam's definition and its emphasis on "nonnormative logics," which I take to pursue an antiessentialist inquiry into structures of power and identity.

The ghost may not always be queer in the way we often imagine lesbian, gay, bisexual, or transgender identities, but in Morrison the apparition inhabits, and perhaps may even be said to attract, a representational field of queer valences around itself, supporting Kathleen Brogan's argument that in contemporary ethnic women's literature "ghost stories are offered as an alternative—or challenge—to 'official' dominant history" (17). In Morrison, the ghost is at the center of queer subterfuge, disruption, and challenge. And there are many of them—everything from old-world hauntings to postmodern erasures, dead or disembodied narrators to fleeting shadows and visions, strange eruptions of sound and music to the indecipherable and uncanny. Morrison's ghosts are at turns fascinating presences, disturbing absences, but mostly provocative embodiments of both and therefore prime figures to trouble the binaries that queer theory seeks to deconstruct.

This project embraces a definition of queering as a broad challenge to all forces of convention and conformity, but it also addresses a very specific nexus of representational and reading practices centered upon the homosexual, lesbian, and bisexual figure. The ease with which queer readings may erase race is the subject of the next chapter, which situates Morrison's work within current debates about queer theory as potentially violent in its impulse to universalize and passé in its potential to effect real social change. Morrison's novels are often works of great theoretical importance in their own right, and Morrison is no less a guide in these readings than Judith Halberstam, Patricia Hill Collins, Trudier Harris, Jacques Derrida, Eve Sedgwick, Barbara Smith, and others.

The way Morrison represents the relationship between (queer) sexuality and black identity is a central concern of *Toni Morrison and the Queer Pleasure of Ghosts*, and both black studies and queer studies inform my approach. Along with the editors of *Black Queer Studies*, I "hope that the interanimation of these two disciplines—black studies and queer studies—whose roots are similarly grounded in social and political activism, carries the potential to overcome the myopic theorizing that has too often sabotaged or subverted long-term and mutually liberatory goals" (Johnson and Henderson 6). To this must be added the fascinating criticism that has emerged on ghosts and haunting by Jacques Derrida, Avery Gordon, and others. In the range of what may be considered merely implied to wildly overt, the twin themes of this book—queer and ghost—structure themselves upon the tension between known and unknown, visible and invisible, familiar and strange.

To queer the ghost, we risk speaking in tautologies. As Nicholas Royle succinctly states, "The uncanny is queer. And the queer is uncanny" (*The Uncanny* 43). But in the doubling much gets revealed about the separate themes of ghosts and queer identities, about our cultural investments in telling stories of haunting and queer transgression, about structures of thought concerning life and death, individual and community, identity and difference. In the convergence of these two themes, moreover, new statements exist and new insights are possible. In *Raising the Dead: Readings of Death and (Black) Subjectivity*, Sharon P. Holland asks "who resides in the nation's imaginary 'space of death'" (4), how are these outsiders silenced, and when, if ever, are they given voice? This book argues that Morrison queers the ghost in order to address some of these silences and to examine the interlocking forces of racism, sexism, and heterosexism.[1]

Along with Marisa Parham's *Haunting and Displacement in African American Literature and Culture*, I see the haunting as not necessarily interesting "because it resonates with the supernatural, but rather because it is appropriate to a sense of what it means to live in between

things—in between cultures, in between times, in between spaces—
to live with various kinds of doubled consciousness" (3). But I also
understand these words as sharing conceptual space with Eve Sedgwick's
definition of queer as "the open mesh of possibilities, gaps, overlaps,
dissonances and resonances, lapses and excesses of meaning when the
constituent elements of anyone's gender, of anyone's sexuality aren't
made (or can't be made) to signify monolithically" (*Tendencies* 8). It
does not take great conceptual leaps to connect the work being done
in queer theory with studies of ghosts and haunting.

The evolution of ghost theory, indeed, runs parallel with the rise
of queer theory—with both fields, interestingly, claiming enormous
thematic and hermeneutical terrain. To take one prominent example,
Jacques Derrida's hauntology—a central concept in ghost theory—asks
us to consider everything as ghost—history, memory, text, and, indeed,
the world as we perceive it. Nothing escapes the problem of presence/
absence. Nothing is without ghost effects. It should not, then, surprise
us that scholars have queered many a ghost, and that queerness itself,
in all its many definitions, gets cast as akin to ghostliness and haunting.
Terry Castle's *The Apparitional Lesbian*, for example, answers its own
question, "Why is it so difficult to see the lesbian—when she is there,
quite plainly, in front of us? In part because she has been 'ghosted'—or
made to seem invisible—by culture itself" (4). And, more recently, José
Esteban Muñoz's *Cruising Utopia* explains that "[t]he double ontology
of ghosts and ghostliness, the manner in which ghosts exist inside and
out and traverse categorical distinctions, seems especially useful for a
queer criticism that attempts to understand communal mourning, group
psychologies, and the need for a politics that 'carries' our dead with us
into battle for the present and future" (46).

We might ask, "What is not queer?" just as easily as Derrida invites
us to ask, "What is not a ghost?" If these are the conceptual tools and
terms for understanding everything, certainly they need to be disciplined to keep them from meaning nothing, but Derrida insures that
his hauntology, a concept that precedes ontology, addresses everything.
It is—not unlike deconstruction—an application of thought and not a
thing in itself, and in this way it conceptually maneuvers like queering, eluding definition and stasis, and, alternatively, emphasizing open
inquiry. "Ghosts," as Colin Davis has observed, "are a privileged theme
because they allow an insight into texts and textuality as such" (17), a
statement that might easily be applied to queering.

It should not surprise us, then, that scholars of ghost theory and
queer theory sound very similar in the extravagance of their claims.

Slavoj Žižek, to cite one current voice, argues that "if there is a phenomenon that fully deserves to be called the 'fundamental fantasy of
contemporary mass culture,' it is this fantasy of the return of the living
dead" (22); and Eve Sedgwick, to consider queer theory's most seminal
powerhouse, boldly claimed that "virtually any aspect of modern Western culture must be, not merely incomplete, but damaged in its central
substance to the degree that it does not incorporate a critical analysis
of modern homo/heterosexual definition" (1). At the convergence of
ghost and queer theories, we might expect further hyperbole and a
doubling of the rhetoric of relevance, but the present study has a more
modest goal: to queer the ghost in Morrison as a way of understanding
its relevance to her work and her time.

It would be tempting to count the ghosts in Morrison's novels
and then offer my readers a firm number of twenty-seven or thirty-two
specters, haunts, phantoms, and visions as a way of suggesting their
prominence in and relevance to Morrison's work; however, the measure
of their importance lies mainly in their elusiveness, their resistance to
naming and fixity, which makes a count not only impossible but missing
the point. In novel after novel, Morrison explores not only epistemologies of ghosts and haunting but their ontology. What are they made of?
What is their relationship to the living? How are they different from us
and from one another? How do they come into being? And how do
our cultural beliefs serve to guide these answers?

To most readers, many of Morrison's specters will be recognizable
as ghosts. Some, like Dorcas in *Jazz*, stare out of photographs, becoming
almost Poe-esque, "in a silver frame waking [Violet and Joe] up all night
long" (13). Bill Cosey, in *Love*, not only gazes out from a gilt-framed
portrait, but Junior is "flooded by his company" and sees "his hand
closing the door" (118–19). Some of Morrison's ghosts speak, such as
Pilate's father in *Song of Solomon*: "Clear as day, her father said, 'Sing.
Sing,' and later he leaned in at the window and said, 'You just can't fly
on off and leave a body'" (147). Some voices, such as that of Florens's
mother in *A Mercy*, come to us as first-person narrators of whole chapters
or hefty passages, and many of the novels feature several ghosts and even
crowds of them. At the end of *Paradise*, for example, there are various
voices and visions that are just as unnamable and unfixed as the identity
of the white woman who gets shot at the beginning of the narrative.
And in *Tar Baby* the night women pour into Jadine's bedroom, "Pushing each other—nudging for space . . . [pouring] out of the dark like
ants out of a hive" (258). Some readers will want to think of them as
figments of Jadine's dreamlife, and even though the novel works hard

at establishing Jadine's wakefulness, the status of the night women gets blurred when they are associated with other dreams. They not only push and nudge one another, terrifying Jadine as they bare their breasts, but they serve to push at the reader's beliefs about the paranormal, anticipating Morrison's most famous representation of a haunt.

Morrison, throughout her writing career, has invited her readers to speculate about ghosts. But each phantom is uniquely rendered, serving different purposes and pushing against clichés of haunting. Many of these apparitions not only confront the cliché of the spooky ghost but also the very shape, definition, and meaning of ghost, such as May in *Love*, who "[b]efore her real death . . . was already a minstrel-show spook, floating through the rooms, flapping over the grounds, hiding behind doors" (82). Morrison's characters often puzzle over the ghostly status of ambiguous figures, such as the "naked berry-black woman," who Golden Gray "is certain is not a real woman but a 'vision' (144) or Beloved, whose (un)earthly form serves as a point of debate throughout much of the novel."[2]

In order to honor Morrison's rich problematizing of binaries of life/death, presence/absence, body/spirit, *Toni Morrison and the Queer Pleasure of Ghosts* examines specters that will not at first seem like ghosts to most readers, such as the haunting music in *Song of Solomon* or the ornate embezzler's house in *Paradise*. Morrison's explorations of ghosts and haunting invite the widest Derridean consideration of ghosts as the master trope for everything from identity to memory to history to reading. But even the thematic considerations of music as ghost or myth as ghost, which may strike some of my readers as applying the term too loosely, frequently provides a tangential reading that addresses more conventional specters as well. There are just so many opportunities in the novels, and so I have tried to suggest the range of thematic considerations, everything from considering whiteness as a figure of ghostliness to a more conventional consideration of the haunted house, albeit recognizing how Morrison, even as (or especially when) she is addressing stock themes and narratives, provides a radical revision of shopworn tropes and strategies of representation.

There are numerous theoretical lenses with which to consider Morrison's ghosts—with many new and exciting scholars working at the intersections of African American studies and queer studies—but I begin with Freud's notion of the uncanny because it has the greatest potential for capturing Morrison's ability to evoke the "familiar strangeness" that Freud located in—among other themes and narratives—the haunted house, the double, the realistic doll, the severed limb, and the dead. In its attention to the convergence of strangeness and familiarity Freud's essay offers, in the words of one scholar, "a significant, wide-ranging presence in our culture, and the tradition of its scholarship lends us an important way of thinking about the history of representation at the turn of the twentieth century."[3] Freud's concept of the uncanny can be felt even in those works that do not address his work, but many of the new theoreticians of race and sexuality find their own early resources, in everyone from Frantz Fanon to Ernst Bloch, and the ghosts of past theories have certainly helped inspire recent work on the intersection of theories of race and sexuality.[4]

The hyperbolic claims for queer studies, race studies, and ghost studies, moreover, share not only a certain extravagance of meaning but also philosophical and ethical positions that might be thought of as a liberationist ethics grounded in the importance of uncovering the repressed in order to release individual and communal potentialities. José Esteban Muñoz's *Cruising Utopia* offers the most unapologetic voice in its "rejection of a here and now and an insistence on potentiality or concrete possibility for another world" (1). But I also find great inspiration in the politically engaged work from many recent theorists, such as Sharon P. Holland, Roderick Ferguson, and Darieck Scott, the latter arguing that he and others begin with the "three now familiar tenets of 'identity' analysis: blackness is a construction, not an essence, which serves to shore up white identity and superiority; categories of race are intimately connected to categories of gender and sexuality; philosophy needs literature to embody, and thereby better envision, its concepts" (258). Not surprisingly, Morrison appears with great regularity in many of these recent philosophical meditations, these adventurous inquiries into race and sexuality.[5]

Muñoz's fierce utopian yearning finds an especially amenable resource in Morrison's queer ghosts, and my interest in queering the ghost aligns most with his notion that "[q]ueerness is a longing that propels us onward, beyond romances of the negative and toiling in the present. Queerness is that thing that lets us feel that this world is not enough, that indeed something is missing." In Morrison, the ghost pushes us beyond the breech of understanding, feeling, and recognition. The ghost, in the shorthand of the present study, queers everything but especially Morrison's capacious exploration of love in all its forms and expressions.

In queering the ghosts in Morrison's novels, I do not propose to uncover static dimensions of the text but dynamic interactions between the tensions in the text and a queer politics of engagement. I do not, in other words, make claims for Morrison's intentions or textual truths but instead consider how Morrison's evocations of ghosts and haunting may be usefully queered, indeed, recognized as always already queer. Some subjects, such as Beloved, serve to challenge heteronormative ways of reading. Many readers will be suspicious of a queering of Morrison's most famous novel and with good reason: the figure of Beloved is exemplary in its ability to resist most readings, especially those that fall along categorical lines, such as heterosexual/homosexual, adult/child, and even living/dead. In queering her ghost, I examine the orthodoxy that has grown around her and the way she resists such containment. Other ghosts, such as the narrator of Love, will yield more to a traditional "outing" in their evocation of performances of the closet and repressed desire.

In a preface to Love, Morrison describes the narrative voice of Jazz as "the book itself, its physical and spatial confinement made irrelevant by its ability to imagine, invent, interpret, err, and change." After creating this unprecedented voice, which many critics praised for its music and formal innovation, Morrison set herself a different task. "In Love, the material (forms of love, kinds of betrayal) struck me as longing for a similar freedom—but this time with an embodied, participating voice. The interior narrative of characters, so full of secrets and partial insights, would be interrupted and observed by an 'I' not restricted by chronology or space—or the frontier between life and not-life" (x–xi). In imagining a "frontier"—even as she banishes it as a barrier—Morrison likens her creation of a spectral narrator as an exploration into unknown places or, rather, the erasure of lines demarking conventional distinctions between life and death. The narrative strategies, which had resulted in the success of Beloved, are left behind for new challenges. Indeed, Morrison's body of work shows exactly this temerity in setting new and impossible challenges even as she continues to investigate the meaning of ghosts, the way haunting works and its relationship to individual and social identities, and the problems, rewards, and dangers of representing the uncanny.

It has been the secret argument of this book that Morrison represents one of the most ceaselessly innovative writers of our time and, indeed, of all time. For forty years, Morrison has set herself new tasks. One only needs to list her many creative projects, everything from librettos to children's books to playwriting to curating a show at the Louvre, to register her intrepid approach to new challenges. If we were to isolate our inquiry solely to the novels, considering them for this same spirit of exploration, we would quickly note the historical range, the thematic reach, and, perhaps most importantly, the formal innovation. To read only *Beloved* or to consider the nine other novels always against this fifth novel is to miss a wonderful opportunity to observe one woman's rich engagement with a wide variety of themes, problems, and formal invention, such as the truly radical nature of *Song of Solomon*'s interplay of aurality as an emergent force within the text against the narrative's ultimate mysteries as dependent on an understanding of oral traditions or *Jazz*'s *sui generis* reinvention of the relationship between narrator and book. It has been my hope that in pursuing a single thematic link across the novels that the reader will not see repetition but rather a crucial aspect of Morrison's history of innovation. To view her return to this theme as repetitive would require a reader to not only ignore her continuous defamiliarizing and radical reinvention of the trope, but it also suggests a specious divide between notions of the ghost as separate from character. No one, for example, would dare accuse her of returning repeatedly to character. Although I am not arguing that all of her ghosts work as fully realized characters, some, such as Beloved and L, certainly do, while others offer a tireless defamiliarization of a trope not unlike Shakespeare's reinvention of the fool or Faulkner's changing scripts of history. As this study has argued, the trope of the ghost already circulates in a queer field, but in Morrison's handling it not only pushes against stock characters but also finds ever new possibilities for challenging heteronormativity.

To honor the formal qualities of haunting, I create ghostly pairs for each of my chapters, allowing Morrison to haunt Morrison. *Sula*, for example, serves as a ghostly companion to *Beloved*, guiding us deeper into the closet narratives and the intrepid inquiry into forbidden knowledges. But then I continue to create a chain of ghostly pairs by beginning the next chapter where I left off with *Beloved*, considering how its representation of 124 as haunted helps to elucidate the Convent in *Paradise*, both novels attempting to collapse the distance between human embodiment and structural haunting. And then I continue the chain by beginning the next chapter with *Paradise* as a novel that haunts *Love*, allowing my readings of each novel to lead to another and then another until the book has covered each of her novels in a chain that would look like a zigzag if it were diagrammed. I began this process unsure if my approach could be sustained, but what I discovered is that ghosts—disruptive, otherworldly, transgressive—are easily queered, and Morrison's ghosts lead inevitably toward the most fruitful and provocative challenges to conceptions of love.

With their bodies marked not only by absence but presence, ghosts tease and taunt the queering impulse into attention. They seem to offer endless poses of the spectral body as resisting boundaries. Although not focused on ghosts, Judith Butler may have just as easily been talking about them when she introduces *Bodies That Matter* with a problem: the impossibility of "[fixing] bodies as simple objects of thought. Not only did bodies tend to indicate a world beyond themselves, but this movement beyond their own boundaries, a movement of boundary itself, appeared to be quite central to what bodies 'are'" (ix). Indeed, bodies matter and they matter even more when they are without matter and "indicate a world beyond themselves." This is the project of *Toni Morrison and the Queer Pleasure of Ghosts*: to offer a sustained analysis of ghosts in the novels of Toni Morrison as an avenue for queering those same novels. I believe this focus is essential to understanding Morrison's life-long project of exploring the reaches and meanings of something we simply call love only to contest each other's meanings and surprise ourselves with confusion and contradictions. As tropes, queering and haunting double the hermeneutical trouble and fun.

In *Spectral America*, Jeffrey Weinstock explains that, "[b]ecause ghosts are unstable interstitial figures that problematize dichotomous thinking, it perhaps should come as no surprise that phantoms have become a privileged poststructuralist academic trope" (4). We might easily extend Weinstock's argument about haunting to tropes of queering, which also problematize dichotomous thinking and arguably serves as a "privileged poststructuralist academic trope," one that surely rivals "how phantoms and haunting [have] exerted their influences in literary and popular discourse" (7). If the readings in *Toni Morrison and the Queer Pleasure of Ghosts* risk overreaching, it is in the service of testing the limits of the hermeneutical possibilities of these tropes, which are also methodological approaches.

Scholars have exhaustively considered what would seem to be every major theme in the novels—with a short list including race, masculinity, motherhood, music, politics, myth, history—and from virtually every scholarly position—including Africanist, feminist, new historicist, and countless other approaches. It is, therefore, surprising that there has been no monograph that queers Morrison despite the early promise of Barbara Smith's queer reading of *Sula* in 1977 and the exciting recent work done by Kathryn Bond Stockton on *Sula* and *Beloved*. In more than three decades of active scholarly criticism on *Beloved*, there have been many provocative readings of gender and sexuality, but they frequently stop painfully short of queering the text. Why?

If Eve Sedgwick is correct that "virtually any aspect of modern Western culture, must be, not merely incomplete, but damaged in its central substance to the degree that it does not incorporate a critical analysis of modern homo/heterosexual definition," then works, such as Toni Morrison's most famous novel, *Beloved*, or her eighth novel, boldly titled *Love*, not only invite but demand a queer reading. Once ventured, a queer reading not only seems possible but fills an essential lacuna in our understanding of Morrison's lifelong project to investigate love and its boundaries. In an early interview for *Black American Literature Forum*, she has stated, "actually, I think, all the time that I write, I'm writing about love or its absence."[6] In several interviews, Morrison has described the evolution of the novel *Love* and her decision to "take out all those *loves* and look for other words and other sentences," describing it as "just the most amazing exercise, because now I know why everybody uses the word: because it works."[7] But, in Morrison's words, the novel does not merely explore love but also "the way in which sexual love and other kinds of love lend themselves to betrayal."[8] Here, as in virtually every interview—and certainly every new novel—Morrison can be seen meditating on the limits of love.

When we read Morrison against herself, an early novel against a later novel, I believe new possibilities open up. The queer themes seem to reinforce each other, making the queering of the ghost an act of recognizing patterns and filmy presences. There are eerie ways in which the novels begin to speak to one another as if an early creation exists to haunt a later evocation of the same bizarre image, closet theme, or twist in narrative. Yes, I am reading the novels intertextually, but I also think it is important to consider this play as not indifferent and merely scholarly but instead full of spooky desire. It is my dream that this study will aid other readers of Morrison, and scholars of African American literature and queer studies. But just as Morrison wrote *The Bluest Eye* because she could not find the book she wanted to read, *Toni Morrison and the Queer Pleasure of Ghosts* is the book I wanted to read—a sustained queer analysis of my favorite novelist. I wrote it because I wanted to read it.

Charles I. Nero's searing critique of Morrison's failure to "imagine homosexual relationships among heroic characters" and her "[playing upon] the stereotype of the 'light-skinned' black man as weak, effeminate, and sexually impotent" sits as a cautionary work if not a seriously compromising voice to my celebration of Morrison's queer ghost (232). Have I failed to highlight (or even recognize) the ways Morrison is implicated in heterosexist systems of thought? In calling for a heightened awareness of the sexual politics of African American literature, Nero's powerful 1991 essay ("Toward a Black Gay Aesthetic: Signifying in Contemporary Black Gay Literature") remains an important inquiry into the role of homophobia and heterosexism in "the intellectual writings of black Americans [which has] been dominated by heterosexual ideologies that have resulted in the gay male experience being either excluded, marginalized, or ridiculed" (229). With a prestigious Pulitzer in the late 1980s and a Nobel Prize in the early 1990s, Morrison, no doubt, served as a logical figure to address, but Nero rests his case on Morrison's failure to imagine a full range of sexualities on the plantation in *Beloved* as well as a few isolated phrases from earlier books that may play upon stereotypes without further inquiry. Although Nero finds more overt examples of homophobia in the form of direct quotes from writers like Amiri Baraka and Eldridge Cleaver, his willingness to take on a broader black intelligentsia may be said to use Morrison tactically. More than twenty years later, I celebrate his challenge even as my study seeks to present a very different Morrison, one who has always questioned sexual orthodoxies but has also imagined homosexual characters, such as L from *Love* and Willard and Scully from *A Mercy*, with more clarity and complexity. In the chapters to come, I do consider some of Morrison's early brushes with sexual stereotypes, but not without considering the complex discursive field they respond to, and sometimes—as with the case with chapter 9—considering an early novel in conversation with a later novel.

With such a long history of criticism to draw from, my examination of Morrison's novels cannot help but slip, from time to time, into a study of reception, but any reading of *Beloved* surely has a very rich resource of critical essays, all with their own arguments, agendas, strategies. In chapter 2, "Spirit: *Sula* Haunts *Beloved*," I turn the notion of haunting on its head by imagining what haunts the more famous novel—even as it haunts everything else and even those novels that precede it. The problem of writing in the shadow of this mythic figure became the very thing I needed to address: how can we queer the ghost that everyone knows so well? What are the risks? What is at stake in queering something that already assumes such a solid place in our imaginations? This chapter had to come first in order to set the stage for the other ghostly queerings but also as a way of confronting readerly resistance head-on. This chapter, therefore, does not solely provide a queer reading of the novel but also a consideration of how Beloved/ *Beloved* queers everything she/it rubs up against. A reading of *Beloved* must come first because that is how haunting goes. If you try to ignore it, terrible things will happen.

Over her entire body of work, looking back at the first four novels and gazing ahead to the future works, *Beloved* haunts because it has grown, like a succubus, beyond the words Morrison has written. It has assumed a life of its own. In many ways, Morrison's characterization of the novel as having an agency of its own has contributed to the ways the novel and its ghost have grown mythic over the years, and we, too, must recognize ourselves as collaborators in the building of myth. Chapter 3, "Houses: *Beloved* Haunts *Paradise*," examines Morrison's reconsideration of the haunted house narrative, a popular narrative that Morrison reshapes in order to more fully engage in questions of place and (sexual) orientation. Beginning with *Beloved*, the chapter considers what it means to collapse the distance between inside and outside, interiority and exteriority, spirit and containment. Paul D's arrival at 124 enacts a heteronormative drama when he drives the ghost out of the house and enters as a masculine, patriarchal presence, disrupting the all-female world that Denver fears losing. Despite the powerfully spatial rendition of heteronormativity in these opening pages, the novel returns to the notion of a queer space or orientation and forestalls simplistic interpretations of a (sexual) orientation or a normative reading of any of the characters. The battle for space, the struggle to understand and make peace with its interiority, announces the novel's resistance to fixed meanings of orientation.

This is a strategy Morrison will return to in *Paradise*, and the chapter sees the later novel as haunted by the earlier exploration of space as symbolic of familial and sexual meanings. In *Paradise*, however, Morrison allows us to see this application of meaning through the misogynist perspective of the men of Ruby. But these voices, with classic Morrison finesse, are not only proved unreliable but also representative of cultural and historical forces that tie sanctuary to danger, paradise to exclusions, and female bodies to perversity. *Paradise* is one of many novels haunted by *Beloved*, but it is also probably the richest in pointing to the convergence of racist, misogynist, and homophobic discourses as structured upon certain historical and ghostly configurations of space.

Moving from a consideration of space in *Paradise* to its representation of the interiority of motherhood and its resistance to clichés of black matriarchy, chapter 4 examines ghostly figures who not only counter clichéd representations of black matriarchy but also test the limits of love through an erasure of the line between the living and the dead. "Matriarchy: *Paradise* Haunts *Love*" furthermore considers these novels as part of the trilogy (with *Love* serving as a coda to the trilogy) that *Beloved* begins. There is as much attention to motherhood, the special exigencies of this powerful subjectivity, in these two novels as in Morrison's most famous novel, but in the later novels mothers turn up missing and haunt those who remain behind. If motherhood represents Morrison's most powerful theme for exploring the limits of love, these novels complicate normative conceptions by queering matriarchy.

Love, as this chapter argues, is Morrison's queerest novel, offering three central figures who are queer, though not without making, in Terry Castle's words, the lesbian apparitional, in this case through L's association with matriarchy and the novel's "closet" narrative of lesbian desire as motherly concern rather than erotic identification. In creating a pair between *Paradise* and *Love*, I am following in this chapter a simple chronology of publication, but these two novels also speak powerfully to one another about the unfinished business of the trilogy and its exploration of all kinds of love. The latter novel, therefore, might be seen as a compendium of types of love, but Morrison's introduction, as I consider in the chapter, highlights the novel's germ in lesbian and outlaw identities.

In chapter 5, "Music: *Love* Haunts *Song of Solomon*," I invert chronology and consider the way that *Love* might haunt an earlier novel, *Song of Solomon*. Much has been written about Morrison's third and very important novel, but *Love* helps to clarify some of the most mysterious hauntings in the earlier novel. In this chapter, I take my biggest risks in considering sound as ghost, asking how the "ghostly voicings" help to explore the inordinate pressures placed upon black men as they navigate a terrain riddled with homophobia, misogyny, and violence. These two novels, along with *Beloved*, offer scenes that challenge popular stereotypes of black gangs with more complicated depictions that, for all their painful detailing of violence, also explore mystical spirit forces that help to imagine the black man with agency and possibilities rather than hopelessness.

In examining Morrison's exploration of male violence through her evocations of sound and her allusions to music, this chapter provides an alternative to the many essays that have considered music as salutary in Morrison. In many interviews, Morrison has imagined a much wider field of meaning for black music, and my reading of *Love* and *Song of Solomon* sees music as not just haunting in the sense of memorable but as mystical, supernatural, and no less engaged than Beloved or L in reaching from another plane of existence.

A logical extension to the discussion of music in chapter 5 is the examination of voice in chapter 6. "Voice: *Song of Solomon* Haunts *Jazz*" considers voice as a specter, beginning with the many voices in *Song of Solomon* but locating its queerest point of view in Pilate, the woman who sings the songs of the ancestors, though she does not necessarily slavishly accept their choices. Pilate, indeed, may be Morrison's greatest representation of an escape from the pressures of heteronormativity. Some scholars have seen her as the central consciousness of the novel, and my reading finds community in those arguments. But Pilate's point of view becomes most powerful in its relationship to a shifting narratorial point of view. The openness this creates in the novel is powerful and far exceeds the usual analysis of *Song of Solomon*'s ambiguous ending, and it haunts Morrison's greatest experiment with voice in her sixth novel, *Jazz*.

In the latter novel, Morrison offers perhaps her most elusive ghost, the disembodied voice of a narrator envisioned as a book. It is a tour de force novel that may at first resist everything except the most sophisticated readings of its postmodern play and metafictional conceits. In this chapter, I use *Song of Solomon* to ask whether the narrator might be identified not only with such philosophical and literary abstractions, which receive a most powerful reading in Maurice O. Wallace's "Print, Prosthesis, (Im)Personation: Morrison's *Jazz* and the Limits of Literary History," but also the rather embattled identity position of bisexuality. How does the narrator, in its neutered role as book open to all readers, present characters through a lens of bisexual desire, highlighting such possibilities even in the face of virulent heterosexuality.

Chapter 7, "Blackness: *Jazz* and *Tar Baby*," might have easily served as a fine introduction for this book, had not *Beloved* threatened to assume its prime position by virtue of its popularity. But my examination of *Jazz* and *Tar Baby* considers how Morrison's evocation of a mythic blackness is already queer. As Darieck Scott argues—with credit given to Frantz Fanon—"blackness functions in Western cultures as a repository for fears about sexuality," and, by extension, "blackness *is* queer" (10). Scott offers a powerful reading of *Beloved*, one that focuses on the silences, elisions, and repressions tied to the sexual violation that occurs in the chain gang scene, which is addressed in other passages of the novel and haunts Paul D's consciousness. My consideration of mythic blackness as tied to queer identities finds *Jazz* to be rich with layers of interpretation as the characters try to make sense of the world that already comes to them imprinted with stories that underwrite myths of sexuality and race. The narrator of the novel comments upon the stories but is none the smarter for it, lost in the same quagmire that attaches sexualized meaning to race and racist meaning to sex.

Jazz finds an antecedent, one that is full of ghostly whispers, in *Tar Baby*, which more directly announces in its title an interest in investigating myth. Morrison has said that "the exploration of the Tar Baby tale was like stroking a pet to see what the anatomy was like but not to disturb or distort its mystery" ("Unspeakable" 394), and a sign that she has in fact preserved the mystery may be seen in the many interpretations of the novel and its central trope of the Tar Baby. In thinking of it as haunting *Jazz*, this chapter focuses on the vision in the Paris supermarket, one of the shortest scenes and most minor characters to ever receive such intense scrutiny from scholars. My own offering in this chapter sees the Parisian woman as a seed for considering the novel's many challenges to heteronormativity and a scene that disrupts its own interest in representing lesbian desire, albeit fastening it upon myths of blackness and desires for authenticity and community.

In chapter 8, "Whiteness: *Tar Baby* Haunts *A Mercy*," I return to *Tar Baby* and flip the coin over to examine its representation of whiteness as both fundamentally ghostly, unable to hold its power through strategies of invisibility, and provocatively queer even as it performs heterosexual privilege with ease. Valerian, as Morrison has stated in an interview, is a center of sorts, but the novel has many centers and it wastes no time in orchestrating the challenge from the supposed margins. Valerian, furthermore, grows more complex as his centrality gives way to other centers, and the novel ends with him almost indistinguishable from a ghost, a victim of his own self-displacement from the details of life. His helplessness, which results in his reliance on his trusted servant Sydney, may be seen as a counterpoint to an early scene in the novel that positions him as the outrageous "date" for Son, who seems decidedly less like a surrogate child to Valerian and more like a provocative partner, one who gets sexualized but ultimately proves himself to be unwilling to perform as an exotic black male, certainly not in order to hold up fictions of whiteness.

In considering *Tar Baby*'s representation of whiteness as a ghost before its time (i.e., a living and rather queer ghost), I see it as a seed for Morrison's most overt homosexual pair in *A Mercy*. Although most readers will readily accept Scully and Willard as queer, I am interested in how Morrison extends her considerations of whiteness to these white indentured servants, clearly the center of little more than their own worlds and a representation of whiteness far different from that of Valerian Street. And yet Willard and Scully not unlike Valerian have their ghosts. They appear in the novel almost as reminders of the decentering of whiteness, which already happens if any one of the chain of signifiers, such as heterosexuality, is missing. They are, therefore, paradoxes of whiteness, male but homosexual, white but indentured. Not surprisingly, Morrison associates them with the dead and the living, able to see the ghost of Sir and yet also instrumental in bringing Sorrow's child into the world. Unlike the critique of whiteness that underwrites *Tar Baby*, whiteness in *A Mercy* has an overtly queer face, one that makes homosexuality a direct theme while only associating white queerness with specters and not making it the embodiment of ghostliness. Nevertheless, the two themes are intertwined and invite us to consider Morrison's evolving exploration of race, spirit, and sexual dissidence.

In a career devoted to considering the very limits of love, Morrison, as I have been arguing, often turns to the intertwining tropes of queerness and ghostliness to express those limits or, rather, the erasure of those limits. It is fitting, therefore, for such an argument to culminate in its own risks, and so in chapter 9 I pursue what I consider to be one of our culture's greatest failings—our inability to love, understand, and embrace others, those people whose varied identities have increasingly been included under the umbrella term "transgender." A recent study "brings to light what is both patently obvious and far too often dismissed from the human rights agenda. Transgender and gender non-conforming people face injustice at every turn: in childhood homes [and in every other aspect of life]."[9] Although the rates of poverty, suicide, and abuse are high for all transgender people, transgender people of color dominate the lists of victims memorialized every year during the Transgender Day of Remembrance and through websites like "Honoring Our Dead."[10] Chapter 9 wishes to honor those victims by asking how our most important living novelist registers a cultural anxiety about transgender bodies, perhaps directing us to the very limits of our understanding of gender.

Although there is no population that more powerfully represents our culture's failure to love, understand, and embrace, I do not hope to convince anyone that Morrison has represented this embattled figure directly or even suggestively, but in this chapter I ask whether *The Bluest Eye* and *Home* wrestle with the mutability of bodies in such a way as to invite readers into the very conceptual terrain of the transgender experience and by extension the wider public discourse about such nonconforming, transgressive, undisciplined bodies. Part of this public discourse questions the authenticity of such an existence and levels charges of imposter, fake, and neither/nor. This discourse effectively erases transgender identities even as those marginalized people seek presence, voice, visibility. It is the question of visibility that makes transgender identity all the more vexed within the African American narrative tradition, a tradition that has been so profoundly involved with questions of visibility.

In this last pairing of novels, I do not merely argue that Morrison addresses the mutability of bodies, conceiving this as related to race and gender, but I also read this theme of mutable bodies against an African American literary tradition interested in exploring what it means to be rendered invisible. This chapter, therefore, risks calling forth the dismissed transgendered body in relationship to a tradition of erased black bodies in both narrative and in life (i.e., the passing figure, the invisible man, the zoot suit, the lynched corpse). If this is the queerest ghost in a study of many queer ghosts, it is not just because it may evoke the greatest sense of disbelief or provoke the greatest resistance. It is because it will haunt with its disturbing incompleteness, incoherence, and insubstantiality. And yet, I hope to prove that Morrison's explorations of ghosts cannot help but call forth such a contested cultural site of newly racialized, sexualized, and gendered bodies.

This, then, is a study of Morrison's engagement with the present, a shifting present of the 1960s when she began writing *The Bluest Eye* and a very different world that forms an implied backdrop to her most recent work. Even as she "rips the veil" from fictions, evasions, and ignorance of enslavement and Reconstruction periods in her most famous novel, *Beloved*, she registers—as Kathryn Bond Stockton, Sharon P. Holland, and others have powerfully argued—a very specific politics of the present. History, of course, is not over, and it is interesting to place Morrison's excavations of the past into direct conversation with her engagement with the politics of the present. Whether exploring the 1600s in *A Mercy*, which a *New York Times* reviewer called "her deepest excavation into America's history," or tackling the more familiar late twentieth century in *Love*, Morrison has always had her pulse on the present.[11] Certainly, as many scholars have already amply and powerfully explored, Morrison's work reveals the many ways that history is not dead but alive, or, in William Faulkner's phrasing, "The past is never dead. It's not even past."[12] It is the goal of this study to fully investigate the way the contemporary politics of sexuality, race, and gender fully engage with the ghosts of four centuries of American history as powerfully articulated in Toni Morrison's work.

Chapter 2

∾

Spirit

Sula Haunts *Beloved*

Consciously or not, Morrison's work poses both lesbian and feminist questions about black women's autonomy and their impact upon each other's lives.

—Barbara Smith, "Toward a Black Feminist Criticism"

I love the feistiness of those women.

—Toni Morrison, in Audrey McCluskey,
"A Conversation with Toni Morrison"[1]

Sula anticipates *Beloved*, helping to illuminate the risks taken in creating an epistemologically and ontologically elusive ghost. Commenting on *Sula* shortly after the publication of *Beloved*, Toni Morrison described the titular character as "uncontained and uncontainable," a phrase that powerfully characterizes Beloved as well as Sula. Both cross several boundaries, but most significantly they transgress that ultimate boundary marked by Western dualistic thinking of life and death. At the end of the novel, Sula speaks beyond the grave, a voice the reader is privy to more than the other characters, while Beloved, of course, is fully characterized as a ghostly presence integrated into the lives of the principal characters. Both figures are transgressors of conventional notions of life but also by an aspect of life frequently associated with a primary life force: sexuality. If *Sula*, as Roderick Ferguson has powerfully explored, may be read as a glimpse into the sexual experimentation, anxiety, and racism of the 1970s, *Beloved*—as Kathryn Bond Stockton has provocatively argued—

19

may be considered in relationship to the AIDS crisis of the 1980s. Building upon these two different historical readings of Morrison's novels, I want to read *Sula* as haunting *Beloved*, paradoxically helping to break queer silences while also strangely silencing queer readings. *Beloved*—not to be outdone—haunts back, urging its own rereading of the earlier novel. *Beloved* threatens to eclipse *Sula* as well as all other threats, creating its own act of silencing even as it breaks silence.[2]

In 1987, two unlikely events changed our understanding of the persistent problem and enormous cultural weight of silence. In bookstores throughout New York City, the fifth novel from Toni Morrison—the book she believed no one would want to read—appeared, giving none of its horrors away in its one-word title: *Beloved*. In her review for the *New York Times Book Review*, Margaret Atwood called it a "hair-raiser," and A. S. Byatt, writing for the *Guardian*, confessed to having nightmares about it. *Beloved* is not so easily forgotten. In its first week, it became a bestseller, initiating a national conversation about "unspeakable things unspoken," a conversation that continues to find new possibilities and new revelations, though not without controversy.[3] But those first booklovers in Manhattan, book in hand, knew nothing of what was to confront them as they turned up their collars to the autumn cold, pushed through the glass door of their local bookstore, and suddenly faced a perplexing poster, perhaps affixed to a lamppost or mailbox, marking the everyday furniture of the world with an oversized pink triangle and the slogan "Silence=Death."

"When I first saw the poster," Jesse Green writes in the *New York Times*, "I didn't know what it was."[4] Designed by six men, mostly artists who later became part of the gay activist group ACT UP, the poster sought to address the cultural and political silences that threatened the lives of mostly (so it seemed at the time) gay white men, some of whom undoubtedly read Morrison's novel, perhaps seeing in its ghostly theme a touchstone for their own crisis of existence. At the end of 1987, the dead from AIDS numbered 41,027 in the United States, a number more dramatic in marking an exponential growth, especially in black and Latino communities. Although not immediately registered by the general population (let alone by our president), the spread of the virus and its reshaping of the world were personally and profoundly fathomed by members of an urban subculture of gay men that cut across race and class lines.[5] If we could summon the dead in order to reflect on the serendipitous convergence of two events in the fall of 1987—the publication of *Beloved* and the appearance of the confrontational posters announcing that silence equals death—the young victims of AIDS would undoubtedly be the most receptive audience for Kathryn Bond Stockton's powerful rendering of the novel as not exactly an AIDS book but strangely akin to an entire subculture's concern with untimely death, a silence seen by many to be insurmountable.

I want to begin by locating Stockton's reading in a broader history of reception of the novel, one that attempts to articulate a queer feeling of imminent erasure and silence. If the ghost embodies a repressed history, to queer the ghost is to queer history. In returning to my analogy between Morrison's novel and "Silence=Death," slogan and title might easily be exchanged for one another, so powerfully do they continue to speak across the years about the loss of our dearly beloveds to cultural amnesia. Novel and slogan, furthermore, use one crisis (slavery and AIDS, respectively) to address earlier holocausts (the Middle Passage and Nazi Germany, respectively), and they link historical moments not as cause and effect but as illustrative of each other, inviting two-way traffic and not bound by chronology. In dedicating *Beloved* to those who died in the Middle Passage, the "*Sixty Million and more,*" Morrison addresses, not unlike the poster's reference to the pink triangles worn by the GLBT prisoners in the Nazi concentration camps, historical moment as synecdoche but not teleology. Just as the novel embeds its story within a more expansive history of oppression so, too, does the terse slogan, but one is not privileged over the other. Time, however, has the last word on the relationship between events.

If the slogan, with its terse and strident voice, may be fading even now from our consciousness, it reminds us that *Beloved*—indeed all cultural products—may fade over time. In *Against Amnesia: Contemporary Women Writers and the Crises of Historical Memory*, Nancy J. Peterson powerfully argues that "*Beloved* strikingly demonstrates that historical reconstruction is always already compromised, that any attempt to recover African American history will inevitably be haunted by that which can never be recovered" (63).[6] Invested as it is with the larger desire to speak to the "Sixty Million and more" who died in the slave trade, *Beloved* uses the kernel of the Margaret Garner story to address this loss and may first feel to have very little to do with another silence, another veil, that which addresses an identity position that sometimes gets labeled queer, though not without creating discomfort for some and even inspiring debate and controversy.

In *Black Sexual Politics*, first published in 2004, Patricia Hill Collins avoids the term "queer," considering the problem in a note. Although some people, Collins observes, "see terms such as *gay, lesbian,* and *bisexual* as misleading in that they suggest stable sexual identities," she chooses not to use the term "queer" "because LGBT African American people do not prefer this term" (323). Michael Warner sounds an even more serious concern, representing the term "queer" as "an aggressive impulse of generalization" (xxvi).[7] Collins and Warner, however, cannot avoid using the term—Collins when quoting black queer theorist Robert Reid-Pharr, and Warner, in the course of introducing *Fear of a Queer Planet.* The scare quotes appear and disappear, perhaps signaling problems. But if this seems to sound the death knell for the term, especially as applied to people of color, E. Patrick Johnson and Mae Henderson, in *Black Queer Studies,* recognize the risks inherent in the term but "believe that the term 'black queer' captures and, in effect, names the specificity of historical and cultural differences that shape the experiences and expressions of 'queerness'" (7). Rich with diverse contributions from a who's who in Black Queer Studies, the anthology collects important essays that display the rewards of the "interanimation of these two disciplines—black studies and queer studies—whose roots are similarly grounded in social and political activism [and carry] the potential to overcome the myopic theorizing that has too often sabotaged or subverted long-term and mutually liberatory goals" (6). With these divergent responses to the term "queer" and its theoretical underpinnings as well, queering the ghost at this particular moment in Black and Queer Studies cannot help but consider the history of reception as it relates to the dangers. It is, therefore, the danger implicit in the project of queering the ghost that this chapter concerns itself with, asking what is at stake.

With a profound sense of how the AIDS crisis has permanently changed our relationship to silence, Sharon P. Holland's *Raising the Dead: Readings of Death and (Black) Subjectivity* boldly asserts that "[b]ringing back the dead (or saving the living from the shadow of death) is the ultimate queer act" (103). Her book, this chapter argues, represents a wave of scholarly intervention interested in bringing back *Beloved*/Beloved from the dead, an effort that may seem to many altogether unnecessary and, to deploy an older sense of the word, queer indeed. After all, in 2006 *Beloved* was named by the *New York Times Book Review* "the single best work of American fiction published in the last 25 years."[8] With this preeminent position in our cultural imaginary, how does it in any way need resuscitation? To address this paradox, I invert Holland's equation and ask whether the queer act, specifically queering *Beloved*, saves it from the shadow of death and whether it, conversely, threatens it with a more profound death, the erasure of distinctly African American meanings and importance.

One of the earliest warnings about *Beloved*'s mortality came from Barbara Christian in 1993. In considering the "number of critical essays published on this novel [as rivaling] those written on only a few other contemporary African American novels," Christian worried that "the power of this novel as a specifically African American text is being blunted" (363). There are problems, Christian announces, with being too popular, too celebrated, too canonical, and the ghost must not be unraced or we consign her to a second death. I would like to place Christian's very important concern about criticism stripping the text of its distinctly African American meanings (a concern that Morrison addresses in "Unspeakable Things Unspoken") next to Barbara Smith's early queering of *Sula*. How might these two texts help us understand the present possibilities and dangers for queering *Beloved*? And what is at stake?

Giving voice to sixty million gone is rather serious business, and to queer this painful and sober subject may seem to some offensive and even opportunistic, but I argue it is very much an invitation of the text. Queering the ghost, furthermore, keeps the unfinished business of history unfinished. We must resist the urge, in other words, toward sanctifying this history, and this is exactly the spirit behind *Beloved*, a narrative of sexual degradations—among other things—that too often had a veil placed over them. In queering *Beloved*, we enact a much-needed disruption of prevailing readings that fix the narrative into one heteronormative perspective. It is important to release the full potential of the sexual multivalence of the novel, a multivalence that echoes the most important ambiguity of the text.

As Justine Tally points out, "Much critical appraisal of *Beloved* has turned on the meaning of the eponymous character and whether or not she should be understood as a ghost or simply as a needy young woman who reads and is read by Sethe as the latter's murdered daughter" (51). The ambiguity, as Tally highlights, is clearly intended, and Morrison has conveyed this in interviews. But this invitation to question the titular character's status specifically as a body that is defined across (and disruptive of) the binary living/deceased invites further examination of the depictions of Beloved as an erotic being, perhaps most dramatically represented in the sex scene with Paul D. In representing her as embodying ambiguity, which further gets problematized as unclearly adult or child, the novel invites readers to view her as a Rorschach test. She tells us much about ourselves, which may explain why she is so beloved.

If her status as ambiguous operates along binaries of living/ deceased and adult/child, we might imagine, as Tally does, that "multiple readings of this character . . . can coexist simultaneously" (51). This decidedly postmodern solution to the question of identity invites us, however, to further ask whether a queer reading is not only possible but important to an understanding of the text's invitations. Does Beloved's ambiguity, specifically marked along axes fundamental to visibility (life/death or, stated another way, corporeal flesh and ghostly apparition) and sexual awareness (childhood/adulthood or, rather, pre- and post-pubescence), require us to consider her status as queer? The messy intersection of these categories has long been the subject of other gothic novels, and several recent studies in gothic literature bleed into studies of sexuality. Mair Rigby has argued that, "[s]ince the advent of academic queer theory in the early 1990s, the proliferation of publications addressing queer reading possibilities in Gothic Fiction suggest that Queer Theory and Gothic Studies may be considered complementary fields" (46). It might also be argued that both studies are alive and well, enjoying considerable attention in both literary studies and the humanities in general. Is it merely coincidence that one of the most discussed literary novels of the contemporary era represents the continued relevance of gothic themes? Indeed, many volumes could be filled with the essays devoted to *Beloved* and the gothic. There has not, however, been much queering of the novel. We might ask whether there is something about the sanctity of the theme of enslavement and freedom that either overshadows such concerns or even resists such queer readings.[9]

If there are certain subjects that resist queer readings, we might expect these dangerous subjects to be some of the most fruitful places to go—for queer theory's greatest power is in its disruption of simple or sanctified notions of identity, politics, and representation. What might a queer reading of *Beloved* tell us about the current state of the politics of racial, sexual, and gender identities? George Haggerty's *Queer Gothic* argues that "the cult of gothic fiction reached its apex at the very moment when gender and sexuality were beginning to be codified in modern culture. In fact, gothic fiction offered a testing ground for many unauthorized genders and sexualities" (2). We might view current cultural debates about gender and sexuality also as manifest in neo-gothic novels like *Beloved,* but it is important to not merely examine the novel but to also consider the responses to the novel, which have overwhelmingly embraced gothic readings while resisting the queerest readings (as I show later). It is, moreover, in these varied responses that *Beloved* begins to reveal much about its engagement with sexual taboos.

Diana Fuss has argued that there is a "fascination with the specter of abjection, a certain preoccupation with the figure of the homosexual as specter and phantom, as spirit and revenant, as abject and undead" (3). To queer a ghost, therefore, should not be particularly difficult; after all, ghosts—haunted as they are by a sexualized landscape and the history of the gothic—are easy targets. But with more scholarly attention focused on Beloved than arguably any other contemporary character, queering comes with risks. Scholars and lay readers not only feel they know this ghostly character very well but feel very attached to their versions and, in turn, suspicious of competing notions. It is the kind of attachment that grows with each new interpretation or resource—the movie version we view with disdain or *The Black Book* we embrace as an ur-text.[10] Myth-building is a collective as well as personal project.[11]

But if we are to fully understand the complicated interactions of race and sexuality in the novel, if we hope to keep the mystery of Beloved alive with complexity, and if we wish to release her from hermeneutical stasis, I believe it is important to queer the ghost. Let us begin by turning the business of haunting inside out. Yes, Beloved haunts all scholarship on ghosts (perhaps all creative endeavors related to ghosts as well), but who haunts Beloved if not Sula? Appearing more than ten years before Beloved, Sula is not often thought of as a ghost. Near the end of the novel, she dies of an unspecified illness and then reflects upon her death. Seemingly unaware that she has become a ghost, "Sula felt her face smiling" and then thinks, "Well, I'll be damned . . . it didn't even hurt. Wait'll I tell Nel'" (149). Here we can see Morrison, long before *Beloved*, complicating the line between life and death. Sula haunts herself. She visits mortal concerns upon her ghostly state and blurs the line between life and death.

Placed next to one another, *Sula* is a narrative that develops its titular protagonist as a sexual monster who becomes a ghost while *Beloved* begins with a ghost who gains a human form, one that becomes sexual late in the novel and pregnant in the final pages. Excessive sexuality leads to death in the earlier novel, and excessive haunting—by a baby of all things—results in sex in the later novel. How *Beloved* moves from the ghost as baby to the ghost as sexual creature is particularly interesting, but I first want to consider how *Sula* haunts *Beloved*. Does the novel's flirtation with the ghost story help to advance queer readings of it and its relationship to *Beloved*?

The history of its reception as a queer text is part of that haunting. It is a haunting that finds its strongest voice in the 1977 publication of Barbara Smith's queering of the novel in "Toward a Black Feminist Criticism."[12] Predating queer theory and the critical tools it offers, Smith's short analysis strikes an adventurous note:

> I discovered in rereading *Sula* that it works as a lesbian novel not only because of the passionate friendship between Sula and Nel, but because of Morrison's consistently critical stance toward the heterosexual institutions of male-female relationships, marriage and the family. Consciously or not, Morrison's work poses both lesbian and feminist questions about black women's autonomy and their impact upon each other's lives. (165)

Smith's essay has continued to remain relevant. In 1989, several of the essays in the anthology *Changing Our Own Words* pointed to Smith's essay as "pivotal," and in 1993 Deborah G. Chay argued that "Toward a Black Feminist Criticism" was one of two seminal pieces that "were to become touchstones for subsequent debates and discussions about difference."[13] Despite (or is it because of?) some of the attacks of Smith's argument, the queering of *Sula* remains a key moment in Morrison scholarship, and yet despite the promise of Smith's reading there have been very few queer readings of Morrison over the years.

Smith, it is important to note, has not just moved the discussion along for Valerie Smith and Barbara Christian, contributors to Cheryl Wall's anthology noted earlier, but her voice has also engaged Morrison herself. In a 1986 "informal gathering of Women's Studies students" at Indiana University, Bloomington, Audrey McCluskey asked Morrison to respond to the scholarship that interprets Nel and Sula as having a lesbian relationship: "The first time I heard that and read Barbara Smith's article it was sort of interesting" (39). In this exchange, Morrison does not position herself as the ultimate authority on *Sula*, and her response demonstrates a generosity to outlying textual interpretations. Although she goes on to prove herself a resisting reader to the queering of *Sula*, she demonstrates her awareness of deep structures of heterosexism from which she created her characters.

> I thought at the time that I was writing *Sula*, that this was
> this extraordinary new thing that I was doing and that I would
> do it in such a way that nothing else would matter in that
> book except the relationship between those two women. (39)

Speaking more than a decade after creating *Sula*, Morrison gives us a
glimpse into what motivated her as being the creation of something
"extraordinary" and "new," a representation of the bond between two
women where "nothing else would matter." As readers of *Sula* will
recognize, however, something does finally draw a wedge between the
two women, and that wedge is sex. Sula crosses one line that Nel is
unable to forgive: she has sex with Nel's husband.

It is not inconsistent for Morrison to characterize the relationship
as important to the extent that nothing else matters even as she then
discovers the one thing that will matter. Morrison frequently represents
the "extraordinary" and the "new" by pushing just past the thing itself.
It is this interest in crossing lines that opens *Sula* to queer readings,
and despite Morrison's suggestion that Nel and Sula have a platonic
relationship (a concept implied but not stated by Morrison), the characters and narrative have been constructed upon a representational field
that imagines an intensely close female friendship within a culture that
privileges romantic and sexual relationships over it. Morrison characterizes Smith's queering as an "easy shot" as if aware of this potential
interpretation all along, and yet she also praises the "arrogance" and
"feistiness" of the approach.

> It would have to be about their friendship so it was an easy
> shot to make them homosexual because the friendship among
> women is so discredited. And always subordinate. One of the
> ways to discredit it is to say that they had no choice. So to
> give it homosexual color or thrust—I'm not making any state-
> ments about homosexuality—but it was again to detract from
> the ability [of women to have real friendships]. However, I
> like the *fact* of the kind of effort—to make something out of
> black feminist criticism. I don't know if it'll ever become, but
> I like the arrogance. I love the feistiness of those women. (39)

The writing of *Sula*, of course, took place after the Stonewall riots in
1969 and very much during a time of increasing visibility of gays and

lesbians. If *Beloved* may find a touchstone in the "Silence=Death" posters, the climate that accompanied the release of *Sula* in 1973 might be registered in the removal of homosexuality from the American Psychiatric Association's list of diseases.[14]

At the writing of *Beloved* more than ten years later, much changed, and yet Morrison still sets as her goal an evocation of love between women that crosses lines of social mores and decorum. At the time that Morrison responds to the question about *Sula*, she is two years away from publishing *Beloved*, and she has clearly thought about the question. In fact, it is Morrison, and not her interviewer, who names Smith, and although she dismisses the reading, she also manages to praise the impulse behind it. We can see in this interview that Morrison has clearly thought about the way people will read *Sula*, and it is not too much to expect that she will consider, in a similar fashion, how readers will respond to the provocative paths of love between Sethe, Beloved, and Denver.

With this interview in mind, it is *Sula* and the queer readings of *Sula* that I wish to view as haunting *Beloved*. How do the lessons learned from *Sula* inform the construction of *Beloved*? But I also want to remember that Sula is a ghost at the end of the novel, that the final view into her mind provides one of the most haunting lines in Morrison's entire body of work. It is dramatic irony at its most effecting: the reader understands that Sula (unless she is able to return from the dead) will not be able to share with Nel that "it didn't even hurt." The love she holds for Nel survives death, and the promise of a ghostly return is suggested in her final thought, "Wait'll I tell Nel"; but those readers who do not believe in ghosts will see it as merely a strange and sad parting, death perhaps superseding infidelity and betrayal. At the publication of *Sula*, most readers had not yet been conditioned by the lessons of *Beloved* to expect much from ghosts, and in the early novels Morrison had not yet fully challenged the line between life and death. This scene, however, does give the reader something to think about: Can love survive death, and how?

As if Sula's death could not fully close the novel that bears her name and as if this death would convey the wrong message about the love between Nel and Sula, Morrison follows with two other scenes— one that increases the dramatic intensity and the other that sits quietly on the page. The passage "1941" begins, "The death of Sula Peace was the best news folks had had since the promise of work at the tunnel" (150). The novel moves from the single death to a mass funeral as numerous townspeople die in the bizarre and apocalyptic collapse of the tunnel. It is a scene that invites us to think how cultures tie disparate events together and search for scapegoats. But even this dramatic ending does not close the novel. Morrison instead chooses a quieter ending, one with another burial twenty years later (the death of Eva) and a chance meeting between Shadrack and Nel. Eva's death and Shadrack's presence allow Nel to sense Sula's ghostly presence. The evocation of Sula as a ghost is subtly conveyed by Nel, who sympathetically feels her eye twitch and burn. She then asks as if it were a call that might be answered: " 'Sula?' she whispered, gazing at the tops of trees. 'Sula?' " (174).

The novel stops just short of a rapprochement beyond the grave. For that, we would have to wait for *Beloved*. But it is the very evocation of love between ghost and human that invites queer readings of these two novels. It is not merely the unusual bond between women, but the way that these affections are pushed to the limits or made queer to readers unused to such representations of love. Morrison's project to create something "new" and "extraordinary" cannot help but invite associations grounded in the "old" and "un-extraordinary," and this is the "easy shot" Morrison admits to and cannot help write with an awareness of. This project of writing at the very limits of what we can understand is made even more complicated with the inclusion of the ghost—that symbol of both the new and the old, the extraordinary and the un-extraordinary.

With their bodies marked significantly by absence and presence, ghosts tease and taunt the queering impulse because they offer endless possibilities for imagining bodies as nonconforming and nonnormative. At first, it seems too easy to queer Beloved: so saturated is she in the characteristics we have grown to associate with postmodern queerness. In *Spectral America*, Jeffrey Weinstock argues that "[b]ecause ghosts are unstable interstitial figures that problematize dichotomous thinking, it perhaps should come as no surprise that phantoms have become a privileged poststructuralist academic trope."[15] Beloved, the scholarship tells us, invites complex readings, but as the years have gone by, she has not been as amenable to contradictory readings, so attached have we grown.

What happens, for example, when someone proposes that she is not a ghost? This is the question Elizabeth B. House asks in "Toni Morrison's Ghost," and in an interview Morrison encourages this ambiguity: "I also knew that I was doing something that might not work—having a ghost who may not be a ghost" (Denard 45). In returning to the text, it is not difficult to find several references to a woman who "had been locked up by some white man," and this reinforces the rationalist counternarrative to the story of the ghost. Which should we believe? Ella's story of "what them two done to me" provides Sethe with a rational explanation for "Beloved's behavior around Paul D" (119), but even Ella understands that "people who die bad don't stay in the ground" (188). Morrison allows her characters into the debate between sublunary and paranormal explanations of Beloved's existence, effectively representing the dialogue the book invites readers to enter.

Nevertheless, despite the invitation to see Beloved as an ambiguous figure, most lay readers assume and stay faithful to the notion that she is a ghost. But if we allow ourselves a moment to consider the counternarrative, the very invitation that Morrison makes explicit through the discussion between characters in the novel, then Beloved yields more to queering. One scene in particular presents Sethe in a rare moment of rational distance as if she has just come out of a spell and is now capable of seeing the queer aspect of her relationship with Beloved. It is, moreover, Sethe herself who provides the queer reading of the scene.

In contrast to an earlier scene at the carnival, Morrison drops us into this scene at the Clearing without explaining how or why Sethe has gone there and how it is that her girls have come to follow: "Now she sat on Baby Suggs' rock, Denver and Beloved watching her from the trees" (95). Unlike 124 Bluestone, this natural landscape is by turns a symbol of the wild and savage (the girls are in the trees) as well as the healing and Edenic (Baby Suggs watches over Sethe). Attentive readers will be especially inclined to consider the scene in relationship to Baby Suggs's lectures on loving the flesh, a joyous celebration of the id that stands in contrast to Sethe's reflections at the Clearing, so solidly inflected with the superego: "We must look a sight, she thought, and closed her eyes to see it: the three women in the middle of the Clearing, at the base of the rock where Baby Suggs, holy, had loved. One seated, yielding up her throat to the kind hands of one of the two kneeling before her" (97). Sethe closes her eyes in order to gain distance and see the "sight" of the three of them, and it is a "sight" because there are "three women [alone] in the middle of the Clearing." Even before *Beloved*, Morrison had written many powerful scenes that expressed the range of female affections, and in interviews she has made thought-provoking statements about the importance of honoring friendships, but Morrison also writes with an awareness of how we view, police, and interpret close women's relationships.

More important to my argument, Sethe's awareness of the three of them as a "sight" is preceded by flashbacks to Baby Suggs's sermons where she "did not tell [people] to clean up their lives or to go and sin no more" but instead told them that "in this here place, we flesh; flesh that weeps, laughs; flesh that dances on bare feet in grass. Love it. Love it hard. Yonder they do not love your flesh. They despise it" (88). Baby Suggs's sermon announces its differences with Euro-Christian orthodoxies, and it is in keeping with Morrison's privileging of African American music as a resource for strength and liberation that this specific sermon ends as "she stood up then and danced with her twisted hip the rest of what her heart had to say while the others opened their mouths and gave her the music. Long notes held until the four-part harmony was perfect enough for the deeply loved flesh" (89). It is in the context of the black community's challenges to orthodoxies about flesh and the nature of love ("love the heart") that Sethe's awareness of being a "sight" must be read. But if this is a scene of homosexual panic, it is one that gets dissipated quickly.

Interestingly, Morrison offers Sethe's thoughts on appearances only to shift to the internal feelings of Sethe and Denver, who are frozen in place because they did not know "how to stop and not love the look or feel of the lips that kept on kissing" (97). The scene, in other words, begins with Sethe's awareness of the "queer" appearance of three women together and moves toward a description of a physical act ("Beloved watched the work her thumbs were doing . . .") and the inability to "stop." It is a scene that cannot help but be read as bewitching, dangerous, and queer. To most readers, the "lips that kept on kissing" will feel spooky enough, eerie and perhaps even sexual, but it will ultimately yield to the novel's supernatural themes. The scene, however, grows queerer if there is no ghost. If the novel wishes us to consider the possibility of Beloved being human, it also invites us—along with Sethe—to see the scene as queer.

The three women's affections are presented as unbounded and finally readable to Sethe as inappropriate: "Then Sethe, grabbing Beloved's hair and blinking rapidly, separated herself. She later believed that it was because the girl's breath was exactly like new milk that she said to her, stern and frowning, 'You too old for that'" (97–98). The novel pushes the scene to the very limits of queer visibility only to diffuse it with a reminder of Beloved's status as child-ghost. As a child (or a version of a child) Beloved is arguably made innocent and resistant to queer readings—a subject I return to in the next chapter—but this scene, regardless of our interpretations of the characters, works as a scene of homosexual panic: "She looked at Denver, and seeing panic about to become something more, stood up quickly, breaking the tableau apart.

'Come on up! Up!' Sethe waved the girls to their feet" (98). Morrison calls attention to how this scene works as a tableau but makes unclear what might follow panic and "become something more." We should remember, however, that the women have been locked in a triangulation marked by the gaze (i.e., "Denver watched"; "Beloved watched"; and "neither Denver nor Sethe knew how not to . . . love the look"), and so we might infer that what is at risk is recognition, and that recognition, associated as it is with silence (i.e., tableau vivant) is even more charged with epistemologies of the closet.[16] This may explain the extensive space given to Sethe's thoughts about what had taken place in the Clearing, which culminates in "the ambition welling in her now: she wanted Paul D" (99). The tableau, in other words, gives way to action and desire, though it is strangely characterized as an "ambition" to want. While desire in the Clearing is depicted as difficult to stop, desire at 124 Bluestone is represented as forced.

Built as it is upon removing the three women from their usual world (and therefore not unlike the carnival scene), the return from the Clearing is marked with transitions: Paul D moves out of the house into a nearby shed and Denver moves into "her emerald closet." The novel emphasizes restricted spaces for these two characters even as it prepares to send them further out from 124 Bluestone. In this spatial way, Paul D and Denver are linked. They first go into their closets only to be sent further out into the world. And, significantly, both are depicted as more vulnerable to Beloved's spell. Paul D will be unable to stop himself from having sex with her, and Denver will be presented as unable to stop Beloved from harming Sethe—"so unrestricted was her need to love another" (104). An uncontrollable desire for the ghost may link Paul D and Denver at this point in the novel, but it is Denver's passion that is marked as queer.

At this point in the novel, Beloved has become a sexual creature, and so Denver's desire for her also shifts. Denver begins to seem queerer. It is not just the emerald closet that begins to cast her in this light. Her "need to love another" is specifically tied to the queer closet: her love is not only depicted as passionate, excessive, and even inappropriate, but it is a love that risks hurting her parent: "The display she witnessed at the Clearing shamed her because the choice between Sethe and Beloved was without conflict" (104). The ghost story, as I have argued, lends itself to these queer readings, but queerness itself is envisioned as potentially lethal. In this way, Katherine Bond Stockton's reading of *Beloved* rings true "as a novel born in 1987, in the cybernetic age of AIDS . . . [not as] an AIDS book—not exactly—but to claim its kinship to 1987 in its conception of a viral gothic" (*Beautiful Bottom* 180). How might it evoke the way the crisis specifically impacted two groups, women and African Americans? As gay white men became more and more visible—physically marked by the disease and culturally marked as the source for a new plague, lesbians and African Americans became even more invisible.[17] The political slogan "Silence=Death" had very real meaning to gay men during this plague, but it also had meaning for lesbians and African Americans who remained (or perhaps became even more) invisible.

Morrison's most famous ghost is a compelling symbol of lesbian and black invisibility, a symbol of both innocence and evil and, by extension, the impossibility of interpretation. As Julian Wolfreys argues, "the question of spectres is a question of speaking of that which presents itself or touches upon itself at and in excess of the limits of definition" (x). The novel seems to push the very limits of interpretative ambiguities only to substitute that ambiguity with a scene more easily read as its opposite. Appearing in a single paragraph at the end of the chapter that presents the tableau of three queer women locked in a "prolonged kiss" and a strange embrace and anticipating the next chapter's representation of fellatio, rape, and humiliation is the representation of the heterosexual coupling of two turtles. After Denver follows Beloved into a stream, she "[drags] her eyes from the spectacle of Beloved's head to see what she was staring at" (105). This shift is characteristic of the novel—characters often cannot believe their eyes—but the scene of a male turtle mounting a female turtle stands out as a very readable symbol. The "impregnable strength" of the male turtle's climb onto the female turtle's back may provide a risible association with condoms and safe sex, but it is "the embracing necks—hers stretching up toward his bending down" that offers the compelling image of risk: "No height was beyond her yearning neck, stretched like a finger toward his, risking everything outside the bowl just to touch his face. The gravity of their shields, clashing, countered and mocked the floating heads touching" (105). Still consistent with Stockton's reading of *Beloved* as related in various ways to the AIDS crisis, this scene's focus on shielding and copulation moves us far from the "spectacle" of Beloved and lesbian desire. Even its humorous quality may be seen as essential to shifting the reader's attention from the fraught scene of lesbian desire to other sexualities.

Barely more than a paragraph long, the odd little image of the turtles creates a transition between the women in the Clearing and the much-discussed chapter depicting Paul D on the chain gang. The novel, in other words, moves to the very brink of making female desire visible only to clearly and unequivocally depict a sign of heterosexuality between two animals—animals associated with safety more than passion—only then to present a brutal scene of white guards forcing black slaves to perform fellatio. Superseding lesbian desire is a violent act, one that Paul D, interestingly, escapes when the guard sees him "vomiting up nothing at all" (108). Although we do not see Paul D directly penetrated, the rape serves as a central image of Paul D's time on the chain gang. The horrific rape and brutalization of men, more importantly, replaces the more complex and resisting scene of love between women. It is a scene that overshadows (or makes invisible) the queer love of black women. If it does somehow evoke the 1980s AIDS crisis, it may do so significantly by enacting lesbian erasure by drawing attention to the homosocial, homophobic, and racist world of the white male power structure.

Morrison weaves this unambiguous scene of violence into a narrative that attempts to keep Beloved's (in)human identity ambiguous. As I have argued, Beloved's status as child-ghost provides much of the explanation for the oddest behaviors and helps readers to resist queer readings. Morrison risks much by allowing Beloved to "grow up" and become sexual. The violation of Paul D on the chain gang, however, offers us an opportunity to sympathize with him right before we must then think of his statutory rape of Beloved. Indeed, few people will read this scene as a statutory rape because most readers will continue to think of Beloved as a ghost and one that becomes increasingly dangerous. For the few readers who continue to consider the possibility that Beloved is a crazy girl who was kept in a shed and raped repeatedly, Paul D's actions—despite Beloved's role in seducing him—will seem horrific. The sexual encounter between Paul D and Beloved, therefore, reinforces the dominant reading of Beloved's ghostly state, though it also ironically makes her seem as queer as ever.

Although Beloved goes to Paul D, follows him to his shed, she is not characterized with desire for him but desire for Sethe. This is perfectly consistent with interpretations of Beloved as ruled by a childish desire for mother love, but it also turns strangely away from this reading as Beloved becomes graphic about what she wants.

> "She don't love me like I love her. I don't love nobody but her."
> "Then what you come in here for?"
> "I want you to touch me on the inside part." (116)

When Paul D reaches that inside part "he was saying, 'Red heart. Red heart,' over and over again" (117). If this is a symbol of Beloved's desires or Paul D's knowledge of that desire, it is particularly vague and resistant to anything but a multilayered reading. But it leads to a strange occurrence: Denver, from—one might imagine—her emerald closet, awakens to the trancelike song. The novel evokes a strange orgasm in the "red heart," but it is also the chant that awakens Denver, reminding us how linked the characters are. Denver—rather than Paul D—is the person most in love with Beloved and she awakens to Paul D's chant. She is only physically and not emotionally removed from the sexual act, and the novel creates one of its sexual moments of triangulation between Denver, Beloved, and Paul D.

Denver's awakening, her orgasm by proxy, is interestingly the scene that marks Denver's growing agency, but it also marks the ghosting of her lesbian desire. It is Denver who symbolizes the effort that must be taken to become visible, inviting us to think of her—rather than Beloved—in relationship to Terry Castle's notion of the "apparitional lesbian," a figure who poses the greatest "threat to patriarchal protocol" and the idea of " 'women without men'—of women indifferent or resistant to male desire" (4–5). Of the three women, she is the only one who does not have sex with Paul D or any male. She is invisible by virtue of being represented as nonsexual—a teenager without expressed sexual desires. Instead, the narrative tries to explain her desire as infused by the supernatural (though supernatural desire, as Terry Castle and others have argued, provides a thin veil for exploring "unnatural" desires). As if trying to provide a physical explanation for Denver's desire for her sister, the narrative provides a backstory of Denver consuming some of Beloved's blood, which was on Sethe's breast after she killed her daughter. But this explanation—with its gothic resonance—only emphasizes the queer and sexual aspect of her desires. How might Denver serve as a displacement of other occluded histories, other invisible lives?

Most critics look at Beloved as the ghost of unfinished business, a way of writing into the history of slavery and the Middle Passage, but in her reading of the novel, Stockton asks us to consider a very different time. What happens, however, when we take Stockton's reading of *Beloved* as reflection of the AIDS epidemic and read it next to her second novel, *Sula*? Does such a reading threaten to overturn or compete with the historical readings that have been offered, or may it enhance those readings? In asking this question, I am mindful of Barbara Christian's worry that "at this contemporary moment, a desperate moment for African Americans as a group, the power of this novel as

a specifically African American text is being blunted" (31). In queering
the ghost, I hope to honor the very real hermeneutical challenges of
the text—to highlight its interests in ambiguities, such as human/ghost,
natural/supernatural, normative/nonnormative—but also a very "quare"
black and unstable identity. I borrow the term from E. Patrick Johnson,
a transformation of the word "queer," that serves as shorthand for a
queer practice that "explicitly takes into account suppressed racial and
class knowledges" (10). Published in the wake of the AIDS crisis and
at a point of pronounced challenges to lesbian visibility, *Beloved* may
be said to continue the project begun in *Sula*. It seeks to represent the
very limits of love.

Beloved, I would argue, has been overburdened by the weight of
what she symbolizes: the silent history of slavery and the sixty million
gone. These histories for which Beloved serves as a compelling symbol
must be kept from becoming static and two dimensional. These are the
voices that are too many and too varied to be reduced to one thing
or to be kept sanctified and free of being queered. If Beloved should
serve as a symbol of only one thing, it might be silence itself, which
may be felt in a number of ways and which may reveal a number of
things. Silence is, by its very nature, queer in the sense that it is the
thing that resists being fixed.

Built upon the ambiguity of being mortal or not, Beloved resists
normative readings, eludes simple fixity. No sooner do we queer Beloved
then she disappears. Denver, however, remains as the new possible symbol of longing and queer desire. But Denver resists queering also, not
so much because we grow attached to her the way we do Beloved, but
because Denver serves as a symbol of innocence. It is the next chapter's project to queer that innocence, and it is Denver's innocence—the
evocation of that innocence in *Beloved*—that haunts Morrison's eighth
novel, *Love*.

Chapter 3

༈

Houses

Beloved Haunts *Paradise*

Beginning *Beloved* with numerals rather than spelled out numbers, it was my intention to give the house an identity . . . the way plantations were named, but not with nouns or "proper" names—with numbers instead because numbers have . . . no posture of coziness or grandeur.

—Toni Morrison, "Unspeakable Things Unspoken"

One is only occupied with ghosts by being occupied with exorcising them, kicking them out the door.

—Jacques Derrida, *Specters of Marx*[1]

The first ghost in *Beloved* is a numeral: "124 was spiteful."[2] In beginning her fifth novel in defiance of certain grammatical conventions, Morrison risks confusing readers, those who might ask, Who or what is 124? Distinguishing itself from words and announcing itself as a sign, 124 stands for the house, not merely haunted by a ghost but itself a ghost, personified as "spiteful," "Full of baby's venom," and fully animated. There are many haunted houses in literature, but Morrison personifies the house as an infant before shifting our attention to a "fully dressed woman [who] walked out of the water" (50). If the novel quickly shifts attention from personified house to a haunting woman, this transmogrification, which is implied more than stated, invites us to consider the orientation of the ghost. As the first site of the haunting of Sethe and her family, 124 might be viewed as disembodied, a symbolic severing of the human drama of infanticide from a recognizable body, a displacement onto an inert structure. But the act of personification is so thorough that 124 may be seen as enveloping Sethe, making inert wood anything but dispassionate and collapsing the distance between the house as merely holding or giving sanctuary to the ghost and the house as ghost. The distinction helps us to recognize the emphasis the novel places on orientations to the past, the ghost at turns walking alongside us and at other times housing—with all that this connotes—the present. In exploring these various orientations toward the ghost as embodied or disembodied—represented through human or house—we are invited to consider disidentification, a political and aesthetic act that José Muñoz describes as "a mode of *re-cycling* or reforming an object that has already been invested with powerful energy" (*Disidentifications* 39).

As Gaston Bachelard writes in *The Poetics of Space*, "A house that has been experienced is not an inert box. Inhabited space transcends geometrical space" (47). But in investing the house with the spirit of Sethe's past, Morrison deepens the usual associations of house and inhabitant with the spirits of the past. In personifying the house, Morrison emphasizes spatial orientation to the past, but she also disrupts the more traditional sense of time as linear: the ghost interacts with its inhabitants and they respond. History, for Morrison, defies conventional notions of chronology and enters into a dialogic relationship with the present. This allows her to approach with temerity the missing stories, such as the specific brutalities experienced by female slaves, and she can do this, knowing that these histories may speak back, ask for more, amend the record, challenge the most recent and most generous additions. *Beloved*, in other words, is less important as a fictional document of a single and specific experience than it is a reckoning of all stories as incomplete, partial, and situated in orientations marked by race, class, gender, and sexuality, as well as other identity positions. By investing her revenant with space (the house), she imagines the past (i.e., Beloved qua house) as enveloping the present (i.e., Sethe and Denver).

In its epigraph, *Beloved* announces its orientation toward the countless lost stories of the Middle Passage: "*Sixty Million and more.*" The specificity of the number is immediately revised as "more" and the epigraph finds an echo in the first line of the novel, which also tries to provide a specific number: 124. But this number shifts its purpose as enumeration to its emerging meaning as house and spirit, highlighting the elusiveness of any accounting, especially the accounting for lost stories.[3] If my last chapter considers sexual identity as a story frequently addressed but not fully registered in Morrison's novels, this chapter explores how representations of houses as haunted serve to illustrate sexual orientations. 124, which announces itself as symbol, may provide a wonderful entrance into houses as symbolic of missing histories and queer lacunae: numbers unaccounted for, numbers not fully explained, and numbers that haunt. *Beloved*'s initial symbol is a first effort at telling a story of loss, queer in its challenge to white, Western heteronormative assumptions of what a household holds, how it frames family, and how it speaks to the past and our heteronormative histories.

One of the most powerful symbols in the first chapter, which introduces us to the house as haunted, is a table, a central symbol of family, sustenance, and communion—in many traditions, the central object of the home. When the house begins to pitch, Paul D falls and reaches for "an anchor" (18). If the table is an anchor, the house, by implication, is now envisioned as a ship at sea—with Paul D as crew or captain ready to take control.

> Paul D was shouting, falling, reaching for an anchor. "Leave the place alone! Get the hell out!" A table rushed toward him and he grabbed its leg. Somehow he managed to stand at an angle, and, holding the table by two legs, he bashed it about, wrecking everything, screaming back at the screaming house. (18)

Paul D's orientation to the house—and by extension his relationship to Sethe's ghost—is as adversary. In battling the ghost with a table, Paul D fights back with the central symbol of family and heteronormativity. It is ironic that Paul D, both as newcomer and wandering man, seizes upon the table as an anchor, but it is only Paul D who wishes to battle the unanchored house and establish some normalcy. Sethe and Denver wish things to remain the same and have grown used to the animated house and the spirit it holds. Denver, for example, goes "down on all fours, as though she were holding her house down on the ground," and Sethe, who is tossed by the pitching house, "struggled to get back into her dress" (18). Denver's actions reinforce her desire to hold on to the ghost and Sethe's actions represent her helplessness and passivity; neither one helps, or even encourages, Paul D in his exorcism.

If the house captures our imaginations as an animate, haunted structure, it is the table that serves as a synecdoche for its power as a symbol of the (heterosexual) family. It also redirects our attention from the haunt as enclosing (even entombing) the family to the haunt as finding another center of the familial sphere, one that is defined less by the exteriority associated with four walls and instead shifted to a central object of its interior space, calling our attention to the importance of shifting centers, especially in the face of lost or transformed symbols, such as the unconventional and haunted house. What the space and site of the house cannot provide (i.e., an anchor), the table offers, and, indeed, "Paul D did not stop whipping the table around until everything was rock quiet" (18). Although it is inviting to read this scene as Paul D's installation as the patriarch of the newly configured family, the novel complicates this notion. When Paul D first entered the house, he walked "straight into a pool of red and undulating light that locked him where he stood" (8). He names the presence "evil," but Sethe states that it is just "sad" (8). Denver adds a third interpretation and sees it as neither evil nor sad but "[r]ebuked. Lonely and rebuked" (13). This exchange highlights the role of orientation in the act of interpretation, and it is significantly Paul D, as outsider and man, who provides the only nefarious reading. While Sethe and Denver project their own feelings and desires onto the ghost, Paul D's desires lock him in battle with the ghost. "Must be something you got it wants," Paul D states, seemingly unaware of his own projections, which become more evident when the ghost becomes embodied in Beloved. Continuing to see the ghost through his own psyche, Paul D (hetero)sexualizes the ghost's desire when he says it reminds him "of that headless bride back behind Sweet Home" (13). But he also pluralizes the ghost, seeing it, or rather interpreting them, as stifling: "They won't let you leave?" The accumulation of these associations points to Paul D's fear of family and his desire to supplant the past with something marked by greater freedom of movement, the very freedom that marks his male existence and contrasts so radically the spatially restricted life of Sethe. If Sethe's life is defined by the house, which is the intimate ghost that surrounds, restricts, and even provocatively entombs her, Paul D's life is defined by traveling, and so his entrance into Sethe's queer space—defined as it is by a secret past and "thick love"—serves as a foil and even a judgment for that inward, intimate, and inverted world.

With great clarity, Sethe responds to Paul D's suggestion that she should move away from the ghost: "No moving. No leaving. It's all right the way it is" (15). Despite Sethe's desire for stasis, things will not remain the same; Paul D's presence ensures this. The family structure cannot help but be altered by his arrival into this all-female household, into a building personified as the girl child of Sethe's infanticide, and into the secret and rather queer family drama. Paul D redefines space with a singular weapon of family stability, the table, but the ghost fights back by becoming fully embodied, surrendering its power as container/containment in order to vie with Paul D as a flesh-and-blood object of affection. The ghost has its own ambitions, foremost being its desire to drive all males from its warm center (Sethe's boys have already been driven away) and to rewrite heteronormativity as homo-familiality.

If we are to believe the first line—that "124 is spiteful"—we must look for confirmation not from Sethe and Denver but from males. In the first paragraph, we learn that Sethe's sons moved away: "[when] looking in a mirror shattered it (that was the signal for Buglar); as soon as two tiny hand prints appeared in the cake (that was it for Howard)." Paul D enters the male space vacated by the sons and quickly feels what the other males have experienced. Although he shows extreme caution in entering Sethe's life after so many years, he ignores her claim that the situation is "all right the way it is" and instead expresses his suspicion of the ghost. His arrival promises to bring Sethe back into a world of living, and even Denver notices that her mother begins acting like a girl when she falls into a sexual relationship with the new male figure. Paul D's presence promises to transform 124 into a heteronormative household, a transformation that begins when he banishes the ghost. In "screaming back at the screaming house," he argues, "She got enough without you. She got enough!" (18). In defiance or perhaps denial of Sethe and Denver's comfort with the ghost, Paul D states his case plainly: he presumes to know what is enough for Sethe and he sees no room for this ghost that manifests itself as an undulating and pulsating red light.

The fight scene, which is sandwiched between the intimate scene where Paul D explores the tree on Sethe's back and the passage where they climb the steps to the second floor to have sex, is fascinating as a psychosexual engagement marked by the retreating of the "pulse of red light," a "grinding, shoving floor," and Sethe "[sliding] to the floor and [struggling] to get back into her dress." As the new head of the household, Paul D takes his place not only at the table but wields it against the "unwanted" ghost. As a symbol of the house's center, the table makes a brief but important statement in the novel. While Denver gets "down on all fours, as though she were holding her house down on the ground," Paul D is "holding the table by two legs" (18). The repetition is important, emphasizing that they are both "holding" on to things but very different things, indicating their opposing orientations toward the ghost and toward the pulsating, pitching, and screaming house. If Paul D's life is defined by the haunting memory of the entombment he experienced in a cage in Georgia, Denver's life is shaped by the entombment she experiences in the haunted house. Both structures haunt, but Paul D wishes to escape his ghost while Denver does not and instead knows the ghost as an extension of herself. Both are strangely queer spaces marked by a living death that is further marked by the absence of a heterosexual potential. At 124, Paul D's arrival changes that when he arrives and does battle with a table.

In *Queer Phenomenology: Orientations, Objects, and Others*, Sara Ahmed considers the importance of tables as objects that shape our orientation to the social and sexual world. The home is logically an extension of self, and it is one that is often marked as heterosexual. For example, at large family gatherings the dining room table often spatially marks the heterosexual couplings, patriarchal hierarchies, and gendered norms. In a song called "The Head of the Table," Joan Armatrading suggests that the "head of the table would bend" but only if we challenge it. Denver, in fact, refuses to accept a patriarchal and heteronormative structure, a resistance familiar to many African American households, and the novel speaks to this resistance when it pits Paul D's desires against those of Sethe and Denver. Morrison transforms the table into a weapon with which Paul D does battle with the ghost, but the heteronormative structure does not so easily fall into place. When the battle is finished, a male will sit at the table and the all-female household will be missing its most provocative member: the ghost. But when the ghost returns as a newly embodied young woman, the developing challenges to the instantiated nuclear family will be even more fully represented as a dramatic challenge to heteronormativity.

If the haunted house is marked by misandry, a decided war against all males, Beloved as an embodied spirit becomes more effective through craft and less through force when she has sex with Paul D in order to get rid of him. If Paul D may be said to succeed in getting rid of the animating spirit in the house by wielding a table as a literal and symbolic weapon of heteronormativity, Beloved will wield her own weapon: the taboo of incest (i.e., heteronormativity perverted from within). Paul D will leave the house, vacating his place at the head of the table and installing himself in a shed and later a local church. He refuses to be taken in by any other family, despite the protestations of Stamp Paid, and instead seems to feel chastened by the ghost at 124. Beloved, moreover, is successful in reinstating the house as a sanctuary against pretensions to heteronormativity, and Morrison reminds us at the beginning of the second section that the house is haunted, though perhaps no longer feeling "spiteful," as the first line of the novel announces, but "loud," as the first line of the second section affirms.

It is important to remember that with the arrival of the embodied ghost, Morrison does not dispense with the notion that the house is personified and is itself a ghost—a force to be reckoned with. Each of the three sections, in fact, begins with the same pattern. First "124 is spiteful," then "124 was loud," and finally "124 was silent."[4] As one of literature's most famous ghost stories, *Beloved*'s dual emphasis on types of haunting—one fully embodied and the other dispersed across the familiar structure of a house—raises questions about our cultural assumptions of who or what speaks to the living, through what means, and why. Scholars have written volumes on the ghost as the embodiment of occluded history, psychic need, and collective memory, but what happens when we ask questions of the disembodied ghost or the house that does not just hold ghosts but is itself a ghost? If Gaston Bachelard is right that "the house is one of the greatest powers of integration for the thoughts, memories and dreams of mankind" (2), then what about the haunted house, which seems to overlay one symbol of history with another? Finally, how does this duplication serve to queer notions of history?

In moving between representations of an embodied ghost and an animate haunted house, Morrison highlights questions of presence and problematizes the very project of retrieving history as some kind of finished or fully recounted story. The "Sixty Million and more" that the epigraph refers to—those countless and nameless many who were subjected to the Middle Passage—can never have their stories fully told, and so Morrison seems to point to this problem in beginning with a number that is a ghost. Both epigraph and the narrative's initial symbol point to enumeration as haunting—as all accountings essentially are failed efforts at being specific and offering a full accounting. In shifting from the ghost as structure to the ghost as embodied, the novel reinforces this failure to account for even the single ghost known alternately as 124 and Beloved.

The shift from embodied to disembodied ghost happens sometimes in a single passage. At the beginning of the second section and directly after being reminded that the house is the personification of the child ghost, Stamp Paid, who is so crucial to Sethe's escape to 124, hears "the stepped-up haunting 124 was subject to" (172). When he approaches the door, he hears loud sounds within lowered to "an occasional mutter—like the interior sounds a woman makes when she believes she is alone and unobserved at her work: a sth" (172). In passages such as this, we might see 124 as again likened to a ghost "with interior sounds a woman makes" or as merely housing a ghost, the source of those sth-ing sounds. Just as Morrison keeps the ghostly status of Beloved inconclusive (see the previous chapter), so, too, does she keep the ghostly status of the house itself a mystery. It is significant that it is a man who tries to interpret these "interior sounds." Is it a ghost or the sounds of women? The novel delights in these kinds of ambiguity, and it does so to emphasize the intimate relationship between the two kinds of haunting.

As if the novel will not yield to a single explanation, its third and final section states that "124 was quiet" (239). This begs the question, Is 124 silent because the ghost, either bodied or disembodied, is gone? Or is 124 holding its tongue? How does sound, the novel seems to ask, make the ghost legible? Derrida's notion of hauntology, which extends his philosophical explorations of reading and interpretation, helps us to better understand what is at stake in representations of the ghost through visual or auditory characteristics. In *Specters of Marx*, Jacques Derrida addresses the importance of ghosts to our understanding of presence, coining "hauntology" as a play upon "ontology." The new term addressing Derrida's familiar themes of the trace, which is itself a haunting of what is left out of a concept, a term, writing, and, indeed, everything.[5] It is how we understand the world through binaries, and Derrida wants us to deconstruct this through an exploration of what is missing. Arguably his most provocative and most productive neologism, this term points to the way ghosts haunt all concepts, most certainly our concepts of time and history. As Derrida argues in *Specters of Marx*, "To haunt does not mean to be present, and it is necessary to introduce haunting into the very construction of a concept. Of every concept, beginning with the concepts of being and time. That is what we would be calling here a hauntology" (161). What this concept brings to older Derridean neologisms, such as *difference* and deconstruction, is simply a new metaphor for understanding structural challenges to reading: "[E]veryone reads, acts, writes with his or her ghosts, even when one goes after the ghosts of the other" (139). *Beloved*, for example, leads us back and forth from the embodied to disembodied, and it is this shift that helps to highlight the importance of understanding how ghosts gain presence through human form, begging a series of related questions: How does the haunted house haunt differently than the ghostly human embodiment? What are the different (i.e., queer) orientations of these hauntings? How does structure and body issue different or similar challenges to heteronormativity?

In *Paradise*, Morrison creates a very different haunted structure. Unlike the small, spare, and simple structure of 124, the Convent is large, ornate, and complex. We first see the building through the eyes of the invaders, the men of Ruby bent on massacring the women: "They reached the Convent just seconds before the sun did and had a moment to see and register for all time how the mansion floated dark and malevolently disconnected from God's earth" (18). It is with an eschatological vision, one that causes them to view their own paradise as endangered, that they are moved to action. They see their happiness, even their very survival, as bound to the women, and so they enter the structure with "rope, a palm leaf cross, handcuffs, Mace and sunglasses, along with clean, handsome guns" (3). The building presents only one problem: "Hiding places will be plentiful in the Convent" (3). Morrison finds various ways to return to this theme of hiding places, emphasizing the structure as palimpsest and ghost, a queer space that resists, contrasts, and responds to patriarchy, misogyny, and heteronormativity.

In the first chapter, we learn that it was built many years ago to be a hiding place for an embezzler, who was captured shortly after the completion of the building, and it later became a religious school for Native American girls, remote and isolated, qualities embraced by the nuns but not the children. It is the third group of residents, a loose gathering of unrelated women, that puts the final stamp upon the structure, and it is the hunt for them that most powerfully defines the structure as notable as a place to hide. But where the men see ominous hiding places—with evil lurking around every corner and debaucheries signaled by the state of the rooms—the women have found sanctuary from their violent and painful pasts. Morrison has stated that *Paradise* "was my meditation . . . and interrogation of the whole idea of paradise, the safe place, the place full of bounty, where no one can harm you" (Farnsworth 156), but we might argue that she has already addressed this theme in *Beloved*, which presents 124 as a safe place far away from Sweet Home. A place where both Sethe and Beloved find sanctuary. But *Paradise*, as Morrison goes on to argue, is "based on the notion of exclusivity. All paradises, all utopias are designed by who is not there, by the people who are not allowed" (Farnsworth 156). In mapping these concerns—safe places and exclusivity—on to a structure defined by its hiding places, *Paradise* offers one of Morrison's most powerful challenges to heteronormativity.

The tension between space as shelter and threat, good and evil, paradise and hell finds physical expression in the Convent—alternately called the mansion because of its two very different residents. When the men of Ruby enter and "shoot the white girl first" (3), they begin to look around and are "reminded that before it was a Convent, this house was an embezzler's folly" (3). The building registers both the original lush design of the embezzler as well as its later incarnation as home and school to nuns and their young charges. "The Sisters of the Sacred Cross chipped away all the nymphs, but curves of their marble hair still strangle grape leaves and tease the fruit" (4). As a setting that immediately conveys two very specific and antithetical histories, one built from scratch and the other charged with denial, erasure, and judgment, this introduction to place—more detailed than any other setting in Morrison's work—presents architecture as a battle between sexual indulgence and religious asceticism, earthly desires and spiritual purposes, wealthy excesses and stern practices. Layered upon this antithesis is the queer world of the throwaway women who now inhabit this odd structure.

While the embezzler and the nuns register—primarily through architectural detail—as ghosts who haunt if not in spirit then through the material objects that have been designed with salacious intent and then later erased, broken, and covered with prudery, the current residents—against this backdrop—appear, ironically, ghostlike. Their presence, moreover, gets tied to the queer structure—its violation of norms and its mysterious depths. Just as the building has many hiding places, so, too, are the women seen as dangerous because they are unknown, unrelated, and mysterious. The men—"They are nine, over twice the number of the women they are obliged to stampede or kill"—will travel "deep in the Convent" (3), a great contrast to the two steps that Paul D takes into 124 before being confronted by the ghost. Instead, this journey "deep in" lingers over the sensations that the men experience: "The chill intensifies as the men spread deeper into the mansion, taking their time, looking, listening, alert to the female malice that hides here and the yeast-and-butter smell of rising dough" (4). At times the descent almost seems sensuous if not sexual. It is the youngest man who self-consciously observes "how the dream he is in might go" and sees colors so bright "[l]ike the clothes of an easily had woman," and "their mission made them giddy" (4). Although Morrison does not linger over the murder, dispensing with the first killing ("They shot the white woman first.") in the first line of the novel, she spends great time with the spatial violation of the structure, detailing the opening of doors, the entrance into strange rooms, and the descent into the cellar.

It is a palimpsest of the structure designed by the embezzler, erased by the nuns, and lived in by the hunted women. If the "rose-tone marble floors" point to the embezzler, and the "chipped away . . . nymphs" register the second residents, ephemeral things—a "name, written in lipstick," "a fedora tilted on the plastic neck of a female torso," "a bouquet of baby shoes"—all point to the current residents (7–8). More than the debauched architectural detail created by the embezzler and in great contrast to the erasure of that debauchery affected by the nuns, the signs left by the women inspire the men to imagine all sorts of satanic occurrences. It is this final layer—what the women have left haphazardly throughout the building—that most disturbs the men. They discover, for example, that "each woman sleeps not in a bed, like normal people, but in a hammock" (7), and each detail confirms their most vicious and queer imaginings of the women. The building, which registers moral extremes even before the women arrive, becomes something unimaginable to the invading men. They invest it with all their anxieties over their own interests in maintaining their town and fulfilling their destinies as patriarchs of Ruby.

When they enter the kitchen, they see that the "table is fourteen feet long if an inch, and it's easy to see that the women they are hunting have been taken by surprise" (5). The table holds all the familiar objects of normalcy—"four bowls of shredded wheat," "scallion piled like a handful of green confetti," and "loaves of bread" (5). But the men see the size and the quantity of things as outrageous, an affront to their own lives. It causes them to think of their own humble beginnings: "From Haven, a dreamtown in Oklahoma Territory, to Haven, a ghosttown in Oklahoma State" (5). Because the dreamtown and ghosttown haunt their actions, "That is why they are here in this Convent" (5). Morgan, one of the twins who will stand as patriarchs of the town, "moves to the long table and lifts the pitcher of milk" (7). In a scene no less symbolically powerful than Paul D's battle with the ghost of 124—and with the table as a central symbol of orientations toward family structures—Morgan "sniffs [the milk] first and then, the pistol in his right hand, he uses his left to raise the pitcher to his mouth, taking such long, measured swallows the milk is half gone by the time he smells the wintergreen" (7). This, as much as anything, begins to signal his complicated relationship to the women and perhaps his growing distance from the murderous men and their mission. He risks communing with the women, albeit in absentia, and his transformation by the events is distinguished from that of his twin. The wintergreen, a herb that is both medicinal and when used in excess is fatal, serves as a reminder of representations of women as healers and witches, but it is too late for Morgan—if this serves to suggest his change of heart—to save the women. He is one of nine men, and the chapter continues to represent the invaders as entering deeper and deeper into the Convent and finding more and more signs of the women's evil doings. Although we are told that the embezzler designed the building in the shape of a bullet, the description of the men's journey deeper and deeper and into darker and darker depths makes the building seem more womblike than anything.

For the men, it is a diseased womb, one that brings only death. Unlike the equations of tomb and womb that Joseph Campbell points to in *The Masks of God*, the men of Ruby see only death and not rebirth. Arnette loses her baby while staying at the Convent; Deek suspects that his wife, Soane, has obtained an abortifacient from the women; and Sweetie hears crying children "among these demons" and tells Jeff Flood, "They made me, snatched me" (130). In addition to these "evil" occurrences, the men tie the misfortunes of their town to the Convent:

> Outrages that had been accumulating all along took shape
> as evidence. A mother was knocked down the stairs by her
> cold-eyed daughter. Four damaged infants were born in one
> family. Daughters refused to get out of bed. Brides disappeared
> on their honeymoons. Two brothers shot each other on New
> Year's Day. Trips to Demby for VD shots common. . . . The
> proof they had been collecting since the terrible discovery
> in the spring could not be denied: the one thing that con-
> nected all these catastrophes was in the Convent. And in the
> Convent were those women. (11)

Most of these signs point to the destruction of the family, many directly related to children, and so when the men enter the Convent they are looking for confirmation of the women as child-killers. "What, [one of the men] wonders, could do this to women? How can their plain brains think up such things: revolting sex, deceit and the sly torture of children?" (8). Although they are never called witches, this scene and the misogynist logic that informs it calls to mind a witch hunt.

Morrison ties the suspense of whether the men will hunt down all the women to the suspense of what they will find in the building:

> Now one brother, a leader in everything, smashes the cellar
> door with the butt of his rifle. The other waits a few feet
> back with their nephew. All three descend the steps ready and
> excited to know. They are not disappointed. What they see is
> the devil's bedroom, bathroom, and his nasty playpen. (17)

And in passages like this, Morrison stops just short of fully describing
what the men see, leaving the journey into this building, this womb
envisioned as tomb, to fully reflect the men's fear, or, rather, their desire
for a suitable scapegoat.

Although the men do not hear the voices of dead children, their
actions—not unlike those of Paul D—may serve to exorcise those spirits.
After their invasion and the murder of the women, the building is seen as
silent. Late in the novel, we learn that Richard Misner and Anna Flood
"returned two days after the assault on the Convent women" (296).
Unwilling to accept the stories that have been told (i.e., "the convenient
mass disappearance of the victims"), they "went to look for themselves"
(303). Continuing a major theme of the novel, their observations highlight the way men and women see and interpret the physical world.

> Richard barely glanced at the cellar floor. Anna, however,
> examining it as closely as her lamp permitted, saw the ter-
> ribleness K.D. reported, but it wasn't the pornography he
> had seen, nor was it Satan's scrawl. She saw instead the tur-
> bulence of females trying to bridle, without being trampled,
> the monsters that slavered them. (303)

Extending the scene beyond the house to the outside gardens, chicken
coop, and grounds, Morrison puts us in mind of death and renewal
with images of

> [s]hriveled tomato plants alongside crops of leafy green
> reseeding themselves with golden flowers; pink hollyhocks so
> tall the heads leaned all the way over a trail of bright squash
> blossoms; lacy tops of carrots browned and lifeless next to
> straight green spikes of onions. . . . Anna sighed at the mix
> of neglect and unconquerable growth. (304–05)

It is, however, the interpretation of a mystical opening that most reveals
their differences. Anna sees the mystical opening as a door while Richard

sees a window. "That's the difference between us," Anna Flood says, "You see a door; I see a window." The text is clear, however, that they both "sensed it, rather, for there was nothing to see" (305). On the drive home, they discuss the vision further, but they are unwilling to really move beyond "focusing on the sign rather than the event," which the text suggests is an invitation to a mystical experience if not an entrance into another world.

The novel spends so much time exploring "signs" and "experiences" as subject to radically different interpretations that the presence of spirits may at first get lost in the flurry of subjective and competing visions of the world. Indeed, the idea of spirits, who have hardly appeared as anything more than haunting sounds that visit some of the residents and visitors, do not at first seem a central concern of the novel. But the "missing" children that haunt the Convent reinforce—if the early incarnations of the building do not convey alone—the loss of a stable heteronormative world. The men are able to stage the massacre because there are no children, only the signs (albeit informed by new and old witch hunts) of sadistic mothers, witches, and deranged lost women. It is in the interest of children—the future of Ruby—that the men feel compelled to action. They are unable, furthermore, to identify with women who do not perform their primary function as mothers. With a pioneer sensibility, these men would only be more disgusted to learn that these women have sought shelter in order to be mothered themselves. Sanctuary—as the men's thoughts of their own town and the founding of their utopia reinforce—is tied to mothers, family, and heteronormativity, everyone performing a very specific and gendered function. Although their history is tied to finding sanctuary, they cannot see past their own histories and are unable to see the women as anything else than foreign, other, threat. They occupy the space that is not utopia or home. Morrison, however, refuses a simple antithesis between the men and the women, and the novel complicates these initial moves throughout.

Not unlike the men, the women are also trapped inside their own histories, and their place of sanctuary, the Convent, also threatens to be a prison. If *Beloved* first represents a table as an agent of change toward heteronormativity, *Paradise* presents imaginary windows and doors as agents of a very individualized change. It is not so much that *Beloved* represents rigid conformity and the clear establishment of heterosexuality. For example, at the end of the novel Paul D, rather than asserting a male prerogative, tells Sethe, "You your best thing, Sethe. You are."

There is the promise of a future for Sethe, and Denver, whom some readers have seen as full of desire for Beloved, which provocatively underscores a lesbian subtext for the novel, also points to an independent future. Both Sethe and Denver have been assisted by the exorcism of the ghost by Paul D and later in the novel by the thirty chanting women, but *Paradise* goes further in viewing women as aiding other women in their journey away from patriarchy and heteronormativity.

Onto the ornate and complex vision of the mansion/Convent, Morrison has the women draw silhouettes of their own bodies. These silhouettes serve as windows or doors into their past, and so the Convent full of crying and laughing babies does finally function as a womb and not a tomb. The women are reborn—if they have, in fact, died in the massacre—and enter a future of their own imaginations—with Mavis reuniting with her daughter, who is now clearly older; Gigi visiting her father; Seneca seeing but denying her mother; and Pallas reconnecting with her infant son. It is, however, Connie, perhaps the most mysterious of the residents of the Convent, who appears with a woman we have not yet been introduced to. In the final moments of the novel, we see Connie with her head in Piedade's lap. This is the final image of a window into a future or, perhaps, an out-of-time experience, and it is a mystical ending, not unlike the open ending of *Beloved*, but it suggests that women can move forward, go through windows and doors and address the past, the ghosts that haunt them.

Chapter 4

∾

Matriarchy

Paradise Haunts *Love*

I don't subscribe to patriarchy, and I don't think it should be
substituted with matriarchy.

—Toni Morrison, in Zia Jaffrey,
"Tony Morrison: The Salon Interview"

We are all haunted houses.

—Hilda Doolittle (H. D.), *Tribute to Freud*

Readers in search of a matriarchal figure in Morrison's novels might look
to *Paradise*, which after all features a figure known simply as Mother.
But Mother, a resident of the Convent during its previous existence
as a religious school and its present incarnation as a home for several
"lost" women, becomes a ghostly presence in the building and loses
the characteristics—involvement, care, and strength—associated with a
matriarch. She resides in the inner recesses of the building, feeble and
near death, while Connie, her most faithful charge, opens the door to
the Convent's new charges, an unrelated series of individuals escaping
desperate situations. Connie, who might be said to carry on the work
of Mother, provides an even more interesting antithesis to the role of
mother. As the new head of the household, she allows women to find
sanctuary at the Convent, but she is too disinterested in the women
to fulfill anyone's expectations for a matriarch. The Convent, therefore,
stands as a female-centered world outside of patriarchy while also everywhere announcing the absence of a matriarchal figure.

53

While Mother remains ghostlike and representative of the past, Connie, who opens the door to these women, is seen as an "ideal parent" only because she is not involved. Described as a "play mother" and a "granny goose" (262), she is dramatically transformed at the end of the narrative: "With the aristocratic gaze of the blind she sweeps the women's faces and says, 'I call myself Consolata Sosa. If you want to be here you do what I say. Eat how I say. Sleep when I say. And I will teach you what you are hungry for'" (262). If this passage begins to cast her in the role of a matriarch, it is as if she were channeling a different person, and even the "women look at each other and then at a person they do not recognize" (262). If Consolata serves as a matriarchal figure at this point in the novel, it is as a conduit for something magical and reparative and not as an extension of realism. Morrison names the trouble that has followed these women to the Convent: "With Consolata in charge . . . [the women] altered" (265) and "[they] were no longer haunted" (266). But what specifically has haunted these women? Each woman, we learn, has a different ghost, a different demon, and so the magic transformation that Connie initiates allows them each to contribute to their own exorcism. While Connie orders them to trace their own silhouettes upon the kitchen floor, each one of them draws onto the figure a personal demon and creates an individualized cure or exorcism. Overturning what first seems to be a scene that positions Connie as a controlling matriarch and the women as obedient children is a very different scenario that characterizes the women as free now to become active agents in their own healing.

This representation of Connie as dramatically and temporarily transformed into a controlling matriarch only to free the women to pursue their own personal destinies highlights the complicated way *Paradise* addresses myths of the maternal, one that imagines new possibilities. The novel presents a world of women not only outside patriarchy but also strangely antithetical to stereotypes of matriarchy. The lack of a strong mother ties these women together, and in the chapters devoted to the Convent's new residents we see what drove each woman to flee, or, rather, what maternal lack kept them from finding sanctuary closer to home. Mavis, in her hour of need, finds her mother to be full of judgment; Gigi is raised by a grandfather and seems to have no mother in sight; Seneca is abandoned at five and thinks it is her sister and not her mother who leaves and never returns; and Pallas's mother, an artist, disappears when Pallas is three, reappears when Pallas is older, but then steals her boyfriend. *Paradise*, we might argue, not only presents

Mother and Connie as the antithesis of matriarchs but also depicts their charges as orphaned and greatly in need of mother figures. The novel, indeed, is haunted by its own withholding of a matriarchal figure, supplying a distorted and mystical matriarch at the end when Connie, who we should note is also orphaned, leads the women toward their own personal reconciliations.

In contrast to the lack of matriarchal figures at the Convent, there is no shortage of patriarchal figures in the nearby town of Ruby, and much of the tension in the novel arises from men asserting their control over spouses, children, and each other. The initial conflict of the novel, moreover, issues from the anger of the patriarchal figures, who view the women as powerful and somehow capable of influencing their townspeople a full ten miles away. When the men enter the Convent with murder in mind, they intend to restore control over the community. Indeed, they meet and plan their war against these women without consultation from the female members of their community.[1] They carry with them distorted ideas of women, sexist notions of gender roles, and personal histories that make them suspicious of outsiders. If the novel offers, in a veiled way, a stinging critique of pernicious myths of matriarchy, it constructs this critique through its noticeable absence of matriarchs at the Convent and a virulent patriarchal structure in Ruby.

Morrison, furthermore, presents the men as caught in a series of equations that link, not unlike the perpetrators of real-life witch hunts, the fear of women's bodies, articulated as a concern with abortion, miscarriages, and deformed births, and with threats to patriarchy, such as homosexuality, female licentiousness, and matriarchy. It is a stew of anxieties, each one seen as connected to the other, but matriarchy is the queer ghost that haunts the novel. In constructing the Convent as a loose conglomeration of women without purpose, Morrison allows us to consider the power of misogyny as a force behind the fear of women and matriarchy. What would a world without men look like? Certainly not free of power. What is the source of fears of matriarchy? Not necessarily—as the story of these men convey—women. One of the patriarchs of Ruby, for example, considers his and his ancestors' journey from "dreamtown" to "ghosttown" and thinks: "That is why they are here in this Convent. To make sure it never happens again. That nothing inside or out rots the one all-black town worth the pain" (5). The men turn to the women as scapegoats to address other fears, and misogyny and homophobia provide a foundation for their actions.

Another townsman (and Morrison keeps the men nameless in the first chapter) sees the women of the Convent as a threat because they are so different: "like none he knew or ever heard tell of" (8). He is not surprised to find "that each woman sleeps not in a bed, like normal people, but in a hammock" and that there are "[n]o clothes in the closets, of course, since the women wore no-fit dirty dresses and nothing you could honestly call shoes" (7). Throughout this first chapter that provides an introduction to the men, their ancestry, and their values, interlaced with their hunt for the women and their journey into the Convent, we see the women through the eyes of men who are threatened by the very idea of women acting outside of certain gendered and sexual conventions. As they move through the building, moving through doorways and into what seem to be countless rooms,

> what alarms two men most is the series of infant booties and shoes ribboned to a cord hanging from a crib in the last bedroom they enter. A teething ring, cracked and stiff, dangles among the tiny shoes. Signaling with his eyes, one man directs his partner to four more bedrooms on the opposite side of the hall. He himself moves closer to the bouquet of baby shoes. Looking for what? He isn't sure. Blood? A little toe, maybe, left in a white calfskin shoe? (7–8)

He is looking for confirmation that these women are antithetical to their proper function as mothers. In place of signs of mothering, he sees infanticide and torture. In a vacuum, one defined by its lack of patriarchy, the men see "throwaway people" (4).

Although Morrison says *Paradise* explores religious love, it is as much about mothers and maternal love as *Beloved*. It is, however, about the absence of maternal love, about missing mothers and the profound effect this has on our destinies. It is this absence that drives Mavis, Gigi, Seneca, and Pallas to flee the past, and it is the absence of mother love that drives Connie, who has been passive for most of the novel, to action. Spurred into action, she becomes a caricature of the strong matriarch, a mystical dictator who leads the women into a healing ritual and through doors that have been previously closed. It is significant that at the end of the novel the undertaker goes out to the Convent and cannot find the murdered women. Women disappear at every turn in the novel. Although the myths the people of Ruby hold of women and mothers remain strong, the substance of the women dissolve, leaving the people of Ruby with a final mystery. As Anna Flood and Reverend Misner explore the empty house, they come upon a crib that is new. Misner asks, "Whose baby was in there?" and Anna Flood assures him, counter to the town's belief, that it was not a crib for Arnette's stolen baby: "He said it again, 'Right,' with the same level of doubt. Then, 'I don't like mysteries.' 'You're a preacher. Your whole life's belief is a mystery.' 'Belief is mysterious; faith is mysterious. But God is not a mystery. We are'" (304). Morrison has said in an interview that she most identifies with Reverend Misner, but it is difficult to believe that she does not embrace mystery, so lovingly does she write mystery into her novels, and *Paradise* seems especially concentrated on myths of matriarchy and how intertwined they are with so many other myths of women.

As the novel circulates these many myths of women and raises the haunting specter of missing mothers, it addresses only in the margins the pairing of lesbianism and motherhood. As I have suggested earlier, this is one of the linkages revealed in the first chapter as the men come upon signs of children coupled with signs of the women's supposed depravity and unnaturalness. A late chapter, bearing the name "Lone" and from this woman's sympathetic point of view, provides an insider's glimpse into the men of Ruby. It is Lone who overhears the men speak "of the ruination that was upon them—how Ruby was changing in intolerable ways":

> Remember how they scandalized the wedding? What you say?
> Uh huh and it was that very same day I caught them kissing
> on each other in the back of that ratty Cadillac. Very same
> day, and if that wasn't enough to please the devil, two more
> was fighting over them in the dirt. Right down in it. Lord,
> I hate a nasty woman. (275)

Although Morrison does not designate which man (or probably men) speak(s), the novel presents a nearly two-page list of grievances that comes back from time to time to linking lesbianism to unnatural mothering.

> What in God's name little babies doing out there? You asking
> me? Whatever it is, it ain't natural. Well, it used to house
> little girls, didn't it? Yeah, I remember. Said it was a school.

School for what? What they teaching out there? . . . Something's going on out there, and I don't like any of it. No men. Kissing on themselves. Babies hid away. Jesus! No telling what else. (275–76)

Homosexuality, therefore, is just one of the many crimes that get linked to satanic mothering, but the men represent it as the most unnatural, most disturbing, most threatening of crimes. As if only starting to explore this forbidden subject through, primarily, the threat of women, Morrison returns to explore lesbianism and motherhood in her next novel, *Love*.

Published more than a quarter of a century after *Beloved*, *Love* appears as a belated and ghostly fourth novel in the "love" trilogy of *Beloved*, *Jazz*, and *Paradise*. While the novels in the trilogy focus on a certain aspect of love (maternal, romantic, religious), *Love* arguably offers a comprehensive study of myriad forms of love. Queer love, however, is its greatest theme, and when it is read against the queer subtexts in *Paradise* and *Beloved*, *Love* invites us to consider how Morrison has been moving toward a more direct treatment of queer love for many years. Morrison not only makes queer desire a central concern of her narrator and two main characters, Heed and Christine, but she also structures the narrative upon queering the ghost and exploring the queer limits of love. Although *Beloved* is the novel in the trilogy devoted to maternal love, *Love*—not unlike *Paradise*—considers the absence of mothers and myths of matriarchy. Indeed, the narrator of *Love* queers the ghost and matriarchy at the same time, serving to emphasize the myths we have of strong women and the importance of finding moral, familial, and social centers. Romen, who is raised by a grandmother and grandfather, represents the benefits of finding a center in a strong family, and the novel does not see his absent mother and father as a deficit. But Romen serves as a central figure of conflict in navigating through moral choices. If his story, specifically his moral dilemma, provides one of the narrative centers of the story, this is counterpointed to the commentary from the narrator, a ghostly and queer matriarch who comments on everyone at Up Beach except, surprisingly, Romen. Morrison disconnects the queer voice of matriarchy from the person most in need, attending instead to the battling women that surround Romen.

Morrison tells us that she began her fourth exploration of love with the story of Romen, who sets Pretty Faye free from a gang rape: "From that initiation into the mysteries and terror of social arrangements evolved the stories of other characters whose vulnerability is turned into shame, into loneliness—the clear sense of having no one on whom one can safely rely" (xi). *Love*, therefore, is about the stuff we forget to mention when we use the word—when we simplify and romanticize it. It is about language and social arrangements.[2] Unlike her descriptions and explanations of *Beloved*, Morrison's various comments on *Love* seem to locate multiple centers, inspirations, and beginning points.

In her foreword, Morrison is quite explicit about finding inspiration in a girl whose "most obvious sign of her behind-the-scrim life—was that she didn't like boys" (x). But she also tells us she began with Romen's "wanton tenderness for a stranger." In an interview, she confesses to almost titling the novel *The Sporting Woman*, after a minor character, Celestial. I am not suggesting incoherence in these various alternative centers but a way the novel eludes having a center, or perhaps, locates its emotional heart in the margins, the hidden, the forgotten. This makes it all the more surprising that scholars have virtually ignored the queer themes. Are these themes so occluded that they resist being read? Deborah McDowell argues that "African American and women novelists with a 'dangerous' story to tell" will often deploy " 'safe' themes, plots, and conventions . . . as a protective cover, underneath which lie more dangerous subplots" (93). With this strategy in mind, I would argue that *Love* makes dangerous themes its very center. The "safer" and more obvious plotlines involve the rise and fall of the black resort owned by Bill Cosey as well as his role in shaping the many lives of the people around him. The novel moves between the resort's heyday in the 1940s and the world of the 1990s. While the narrator, L, provides much of the information about the past, the conflict between Bill Cosey's second wife, Heed, and his granddaughter, Christine, propels the narrative set in the present forward. Christine and Heed are the same age when Cosey marries the eleven-year-old preteen, and the lifelong hatred eclipses one of the most profound loves that the novel wrestles with. But none of this—not the intergenerational marriage or the love eclipsed by hatred—reveals the really dangerous work of the novel.

In speaking of the risks of writing about and titling her novel *Love*, Morrison highlights the paradoxical attraction and resistance to using "the most empty cliché, the most useless word" for her title, confessing to being worried by but also fascinated by her concern.[3] Intrigued by the push and pull of this empty word, Morrison also chose to name her narrator "Love," producing two puns, as I delineate later, relevant to queer theory and made queerer by the figure of the ghost. These puns, tied as they are to the narrator, help to provide an unfixed center, one that embraces the many outsiders of this novel.

While *Beloved* presents its ghost, albeit ambiguously, as central, *Love* withholds information about the otherworldly status of its narrator. In a radical departure from the structure of the more famous novel, *Love* does not reveal that the narrator is a ghost until the final pages of the novel. Morrison's eighth novel, in other words, works hard to disrupt the assumptions of its readers. Nevertheless, it is "impossible not to read *Love*," as Anissa Wardi artfully states, "intertextually with *Beloved*, as Love/love, linguistically and thematically, are part of Beloved/beloved" (201). Part of this intertextual play involves *Love*'s effort (and relative success) in distancing itself from *Beloved* even as it invites readers to consider the linguistic and thematic relationships. In boldly taking a part of *Beloved* for its name, *Love* risks and even invites the very thing it tries to disrupt: being compared to its famous sister.

In being called to read intertextually, perhaps the most important question we can ask is how the later novel addresses *Beloved*'s focused exploration of maternal love. In the course of the later novel, we are introduced to mothers who are missing, negligent, dead, or distracted, but none of these incidental characters receives great attention. So remarkable is the lack of mothers, we might argue that the novel inverts *Beloved*'s attention to excessive maternal love with mothers *in absentia*. If there is any matriarchal figure, the narrator is perhaps the greatest contender.[4]

As the cook to Cosey's resort, L oversees food, comfort, and the children, Heed and Christine. Reversing the narrative of *Beloved*, it is the matriarch and not the child who is the ghost; and it is her hunger, her desire to feel loved, and her obsession with the past that provide the greatest haunting. "I know I need something else," L says in her initial monologue, but even this direct articulation of a "want" does not prepare us for how big and disturbing those needs are. Not unlike Beloved, L asserts her will and, in the closing moments of the novel, her desires are literally depicted as resting upon the tombstone of the past. "I sit near her," L says of Celestial, "once in a while out at the cemetery." And in this closing reflection, we see much of the otherworldly and queer desire reminiscent of Beloved.

It would be unfair to push the comparison much farther, but this intertextual reading opens us to considering how Morrison uses the ghost to explore the queer limits of love. As I have argued in the previous chapter, both ghosts serve to manifest the work of love as not ended. I do not see this as conflicting with Marisa Parham's *Haunting and Displacement in African American Literature and Culture*, which sees haunting as not necessarily interesting "because it resonates with the supernatural, but rather because it is appropriate to a sense of what it means to live in between things—in between cultures, in between times, in between spaces—to live with various kinds of doubled consciousness" (3). It is our job to consider what "in between spaces" L gives voice to.

Not unlike Beloved, she serves as the cipher of the text. Who is she and what does she want? We learn as much from what she conceals as what she reveals, but there is one secret that the novel teasingly withholds—her name: "Some thought it was Louise or Lucille because they used to see me take the usher's pencil and sign my tithe envelopes with L. Others from hearing people mention or call me, said it was El for Eleanor or Elvira. They're all wrong" (65). The secret of L's name gets cast as resistant both to spoken or written cues, and it is only late in the novel that she reveals that: "If your name is the subject of First Corinthians, chapter 13, it's natural to make it your business" (199). L answers the riddle of her name without ever speaking the word, and in this way Morrison constructs the two puns relevant to queer theory.

With the twin revelations of L's name and her ghostly state, readers should recognize that "Love is Dead." The ironies abound in this occluded pun, which only comes together late in the novel. But Morrison also invites us to consider that "Love," the character, does not ever speak her name, and this will put many readers in mind of Lord Alfred Douglas's reference to homosexuality as "the love that dare not speak its name." The latter pun associates *Love* and its titular narrator with problems of legibility, nomination, and visibility while the former calls into existential crisis the unnamable. If Love is dead, what of desire?[5]

Morrison, of course, has already powerfully explored the desires of the dead in *Beloved* and so the existential crisis in *Love* gives a nod to that earlier book while not fully answering its own questions about the limits of love. In its withholding of L's status as ghost, the novel, furthermore, does not allow us to fully consider the narrator's existential crisis until the end. Instead, we read L's early monologues without the knowledge of her ghostly state, and this will invite many readers to read L in relationship to stock figures of the judgmental and controlling black matriarchal figure, a figure that for many, as Roderick A. Ferguson points out, was associated with "[regulating of] a range of racialized gender and sexual formations" (125).

In his extraordinary reading of *Sula*, Ferguson documents how "[b]lack lesbian feminists' engagement with *Sula* [primarily in the 1970s and 80s] represented a process of negation in which an apparently non-political literary text about two black women became a resource for epistemological and political practices that could express alternatives to existing social movements" (126). In the closing argument of *Aberrations in Black: Toward a Queer of Color Critique*, Ferguson goes on to recognize our "historic moment [as] characterized by the normalization of racialized class formations," which require "modes of analysis that can address normativity as an object of inquiry and critique" (148). *Love* provides that critique: it is not just a compendium of representations of love but especially gives weight to nonnormative desires. It may begin with the judgmental voice of L, but it ends with this now contextualized by her own outlaw desires. Morrison artfully gives voice to the bookend expressions of judgment and outlaw desire through extralinguistic sound.

In the opening line of the novel, the enigmatic narrator hums. She hums because "[t]he women's legs are spread wide open" and she hums, we learn at the end of the novel, because she wants "[s]omething just for me" (202). But what is it that L wants and does it conform to normative desires? *Beloved*, as I have been arguing, prepares us for this kind of intense desire from the grave, but because Morrison now has the dead serve not simply as protagonist but narrator and because she withholds the key information of her ghostly status, it is the role of secrecy and not ambiguity that becomes key to understanding the role of the ghost in telling this story about love.

If Morrison seems to be exploring the trope of the closet, she also does much to disrupt what Marlon B. Ross powerfully critiques as a paradigm that too frequently erases race and other identities. Indeed, L's secrets are many and not just her queer desires. Ross highlights exactly this multivalent understanding of identity when he argues that "[w]hen the question of telling loved ones what they already know does become an issue, it can be judged as superfluous or perhaps even a distracting act, one subsidiary to the more important identifications of family, community, and race" (180). For Ross, "The question is not whether or not the closet can be made to apply to African Americans . . . [but] what happens when the closet is applied *as though* its operation has no dependence on racial-class thinking or no stake in acts of racial-class discrimination and exploitation" (182–83). With Ross's injunction in mind, it is important to investigate the way *Love* offers layers of secrets, layers of identity positions, rather than any "spectacle of the closet."[6]

Although there is no "spectacle of the closet" in *Love*, no scene recognizable as a coming out, Morrison layers the secret of queer desire with the ghostly closet, essentially upstaging the supposedly "central" queer trope with other identifications. This ghostly state, furthermore, comes with other secrets, such as the revelation of L's role in keeping Christine and Heed together. L, therefore, is invested with more than a universalizing queer identity, one that participates in myths of independence from community. Instead, L's "closet," if it can be called that, is tied very closely to African American cultural traditions that embrace, no matter with how much resistance, the black matriarch and her important role in keeping family and community together.[7]

In alternating L's humming narration with a third-person omniscience, *Love* does much to foreground issues of the individual and its relationship to community. Questions of presence/absence and present/past are highlighted through the different narrative points of view, which receive a visible marking through typography: L's words are in italics; the omniscient narration is not. But Morrison also collapses these points of view by sometimes placing both points of view in a shared chapter and other times offering single points of view in a single chapter. In this way, the novel provides a logical sign of narrative order only to disrupt it. In a similar fashion, it offers L as a central narrator only to place her centrality in question with the late revelation of her ghostly state, inviting readers to question her narration and its relationship to the present tense of the novel. Morrison invites us to question the ontological limits of omniscience.

L, however, does not simply serve as an agent of deconstruction but a trope for queer desire. Despite her claims to be discreet, she paints a sensuous picture of "inner thighs" and "tongues [working] all by themselves with no help from the mind" (3). This latter image of tongues working all by themselves may be a metaphor for loose talk, but in the context of the image of the brazen women's legs, it certainly invites a more libidinous reading. So, too, might we interpret the humming as not discretion but her irrepressible desires given sound. When she describes her humming as "words [dancing] in my head to the music in my mouth" (3) and "the movie music that comes along when the sweethearts see each other for the first time" (4), she invites a psychoanalytical reading. But L also describes her hum as "mostly below range, private; suitable for an old woman embarrassed by the world; her way of objecting to how the century turned out" (4). The irony, of course, is that L, as the reader's confidant and narrator, is not private with us. In confessing her discretions, she is not discreet. In describing her disdain for brazen women, she conveys the opposite. When the novel reaches its final line—"I want something back. Something just for me. So I join in. And hum"—L's disingenuous or perhaps unconscious notion of humming as a withholding gets recast as sensual engagement.

This repressed longing gains more weight next to the only passage where L speaks directly about a love object.

> The ocean is my man now. He knows when to rear and hump his back, when to be quiet and simply watch a woman. He can be devious, but he's not a false-hearted man. His soul is deep down there and suffering. I pay attention and know all about him. (100)

The ocean, typically associated with the feminine, never seems fully male or female in L's musings despite her claim that he is masculine. She offers several images of lovers coming out of the ocean, but it is only Celestial, Bill Cosey's sporting woman, who captures her eye as "she got up, naked as truth, and went into the waves" (106). L spends much time with her description of Celestial as "she stretched, raised her arms, and dove." The profundity of recollection is emphasized when she says, "I remember that arc better than I remember yesterday." As if having a sexual experience, L describes how she "held [her] breath as long as she did" and when "[Celestial] surfaced . . . I breathed again . . ." As if the reader is a witness to her displays of longing, L further states: "I don't deny her unstoppable good looks—they did arrest the mind . . . ," and in response to the unintelligible sound that Celestial makes as she "rose up slowly [from the sea] and took on the shape of the clouds dragging the moon," L tells us that "it was a sound I wanted to answer" (106).

In the final tableau at Bill Cosey's grave, L, despite the reader's recent awareness of her ghostly state, never seems more embodied when she is standing next to the ethereal Celestial and never seems more painfully audible than with her final hum. I am aware that Morrison repeatedly examines heterosexism's threat to female bonds, all female bonds, but what is important to note in *Love* is not just the invitation to read characters like L as queer but the queering of narrative form. L's hum, so full of desire and repression, is the gloss with which readers are invited to consider the limits of omniscience and the importance of embracing those whom it silences. Silence, in the slogan of AIDS activism, equals death, but in *Love* death does not equal silence.

L both reveals and conceals information, but the secret that may most relate to her queer identity concerns the love between Christine and Heed. In her opening disquisition on loose women, L refers to Christine and Heed as the "Cosey women." It is a phrase that puts the reader in mind of women cozying up to one another, but L distinguishes them as violent and sure to kill one another. This intense love/hate relationship between the two women becomes clearer with the significant interruption of their friendship when Bill Cosey marries the eleven-year-old Heed. Cosey's granddaughter had been a friend to Heed, but the relationship gets strained with this dramatic change, which essentially transforms her friend into step-grandmother. The opinionated narrator, who as head chef to the Cosey business has much to say, delivers a more poignant explanation of the problem: "The way I see it, she [Heed] belonged to Christine and Christine belonged to her" (105).

In explaining that Cosey "chose a girl already spoken for," L casts the childhood friendship as a romantic relationship, but many readers invested in myths of childhood innocence will dismiss L's characterization of the relationship. In the third-person narration of "Phantom," the final chapter of the novel, the account of the two girls does seem to highlight their innocence and how it ends with Heed's marriage to Bill Cosey, but the relationship, filtered through the third-person narration, remains somewhat romantic and not very different from L's characterization.

Moving between the past and the present, Morrison integrates the account of their early friendship/romance against the final confrontation/embrace of the two women. Brought together by Heed's mortal fall, the ghost of Heed says, "I wanted to be with you. Married to him, I thought I would be." And Christine confesses, "I wanted to go on your honeymoon." When Heed says that she wishes her friend was there at the honeymoon, Christine asks, "How was the sex?" (193). With the dialogue shifting from moments characterized by innocence and at other times experience, the adult women resort to "their most private code," which is given the name "Hey, Celestial" and used when they wish to "acknowledge a particularly bold, smart, risky thing" (188).

In this way, the most significant characters in the novel, along with L, are linked to the minor character Celestial, the one that Morrison almost named the novel after. "I think the idea of a wanton woman," Morrison argues, "is something that I may have inserted in almost all of the books. A kind of outlaw figure who is disallowed in the community because of whatever reason—her imagination or her activity or her status, whatever" (Houston 230). Morrison invests this figure with a freedom that the other women long for, and it may be envy of Celestial, a desire for her independence, that provides one of the many missing centers for the novel. If L's voice begins and ends the novel, her humming tries to "join" one of Celestial's "down-home raunchy songs that used to corrupt everybody on the dance floor" (201–02). It is as if L is asking to be corrupted. She may begin the novel announcing that she hums in order to be discreet, but at the end she is humming alongside the novel's most pronounced symbol of indiscretion.

L, in short, does not know herself. She may know something about the subject of First Corinthians, but she cannot be trusted to speak truthfully about herself. Love is not only dead but blind. The novel may present itself as a study of all sorts of love, as many critics have reasoned, but it is also very interested in exposing the ways that love resists knowing. By beginning and ending with an unreliable narrator, a narrator who does not merely try to fool the reader but who deceives herself, Morrison provides a study of love that announces its interest in masks. What better way to investigate love's prevarications than to provide a narrator who knows more about others than herself. She may announce that her man is the ocean, but the music she makes in the cemetery suggests a very different desire.

In imagining so much wisdom and so much repression as embodied by the dead, Morrison structures the forbidden desires as speaking across the divide of death and life. Junior, the greatest outsider in this community, accidentally hears L's name as Hell, and here we see Morrison continuing to have fun with L's name by linking "Love" to "Hell." Indeed, L, or Love, truly grows in this moment as the libidinal opposite to Celestial. But Junior is not correct: L is not Hell—not in it or of it. She is the most human ghost Morrison has created, defined by her judgments and desires and her inability to find even greater self-awareness in death. Her stasis serves to contrast the final transformation of the two characters, Heed and Christine, who are most defined by being stuck in the past and ruined by the actions of Bill Cosey.

In its exploration of the very limits of familial love, *Beloved*—so my previous chapter argues—depicts scenes of homosexual panic, displaced heterosexuality, and queer desires. But *Beloved* does not easily yield to as much as it resists queer readings, and those points of resistance may prove illustrative to a reading of *Love*. Although *Beloved* may introduce a ghost who is both child and adult, creating a wedding that strains simple equations of innocence with childhood, *Love* deploys the figure of the ghost in order to address cultural assumptions about childhood, innocence, and same-sex desire. In extending its reach into the limits of love, this later novel does not abandon familial love as the arena for queer desire but more powerfully uncouples innocence and childhood.[8]

Love takes enormous risks in challenging cultural beliefs about the nature of childhood as a period of innocence, and in this way it provides a narrative companion to recent scholarly work done on childhood, such as James Kincaid's fine intervention in myths of childhood as bound to innocence and Kathryn Bond Stockton's fascinating exploration of childhood as queer.[9] At the heart of *Love* is a desire to investigate the myriad assumptions, definitions, and conceptions of love, and so it would make sense that the novel would find the most extreme articulation of that in the figure of the queer child. This is the project *Beloved* only hints at addressing but finds it fullest exploration in Morrison's eighth novel.

Near the end of *Beloved*, Denver's soliloquy chapter may provide the most compelling excuse for Beloved's behavior as the actions of "a greedy ghost" that "needed a lot of love, which was only natural, considering" (209). Here and throughout the novel, Beloved's status as murdered child is kept in the reader's mind. This notion of the "natural" haunts the novel, which tries to explain the unimaginable (i.e., infanticide) through the natural (i.e., mother love). In many ways, *Beloved* may participate in a larger cultural conversation about the nature of motherhood and childhood. The counterdiscourse to the cult of motherhood has grown stronger over the years and childhood has also been queered. I would like to argue that *Beloved* haunts *Love* exactly through this conversation about the naturalness of motherhood. *Love*, we might say, queers motherhood and childhood both.

In moving toward its dramatic ending, *Love* reveals not one character as queer but three. L, as I have argued earlier, reveals her desire for Celestial and articulates her need for "[s]omething just for me." This articulation, more importantly, appears on the heels of the scene between Christine and Heed, a scene that is filtered through Romen's point of view as he searches for them in the resort: "Both look asleep but only one is breathing. One is lying on her back, left arm akimbo; the other has wrapped the right arm of the dead one around her own neck and is snoring into the other's shoulder" (195). It is an intimate scene between the living and the dead, and Morrison follows this intimate tableau with a last conversation between the women. In this conversation they are speaking to one another as they could not do before one dies. Or is it the secret language, which they call "idagay," that allows them to address the hurts of the past and reawaken their intense love for one another? Both death and their secret language should remind us of the puns built into L's name, the queer tropes that bind L to Christine and Heed. But it is only Christine and Heed who can move forward, exorcise the spirit of Cosey, and rediscover love on the other side of this exorcist:

> He took all my childhood away from me, girl.
> He took all of you away from me. (194)

This exchange, full of confession and love, takes place just as the two women are "exhausted, drifting toward a maybe permanent sleep" (192). In this short exchange, Morrison evokes their innocence and queerness at the same time, providing the greatest risk in exploring the limits of love through the queer child.

Chapter 5

ᵔᵕ

Music

Love Haunts *Song of Solomon*

There are musics that haunt us like a phantom limb.

—Nathaniel Mackey, *From a Broken Bottle
Traces of Perfume Still Emanate*

the isle is full of noises,
Sounds and sweet airs, that give delight, and hurt not.
Sometimes a thousand twangling instruments
Will hum about mine ears; and sometime voices,
That, if I then had wak'd after long sleep,
Will make me sleep again . . .

—Shakespeare, *The Tempest*, III.ii.133–38

In *Different Drummers: Rhythm and Race in the Americas*, Martin Munro contributes to the wonderful work done on music as a cultural system by examining how race is marked by rhythm across the Americas. In delineating his field of interest, Munro chooses to view rhythm as "a malleable concept that may be applied to other patterns of repetition and regularity, be they natural (the rhythms of the body, time, and the seasons) or manufactured (rhythms of work, machinery, industrial time, everyday life" (6). He might easily have extended his reach to consider the revenant as rhythm, asking how narratives of haunting deploy African American musical forms. Rhythm, Munro's book carefully delineates, is bound to spiritual experiences and subjectivity, and the ghost as repetition, a rhythmic return, offers an interesting parallel. But what

69

is the thing lost and how do we register it if it floats free from bodies, appears as a disembodied ghostly emanation? What happens when music, sound, rhythm represent supernatural forces?

This chapter moves beyond traditional understandings of ghosts to ask whether Morrison's representations of the ghostly emanation might be fruitfully considered part of the "spectral turn" that Jeffrey Weinstock sees as arising "out of a general postmodern suspicion of meta-narratives" (5). Full of sound and rhythm, which neither precede the entrance of an apparition nor indicate anything outside of itself, the ghostly emanation is unlike conventional representations of an eerie and haunting music, tied as they usually are to visible or invisible ghosts, and instead the music circulates and hovers over the protagonist as neither a good nor evil force. It is as if this music serves to counterpoint the unspeakable as well as indicate something outside the sublunary violence and trauma uniquely endured by the embattled black men in Morrison's fiction.

. It is difficult to resist popular notions of music as freeing and ask, instead, whether there might be something more complicated happening with Morrison's ghostly musical emanations. What are these emanations and how do they resist being read as ghosts? In some of her most provocative scenes of violence, Morrison presents sound and music as a ghost that is not issuing from a specific dead person but floating free of bodies; neither visible nor invisible as a singular object of haunting but disembodied and dispersed but also otherworldly. Although this music seems to have no attached source, it is tempting to read it—as we might interpret a ghost—as full of spiritual need and unfinished business. These jazz sounds, these ghostly emanations, are as complex and contradictory as the more embodied ghosts of the titular Beloved and L, but they point to a musical heritage—blues, jazz, spirituals—full of subversion.

Literary representations of the spirit world more often than not imagine a single embodied ghost, one where the body may be invisible but still imagined as fully unified, but in giving expression to something much less singular—more like a jazz ensemble—Morrison expands our cultural mythology of the visitation. These unique expressions of the spirit world might be thought of as a Greek chorus (an appropriate contrast to the solitary voice of most ghosts), but it is a chorus deconstructed by the complex meanings of jazz. Morrison—with her great knowledge and interest in the classics coupled with her great affection and respect for jazz—may be provocatively reinventing the Greek chorus as jazz orchestra. Although the Greek chorus offers a homogenous voice, one that may offer commentary and provide background information, the jazz ensemble suggests the possibility of individual expression and interaction. While the association with a Greek chorus encourages us to think of Morrison's ghostly emanations as communal and unified voicings, the jazz inflections complicate these assumptions and encourage associations with difficulty, dissonance, and contradiction. With such different forces behind it, the ghostly emanation may finally resist interpretation and that may be the point: music resists what language seems to offer, answers. This is the resistance to metanarratives that Weinstock highlights, going on to argue that the "usefulness of the ghost in the revisioning of history from alternate, competing perspectives is one reason why tales of the spectral have assumed such prominence in contemporary ethnic American literature" (5). Morrison, of course, is an extremely important voice in this wave of spectral literature, mentioned if not fully explored in nearly every monograph on spectral America, though scholars primarily focus on *Beloved*. It should not surprise us to find ghosts appearing throughout her novels, even in the disembodied ghostly emanation that appears, at first pass, merely like ornament, background music, or a metaphorical conceit for conveying emotion.

Hardly legible as ghost, these emanations visit some of Morrison's most embattled males—Paul D from *Beloved*, Romen from *Love*, and Milkman from *Song of Solomon*—as they enter their greatest moments of crisis. These scenes specifically position the individual male in crisis against a backdrop of "the male gang," a phrase that needs to be placed in quotes to highlight its fictive nature, tied as it is to racist stereotypes of black youth that the media has always promulgated with great vigor and promoted with great blindness during the years Morrison would have been writing *Song of Solomon* and *Beloved*. Morrison's representations of black men in crisis may be seen as a response to some of these myths of black gangs.[1] Morrison not only examines the allegiances of black male youth, sometimes allowing them to step within the sphere of myth, but also counterpoints narratives of black youth with the haunting sadism of white male gangs, such as the white guards who terrorize Paul D in *Beloved* and the white youth, two teenage boys and a girl, who terrorized, brutalized, and murdered Emmett Till. Morrison begins *Home* with her most clearly defined scene of lynching, directly representing an all-too-common occurrence that haunts America to this day and stands as a painful and ironic counterpoint to media stereotypes of black gangs. Morrison, this chapter argues, deploys the ghostly emanation to directly complicate our responses to the idea of gangs and our facile responses to male violence.

It is not coincidental that Morrison explores gangs and popularized fears of gangs in her most fully realized male characters. Never one to shrink from large cultural concerns, Morrison explores black male identity through different conceptions of what it means to be in a gang, and in creating some of her most graphically horrific scenes she seems to ask, through the ghostly emanation, what kind of spirit will speak to these embattled males as they struggle to hold on to their humanity. Music in these scenes marks a certain transcendence from the physical world while reminding us of sound's ephemeral, indeed ghostly, nature. Furthermore, these ghostly emanations, which counter certain silences, queer the text by offering not commentary or judgment of homophobia but sound unhinged from the limitations of words. "Sounds," Munro emphasizes, "are the most important stimuli that human beings experience, but they are also the most evanescent, dissipating quickly into nothing. . . . Sound is therefore something that is not only heard but felt, with palpable physical effects" (4). Upon venturing into the most violent male worlds, Morrison turns to the ghostly emanation to "speak" to the most unspeakable acts and to register, through music, cultural anxieties tied to homophobia. She offers music as an emotional touchstone for the reader if not her protagonists in the scene of a chain gang in *Beloved*, a gang rape in *Love*, and gang violence in *Song of Solomon*. These scenes, however, cannot be fully understood without first considering the dominant strain of analysis that reads Morrison's music as salutary. It is this healing music that haunts (or offers the trace) to the ghostly emanations that overlay violence and virulent homophobia.

The quintessential text of music as salutary can be found at the end of *Beloved* when thirty women come to exorcise the spirit of Sethe's murdered child. The music these women create is healing, and scholars have noted the way this passage sings to its readers. It is not surprising that this scene holds such power for scholars of aural aspects of text. Here Morrison empowers women and community with a godlike force capable of creating a "wave of sound wide enough to sound the deep water and knock the pods off chestnut trees." The near-miss of "Gods" instead of "pods" may put readers in mind of how these women—with their "wave of sound"—provide a spiritual force outside traditional religious institutions not unlike the Clearing sermons. Indeed, this "wave of sound" causes Sethe to "[tremble] like the baptized in its wash" (261). Scholars have mined this scene for polyphony, black sermonic traditions, and jazz innovations, and the passage has been seen as affirming the power of sound and song.

In discussing the healing qualities of black music, Morrison has specifically stated, "My parallel is always the music . . . the music is the mirror that gives me the necessary clarity" (Gilroy, "Living Memory" 181), and scholars have built upon Morrison's argument to further link her music to communal empowerment, personal transformation, and even transcendence. "Any lack of musical expression," as Aoi Mori states, "seems to have a serious effect on Morrison's characters, preventing them from developing an identity and cultivating a communal relationship with other people" (91); and "[m]usic in Morrison's writing," according to Roxanne Reed, "[w]hen coupled with the maternal . . . [brings] communal salvation" (68). But what about when music is coupled with male violence? Do our preconceived notions about the productive function of music—and black musical forms in specific—conceal as much as they reveal? How do we make sense of doves cooing to rape? And how does the ghostly intrusion of a trumpet blare signal a force that does not heal but addresses the sexual politics of masculine communities? How does the disembodied refrain "Everybody wants the life of a black man" speak not only of aggressive desire but same-sex desire?

In contrast to the thirty women who sing a communal and healing song, we might consider Paul D in the chain gang from the same novel. Alan J. Rice has argued that the "best illustration of Morrison's acknowledgment of the sturdy strength of the musical tradition and its central place in her people's history comes in *Beloved* when Paul D. is imprisoned in a chain gang" (163). Rice considers the syntactic parallelisms, call-and-response patterns, and collective musicking of this scene, exploring the "structure [of] her text" with its meaning. For Maggie Sale, the chain gang scene is "analogous to a single song," one that creates a progression not different from the blues, when it refers to " 'one thousand feet of the best hand-forged chain in Georgia' [which] becomes 'dance two-step to the music of hand-forged iron' [which] becomes 'they chain-danced over the fields' " (107–08). Both critics locate much of the musical work in repetition, call and response, and improvisation, and both scholars see the text as empowering in its use of African American musical traditions.

Is Morrison in danger of aestheticizing violence in her descriptions of the prisoners "[dancing] two-step to the music of hand-forged iron" (108), "Singing love songs to Mr. Death" (109), and listening to the

" 'Hiiii!' at dawn and the 'Hoooo!' when evening came"? In associating her most violent scenes with music, Morrison relies on African American cultural traditions to provide a more complicated association that resists aestheticization. For example, the musical references invite readers to consider the subversive force of slave songs and spirituals, which contained the seeds of rebellion, resistance, and counternarrative.

In *The Songs Became the Stories: The Music in African-American Fiction (1970–2005)*, Robert Catalliotti reminds us that "the insider codes and double entendres of lyrics and tales enabled communication and organization, despite the imposition of rigid restrictions, and ultimately were tools of subversion and resistance used for the attainment of freedom" (xi). Readers aware of this well-documented history will associate the music in the chain gang scene with something far more important than ornament or even tool for conveying emotion but a tie to ancestry, community, humanity.

Beloved indeed is interested in not only humanity but specifically how black male slaves fought to retain their masculinity, their sense of being men. The flashbacks to Sweet Home, for example, present various scenes where men are emasculated by—among other things—their constrained relationships with women and, ultimately, the ownership of wives and mothers by white men. Halle witnesses the rape of his wife, and Paul D has a bit placed in his mouth and sees that a rooster has more freedom than he. These scenes of degradation, tied as they are to emasculation, culminate in Paul D's failed escape from Sweet Home and his ultimate restriction and victimization in a chain gang. This scene, which follows the chapter focused on Beloved's queer embrace of Sethe (see chapter 3), represents Paul D's experience as being buried alive: he and forty-five men "share that grave calling itself quarters" (106). It is a short but powerful scene that serves to explain one of the things, if not the most haunting thing, that Paul D places and keeps locked "into the tobacco tin lodged in his chest" that "nothing in this world could pry . . . open" (113).

Paul D, haunted as he is by the things locked in his chest, serves as a foil for Sethe, who has a more singular and embodied ghost. With the tobacco tin envisioned as part of him, Paul D houses his own ghost, serves as his own ghost, and gets likened to a ghost throughout the novel. For Sethe, he brings "another kind of haunting" (96), and his eighteen years of freedom are marked by an endless walking that marks him with the restlessness of a ghost. But it is in the chain gang scene that Morrison most likens him to the living dead: "Life was dead" (109).

Morrison details the living tomb that Paul D and forty-five other men must endure, likening their experience to being buried alive. The cages sit inside ditches, "three feet of open trench in front of him with anything that crawled or scurried welcome to share that grave calling itself quarters" (106). When the men escape, they are likened to "the unshriven dead, zombies on the loose," and they "trusted the rain and the dark" (110). When they appear alive at all, it is when they are laboring and singing work songs.

When the men are permitted to "rise up off their knees," they "dance the two-step to the music of hand-forged iron," and "[w]ith a sledge hammer in his hands and Hi Man's lead, the men got through. They sang it out and beat it up, garbling the words so they could not be understood; tricking the words so their syllables yield up other meanings" (108). When they are back in their underground cages, the boxes that separate each man from the other, the chain links the men together. The chain, the very tool of enslavement, also becomes the conduit for communication, and their escape is characterized as not unlike the music, the rhythmic awareness, that ties them together when working, the "power of the chain" binding them together and allowing them to follow Hi Man's lead. In coming out of this living tomb as zombies, Morrison reaches for a metaphor to describe not only their past but their future, but she also ties Paul D to Sethe as also haunted, though with a difference. She provides a symbol of Paul D's self-haunting as the "tobacco tin lodged in his chest" (113). Introduced earlier, the chapter devoted to the chain gang ends with a reminder of Paul D's personal symbol of haunting: "It was some time before he could put Alfred, Georgia, Sixo, school teacher, Halle, his brothers, Sethe, Mister, the taste of iron, the sight of butter, the smell of hickory, notebook paper, one by one, into the tobacco tin lodge in his chest. By the time he got to 124 nothing in this world could pry it open" (113). Paul D's tin box, which becomes a part of him, serves as a metaphor of how he will carry his haunting inside, unwilling to share it with anyone.[2]

Of the list of memories, the first—Alfred, Georgia—refers as vaguely as possible to Paul D's time in the chain gang. The horrors of the chain gang, however, begin with a surprisingly twentieth-century image of anxiety—male rape. The scene alludes to the white male guards forcing the black male prisoners to perform fellatio at gunpoint. "Want some breakfast, nigger?" one guard asks, and the text never fully describes the act, except by omission: "Occasionally a kneeling man chose gunshot in his head as the price, maybe, of taking a bit of foreskin with him to

Jesus" (108). This, of course, emphasizes the cost that some men will pay to avoid further dehumanization, particularly this culturally symbolic, extreme form of emasculation. It is significant that Morrison does not show Paul D subjected to this ultimate emasculation. We learn that he is spared only because he vomits when it is his turn. As a memory that haunts him, we never learn whether he was spared future attacks.

The rapes, however, are presented as continuous, both indiscriminate violations (i.e., "they waited for the whim of a guard, or two, or three") and also sexual acts directed at individuals (i.e., "Or maybe all of them wanted it. Wanted it from one prisoner in particular or none—or all"). Morrison chooses an odd image (or, more importantly, sound) to convey the haunting qualities of homosexual rape. The first of three references introduces the initial rape: "Chain-up completed, they knelt down. The dew, more likely than not, was mist by then. Heavy sometimes and if the dogs were quiet and just breathing you could hear doves. Kneeling in the mist they waited for the whim of a guard . . ." (107). The doves, however, bring neither song nor consolation, and in the next reference Paul D hears the sound of the guard as he rapes the man next to him as "soft grunts so like the doves' " (108). If the unlikely analogy creates power through defamiliarization, it also foreshadows a more peaceful future and perhaps may even suggest a supernatural force ready to intercede in the horrors of the chain gang.[3] The scene's final reference to the doves follows the empowering description of men singing work songs in order to make "them think the next sunrise would be worth it," and it is no longer sound of the doves but the absence of the doves from sight that foreshadows a release from this inhuman existence. As with so many of Morrison's evocations of ghosts, there is a logical explanation for the disappearance of the doves—"it rained"—but the disappearance, and perhaps their earlier cooing, foreshadows a release from this living death.

If we read the doves as a ghostly emanation, their presence does not really seem to affect the prisoners. It is, instead, a counterpoint to the music the men sing. The music the men sing offers them a tool for emotional release, escape really, but it also trains them to hear the rhythm of their shared experience and later their shared effort to escape together: "For one lost, all lost" (110). As a bearer of history, the music of the work song, full of subversion, is a powerful enough ghost, but the sound of the doves, which after all, gets cast as something the men hear, is also full of the subversive, haunting in its indecipherability and ghostly in its effect on readers who must make sense of the incongruity of "doves" and "rape." If this incongruous sound, briefly referenced three times in the scene, serves to indicate something otherworldly, it does not do so in the form of a traditional ghost—neither embodied nor purposeful. When Morrison refers to the doves in a later section of the novel, it becomes clearer as a symbol of dangerous desire: "Listening to the doves in Alfred, Georgia, and having neither the right nor the permission to enjoy it because in that place mist, doves, sunlight, copper dirt, moon—everything belonged to the men who had the guns" (162). In his mind, Paul D hears the guard's "soft grunts so like the doves'" but also vomits from the sight of the rape. Tied as it is to the earlier cooing the guards make while raping the slaves, the later reference to doves more fully explains that "these 'men' who made even vixen laugh could, if you let them, stop you from hearing doves or loving moonlight. So you protected yourself and loved small" (162). It is one of Morrison's most incongruous and risky metaphors for love, the sound of doves' cooing that is not unlike the sound of white guards raping slaves. In his constricted world, Paul D almost loses his mind, conflates this beautiful sound with this horrific act, but the doves also serve as a ghostly emanation, sound floating over the scene and later disappearing, a supernatural force that hovers over the violence and allows Paul D to understand more fully love (and the forces against love). He recalls this greater understanding as Sethe tells her story of escape, and he can relate to it, knowing that it is important "to get to a place where you could love anything you chose—not to need permission for desire—well now, that was freedom" (162).

If the doves indicate a ghostly emanation, one that indirectly raises the specter of homophobia, tropes of emasculation, and limitations to the meaning and the object choice of desire, it does so rather indirectly. Morrison, however, more fully represents the ghostly emanation in other scenes of male violence, though switching from the depiction of a white male gang, the guards in *Beloved*, to black gangs in *Love* and *Song of Solomon*. Never one to shrink from large cultural concerns, Morrison explores black male identity through different conceptions of what it means to be in a gang, and in creating some of her most graphically horrific scenes she seems to ask, through the ghostly emanation, what kind of spirit will speak to these embattled males as they struggle to hold on to their humanity.

In *Love*, Morrison creates the scene of a gang rape with shocking graphic detail, and the viewpoint shifts from the novel's initial narrator, L. Many readers, however, will be surprised to discover that it does not shift to the point of view of the victim of the rape but instead to one of the male aggressors. Few writers are willing to risk such an unsympathetic point of view, but Morrison actually asks us to consider Romen's humanity alongside his complicity. Although Morrison has him stop short of fully participating in the rape with his "belt unbuckled" and "anticipation ripe," he is a witness to and therefore complicit in the rape of Faye by six others (46). Morrison not only asks us to sympathize with Romen, but she continues to place Romen in ethical positions throughout the rest the novel, inviting the reader to consider his struggle against evil forces.

In the rape scene, Morrison asks us to consider masculinity as on a journey toward two very different destinies, "the Romen he'd always known he was: chiseled, dangerous, loose" (46) and the one who emerges at the moment he "punked out" and rescued pretty Faye. Romen can only belong to one of two groups—the violent male gang or the larger community of life and humanity. Morrison represents one of her most important male characters caught in a battle between various versions of himself, one who is bound to an unwritten contract with Theo and his gang (the pressure of peers) but also one who has not steeled himself against the humanity of others, specifically women. It is, therefore, significant that Morrison represents this youth's ghost as a disembodied musical emanation, but not necessarily with his best interests in mind. Music, in this evocation, does not necessarily have Romen's best interests in mind.

When Romen steps up to take Theo's place, he "watched in wonder as his hands moved to the headboard. The knot binding her right wrist came undone as soon as he touched it and her hand fell over the bedside." This is a scene of a disassociated sensibility. Romen, who provides the point of view for this section, "watches in wonder as his hands moved to the headboard." When he finishes executing this seemingly unwilled release, he "picked up her shoes, high-heeled, an X of pink leather across the front," and he then hears the "whooping laughter—that came first—then the jokes and finally the anger." Not unlike the doves cooing, Morrison highlights the interpretation of the listener. As Romen breaks with the gang in order to help this stranger, Romen leaves the world of sound only to feel betrayed by sight: "He thought her name was Faye or Faith and was about to say something when suddenly he couldn't stand the sight of her." In filtering everything through Romen's point of view, Morrison heightens the visual and auditory world for Romen, but it is the auditory world that most threatens to betray him.

As Romen walks away from Faye and her friends, he heard "their shrieks, their concern, as cymbal clashes, stressing, but not competing with, the trumpet blast of what Theo had called him: the worst name there was; the one word whose reverberation, once airborne, only a fired gun could end" (47). Morrison does not tell us what this name is (one of the many silences she creates), but instead describes it as a trumpet blast that even the cymbal clashes of concern could not compete with. The passage emphasizes that the cymbals do not (or perhaps cannot) compete with the trumpet blast, and the irony is that Morrison does not provide the actual word and instead represents the epithet, which she silences—or rather substitutes with pure sound, the trumpet blast. It is tempting to read the trumpet as a phallic image, but more importantly it serves to counterpoint an evocation of blaring sound against silences in order to create a scene fraught with auditory extremes. It is difficult not to read the "one word . . . only a fired gun could end" as an epithet for a homosexual man—"faggot" or "queer." In having Romen imagine himself as having "punked out," the prison slang ("punk") for another man's bitch, Morrison already suggests that the scene will address homophobia, but in removing the actual epithet and substituting the sound of a trumpet blast, Morrison imagines music and sound as a ghostly force, one with the power to influence Romen.

Morrison suggests dramatic shifts in volume as the scene counterpoints Romen's interior monologue—full of rhetorical questions and inner musings—against the repeated references to the gang as a trumpet. There are six references in all, of which here are three: "even when he didn't stare back or meet their eyes at all, the trumpet spoke his name"; "the trumpet spat"; "there was another word in the trumpet's repertoire" (48). The antiphony between the derisive horns in his head and a troubled interiority serves to develop Romen as a bifurcating character. Morrison provides an explicit description of two Romens: "[a] fake Romen, preening over a stranger's bed . . . tricked by the real Romen, who was still in charge here in his own bed, forcing him to hide under a pillow and shed girl tears."

Ending not with either Romen but the trumpet sound, the internalized hatred of the gang turned into a brassy jazz explosion, Morrison resists closure. This description of the sound, which Morrison associates with violence, also comes in the form of a fragment, which further refuses closure: "The trumpet stuttering in his head" (49). With this final repetition, Morrison seems to suggest a continuing tension more than finality, and she most surely invites readers—with the six repetitions of the trumpet sound—to imagine the repetition to have a life of its own and not merely to provide evocative metaphors for the gang's taunts.

In associating the trumpet sound with the bifurcation of Romen, Morrison invites us to hear certain jazz innovations as well as the multiplicity of voices. She perhaps even invites her readers to enter the silences between the trumpet braying and Romen's interiority in order to allow us into the "gaps and silences" as a way for readers to consider whether there can truly be two Romens and, perhaps, whether one of them is worthy of our forgiveness. In a novel that begins with a humming, disapproving narrator, Morrison represents the most disturbing act of violence against women with a classic jazz sound, one associated with violence. In its evocation of trumpets stuttering against cymbals clashing against the silent musings of "the real Romen who had sabotaged the newly chiseled, dangerous one" (49), Morrison invites us to hear a jazz that is difficult, perhaps cacophonous, full of surprising shifts from silence to explosive sounds, expressive of something that is neither healing nor liberating but a battleground, one full of ghostly soundings.

The progression of the six descriptive phrases for the trumpet sound, which itself enacts a sort of improvisation that Maggie Sale might call a simple song, and the counterpointing of Romen's interiority against these sounds, which create wild shifts in the reader's impression of the aural qualities of the text, feel very much like the jazz aesthetic that Paul Gilroy argues involves the audience/reader. In confronting the painful story of gang rape, Morrison finds an alternative to asking readers to identify with either victim or perpetrator; she invites readers to enter a jazz rendering of ricocheting extremes of experience while imagining forces that act upon a young man, contest for his soul and not always with the most virtuous purposes. It is a narrative technique that she uses in many of her novels: asking musical forms and analogies to provide a model for breaking with a single point of view, a central voice, and even a simple ethical viewpoint.

Morrison may have first considered the disembodied vocal emanation in *Song of Solomon*, which also features a gang, the men of Shalimar, and their attack on Milkman. As Milkman first enters the town store, he is aware that "he'd struck a wrong note." Although Milkman understands that he has insulted them, he continues to offend them.

Morrison represents small-town gang violence as a response to Milk-man's northern ways, which "was telling them that they weren't men" (266). The quick back-and-forth dialogue of the dozens shows Milkman as fully willing to counter their statements about Northern pricks with his own sexualized bravado. When the men make insinuations about how the Northern "pricks is different," the first man stating that they are "[w]ee, wee little," Milkman does not back down.

> "I wouldn't know," said Milkman. "I never spent much time smacking my lips over another man's dick." Everybody smiled, including Milkman. It was about to begin.
>
> "What about his ass hole? Ever smack your lips over that?"
>
> "Once," said Milkman. "When a little young nigger made me mad and I had to jam a Coke bottle up his ass."
>
> "What'd you use a bottle for? Your cock wouldn't fill it?"
>
> "It did. After I took the Coke bottle out. Filled his mouth too."
>
> "Prefer mouth, do you?"
>
> "If it's big enough, and ugly enough, and belongs to a ignorant motherfucker who is about to get the livin shit whipped out of him." (267)

Milkman survives the fight, though "he probably would have had his throat cut if two women hadn't come running in screaming," which provided "enough lull for Mr. Solomon to interrupt the fight" (268). With this scene emphasizing Milkman's mouth and throat as agents of aggression ("he'd struck a wrong note") and an object of violation ("stick that cocksucker"), *Song of Solomon* presents Milkman, who after all got his name from inappropriate sucking on his mother's breast, as in danger because of his mouth. It is, however, in the next scene with the village elders that Milkman as voice, as throat, comes to a climax. Still bleeding, he is invited to go hunting. At King Walker's gas station, the men decide to dress him in appropriate clothes. Having survived the fight with the younger men of Shalimar, Milkman subjects himself to this dressing—with the men "laughing all the while at his underwear, fingering his vest" (271). In contrast to the scene with his peers, this scene with the village elders with its more intimate physicality never gains the same sexual tension. It is only on the hunt, when Guitar arrives, that Milkman's throat and physicality are again emphasized.

In contrast to the previous scene with his peers, the sexualized potential of the scene with the elders never develops until they enter the woods and Milkman recognizes that these men are in touch with the natural world in a way that he is not. "What did [Calvin] hear that made him know something unexpected had happened some two miles—perhaps more—away, and that that something was a different kind of prey, a bobcat?" (277). In this scene, Morrison continues to find analogies in music, and the text announces its aural qualities as Milkman tries to make sense of the "low *howm howm* that sounded like a string bass imitating a bassoon [that] meant something the dogs [understood] and executed. And the dogs spoke to men: single-shot barks—evenly spaced and widely spaced . . ." (278). There are so many sounds that Milkman must make sense of: "those rapid tumbling barks, the long sustained yells, the tuba sounds, the drumbeat sounds, the low liquid *howm howm*, the reedy whistles, the thin *eeeee*'s of a cornet, the *unh unh unh* bass chords. It was all language. Before things were written down. Language in the time when men and animals did talk to one another" (278).

This scene presents language and music and extralinguistic sound all in a rush and overlapping. Milkman's survival in the previous scene depended on his physical strength, but here it is specifically linked to his ability to translate and decode sound, music, and language all together. The scene culminates with Milkman metaphorically as instrument when Guitar slips a wire around his neck and Milkman relaxes for a second and "in the instant it took to surrender to the overwhelming melancholy he felt the cords [note the pun on musical chords] of his struggling neck muscles relax" until he is filled with "such sadness to be dying, leaving this world at the fingertips of his friend" (279). In this tableau, Guitar places his "fingertips" on his friend as if Milkman were a guitar to be played, and then his friend wraps a wire (A guitar string? A visual pun on this friend as weapon?) around his friend's neck as if he were ready to play him like an instrument, but Milkman—in this powerful scene laden with pure sounds and musical references—decides to live and not simply be played. If this scene serves to represent Milkman's will to live, a noticeable transformation, the third scene presents a startling proxy for his near death, and Morrison delays the sense of transformation with a strange music.

The hunt yields not the death of Milkman but a bobcat. In the ritual of skinning the bobcat, Morrison interweaves italicized refrains that begin with "Everybody wants a black man's life." Indeed, the refrain positions Milkman's interior monologue as identifying with the cat, which the men castrate and skin from "scrotum to jaw" (282). In the extended scene of skinning, Morrison includes nearly a dozen italicized phrases, which might be viewed as floating lyrics. One odd phrase even signifies on a 1968 hit by the First Edition (not the New Edition): "I Just Dropped In to See (What Condition My Condition Was In)." In Morrison's rendering of the lyric, the singular "my" is replaced with the plural "our," signifying on the individualism of the Kenny Rogers song. "It's the condition our condition is in" comments upon blackness and not merely the condition of one black man. Morrison, furthermore, does not make clear whether these italicized lines or lyrics are Milkman's interior thoughts or a more distanced musical riff upon his emotional state as he watches the bobcat eviscerated.

Susan Neal Mayberry's wonderful reading of *Song of Solomon* suggests that the words belong to Guitar, and I don't find this inconsistent with my reading of the disembodied nature of the lyrics. They might be thought of as voicings from Guitar, though not specifically bodied but hovering over Milkman almost as a ghost. Other readers may interpret these phrases through the prevailing conventions for interiority, even seeing Guitar's voice as internalized by Milkman, but this also allows something more communal in nature. The ghost, in other words, need not seem distinct from the protagonist or his antagonist, but I would suggest that Morrison invites us to hear something bigger than interiority, something more communal and ghostly. These jazz voicings point to contradictions and mysteries related to love, life, and the black man. They stand-out not only as italicized text but also free of dialogue tags and floating separate from the scene of the men carving the carcass of the bobcat. "*It is about love*," one line reads, "*What else but love?*" (282), but perhaps the song's greatest gesture to rhythm comes in the final refrain "*What else?*" (282). This short question appears in three separate lines with the last line repeating the refrain three times and never fully feeling as if it solely belongs to Milkman or Guitar but something bigger than the two of them. It is as if the lyrics—not really part of the scene but somehow strangely related—function to represent not just Milkman's disassociated state, and not just Guitar's quest for justice, but something radically different—a larger communal chorus.

If this is Milkman's or Guitar's voice, it shows each of them with greater self-reflection than ever. It is more believable that this question represents a larger communal sentiment, one that lends itself to the title of Susan Neal Mayberry's book *Can't I Love What I Criticize? The*

Masculine and Morrison. Indeed, many readers will first come to the monograph and assume the quote to be Morrison's sentiment rather than Milkman's or Guitar's, and I would like to suggest all of these possibilities, a vision of communal jazz sounding. If we go one step further and see this communal voicing as a ghost, the scene makes more sense as a queering of the male community at Shalimar, a recognition of the homosocial world of the men as they reach in and give the heart of the bobcat to Milkman. The homophobia that drives the fight in the town store highlights one of the social forces that Morrison continues to explore as she represents Milkman's acceptance into the community. The scene counterpoints the direct statements of the jazz soundings ("*It's about love. What else?*") to the highly symbolic and suggestive ritual with the men and the bobcat.

> Now Luther went back into the stomach cavity and yanked the entrails out altogether. They sucked up like a vacuum through the hole that was made at the rectum. . . .
> "What are you going to do with it?" asked Milkman.
> "Eat him!"
> A peacock soared away and lit on the hood of the blue Buick. (282–83)

A suitable break in the highly symbolic language of the scene, it is the ghostly emanation that offers commentary but no answers. The final stuttering line ("*What else? What else? What else?*") is not unlike the out-of-body stuttering that Morrison creates in *Love*'s violent scene of a gang rape. But the stuttering in *Love*, the trumpet blast, is even more disturbing as a call to the "dangerous, newly chiseled" Romen while the "*What else?*" that hovers over Milkman already seems sympathetic, though haunting.

I began this chapter with the argument that Morrison's representations of gang violence provide a contrast to the usual subject of scholarly approaches to Morrison's music and that they do not, rightly so, represent music as empowering, healing, or communal. The gang fight in *Song of Solomon* and the gang rape in *Love* may not be scenes that invite us to consider the beauty of music but instead its unflinching willingness to confront the harshest realities and the most painful subjects. Morrison has argued that "classical music satisfies and closes. Black music does not do that. Jazz always keeps you on the edge. There is no final chord. There may be a long cord, but no final chord.

And it agitates you" (McKay 411). If these scenes of male violence in Morrison's novels are to be seen as something more than unflinching, something—for example—transformational, it is in their ability to agitate. This is the participatory reading that Morrison expects and the music that agitates for it.

Chapter 6

∾

Voice

Song of Solomon Haunts *Jazz*

Being haunted draws us affectively, sometimes against our will and
always a bit magically, into the structure of feeling of a reality we
come to experience, not as cold knowledge, but as a transforma-
tive recognition.

—Avery Gordon, *Ghostly Matters:*
Haunting and the Sociological Imagination

There can be little doubt that shouting is a survival of the African
"possession" by the gods. In Africa it is sacred to the priesthood or
acolytes, in America it has become generalized. The implication is
the same, however, it is a sign of special favor from the spirit that
it chooses to drive out the individual consciousness temporarily and
use the body for its expression.

—Zora Neale Hurston, *The Sanctified Church*

Song of Solomon makes voice its central if not obsessive concern, layering one voice upon another, allowing each to haunt, echo, and queer
one another, building to a dramatic ending. In the history of the novel,
few endings do as much to stop short of the fulfillment of the reader's
expectation for closure, creating a vacuum for the many voices of the
novel to enter. Milkman, the protagonist, certainly hovers closely to the
narrator's voice, which follows his point of view, but the narrator's voice
also distinguishes itself with commentary on the nature of flight, the
great theme of the novel. Milkman's great-grandfather, Shalimar, one

of the most important ghosts in the novel, can also be heard in the final sentence: "For now [Milkman] knew what Shalimar knew: If you surrendered to the air, you could *ride* it" (337). Pilate's voice, perhaps the queerest voice in the novel, also can be heard in the music and mysticism at the end if only as a haunting echo. The dramatic ending, which holds the fate of the protagonist literally up in the air, queers our expectations for closure and invites readers to listen to the voices haunting it, but the layered voices at the end only make sense if we consider what leads up to it.

We might logically begin with Pilate, who is a lively voice for the ghosts that haunt the Dead family. She sings their songs. The ghost of Pilate's father, for example, tells her "Sing," and she does, beautifully carrying the history of her people in song, but offending many along the way. She is the "singing woman" in the opening scene, wielding a powerful contralto that embarrasses her brother and causes half the crowd to snigger. Singing in public—in the words of her brother—makes her "like common street women!" (20), and his analogy, in the crucible of misogyny, connects her gift with crimes against social norms and her sex. Milkman, who has been told to stay away from Pilate, also forms his judgment in sexist, middle-class, and homophobic terms, thinking of her as "a silly, selfish, queer, faintly obscene woman" (123), his "queer aunt" (37), the woman who "ain't got no navel" (37). She wears a knit cap pulled down over her head, sells moonshine, and wields a knife like a man, but her noncompliance with gender norms is not as defining as her lack of a navel, a sign of her preternatural being. She is the Tiresian prophet who sings throughout the novel, a figure that straddles worlds defined by gender, sexuality, and mortality, and when she sings, it is as if we are listening to the dead, her voice carrying not only the stories of ancestors but also a queer defiance of norms.[1]

Although her public singing causes half the crowd to snigger, the other half listens "as though it were the helpful and defining piano music in a silent movie" (6). The analogy, evocative of another era, imagines sound divorced from the thing it helps define, for the piano must race to keep up with the emotional tempo of the film, and it is a passionate but inarticulate substitute for speech, a reminder of the open mouths that yield no sound. Pilate, similarly, heightens our awareness of missing voices, those of the ancestors, and her voice, in turn, haunts the novel. She is the spiritual center of the novel, the voice that lurks behind the narrator and the queer answer to conventional iterations, such as the homophobic discourse examined in the last chapter. As the queer center of the novel, Pilate sings of alternatives, her voice filled with prophecy and forbidden knowledge.

In the previous chapter, I examined how music appears as a ghostly emanation attending moments of crisis and violence. The present chapter is a ghost to the last one, which has unfinished business: the accounting of sound, specifically voice, as ghostly and queer. Pilate not only serves as a counterpoint to the representations of homophobia examined in the last chapter, but she presents an alternative way of being, and her voice, laden with mystical meaning, is represented as otherworldly, hardly issuing from a live body but a spirit. As Macon Dead approaches Pilate's house, he imagines "her face would be a mask; all emotion and passion would have left her features and entered her voice" (29), and Milkman later considers that same face to be "like a mask" when she becomes silent and serious (48). This recurring characteristic is consistent with Susan Neal Mayberry's assertion that Pilate is a shape-shifter, one who will eventually take on the form of Circe. But it also continues to represent sound as divorced from its source—like the "defining piano music in a silent film," a ghostly evocation of sound from the living dead.

Irony, indeed, is built into the family name of the protagonist, Dead, and when Pilate tells Milkman, "Ain't but three Deads alive" (38), her "miscalculation" invites us to consider what she means by "alive." In pointing to the spiritual death of Milkman's family, Catherine Carr Lee joins a host of critics who address the rich interpretative possibilities of the Dead family name.[2] The Deads, both living and ghostly, speak in this novel, but it is Milkman who is frequently characterized as raising his voice. He shouts in his first confrontation with Pilate, raises his voice with the ghostly Circe, and, in the final scene of the novel, bellows to Guitar across the valley only to hear his words echoing back. Milkman's shouting does not haunt but instead attracts haunted voices. Upon the occasion of his birth, someone asks, "Did he come with a caul?" and a second busy voice says, "You should have dried it and made him some tea from it to drink. If you don't he'll see ghosts" (10). A third voice asks, "You believe that?" The second section of the novel seems to answer this question.

In the second half of the novel, Milkman meets Circe. Upon entering her decrepit abode, Milkman recalls dreams he had as a child, "dreams every child had, of the witch who chased him down dark alleys, between lawn trees, and finally into rooms from which he could not escape" (239). When Circe comes to the top of the stairs, Milkman cannot resist her, though "he knew that always, always at the very instant of the pounce or the gummy embrace he would wake with a scream and erection. Now he had only the erection" (239). In one of Morrison's deft jumps, this provocative line is followed by Milkman closing his eyes "helpless to pull away before the completion of the dream" (240). Although we should infer that a scream would complete the dream, the sexual intimations are obvious, linking the forbidden and desire and imbuing the scene with a queer cast, one that links the otherworldly to desire.

What makes Milkman "surface from [the dream] was a humming sound around his knees . . . a pack of golden-eyed dogs," but "reality" seems no less dreamlike:

> "Come, come," [Circe] said to Milkman. "In here." She took his hand in both of hers, and he followed her—his arm outstretched, his hand in hers—like a small boy being dragged reluctantly to bed. Together they weaved among the bodies of the dogs that floated around his legs. She led him into a room, made him sit on a gray velvet sofa, and dismissed all the dogs but two that lay at her feet. (240)

Like Pilate, Circe both disgusts and entrances Milkman, and the awful stench that surrounds her is reminiscent of the odor that comes from Pilate's house (36). Circe's voice, however, stands out as her most bizarre and haunting characteristic. Not unlike the most distinguishing feature of Pilate, Circe's voice is at odds with her face.

Milkman reasons that Circe "*had* to be dead. Not because of the wrinkles, and the face so old it could not be alive, but because out of the toothless mouth came the strong mellifluent voice of a twenty-year-old girl" (240). The disparity between what Milkman sees and what he hears creates a haunting that is no less powerful than Pilate's powerful contralto. Circe is not the specter Milkman expects, and "[i]t was awful listening to that voice come from that face" (241). Although he speculates that "[m]aybe something was happening to his ears," Milkman decides to interrupt the sound of the haunting voice with "the sound of his own voice . . . to take a chance on logic" (241). In hearing his own voice as the bearer of logic and in calling it forth to displace the maddening sound of Circe, Milkman privileges speaking over listening, denial over acceptance, and the familiar voice of the Dead (the puns being endless) over the strangely youthful voice that issues from this wizened woman. He is reassured to know *his* voice has not changed. "Now he needed only to know if he had assessed the situation correctly." Milkman's rational mind, however, cannot make sense of Circe, who must be dead but stood there talking to him with a young woman's voice.

Here and throughout *Song of Solomon*, voices haunt not simply because they issue from specters but because they queer expectations. The conversation with Circe, moreover, marks one of the most significant points in Milkman's journey toward a new understanding, an escape from the confinement of his middle-class, heteronormative family. And yet he hardly knows what is happening to him. Aware of an almost mystical transformation at the same time that he is characterized as still stuck in the past, Milkman is caught between old ways of thinking and new possibilities. Nevertheless, he cannot help but see Circe through the stereotype of the loyal darky—which recalls his disgust with Pilate's mammy act at the end of section 1—and he is unable to interpret her story of not only enduring but prevailing.[3]

The narrator tells us that "Milkman had no trouble letting his words snarl" (247), but Circe meets his tone with words that are more pointed: "You don't listen to people. Your ear is on your head, but it's not connected to your brain" (247). Despite her uncompromising criticism, Milkman leaves feeling gratitude to this woman who has filled in so many of the pieces of his history, and we sense that "maybe something *was* happening to his ears" (241; emphasis added).[4] Milkman, however, continues to prove himself prone to misinterpreting others and hitting the wrong note (see the last chapter) as he leaves Circe and continues on to Shalimar.

Throughout the novel, the thing that happens to Milkman's ear is the thing that happens to the reader as well. We must do more than follow the words on the page; the novel seduces us into listening for the sound—rhythm, music, intonation—or the full meaning of the written word will be lost. *Song of Solomon* is a novel deeply concerned with this relationship between oral and literate traditions, not necessarily privileging one over the other as much as uncovering the way that the hegemony of rationalist literate traditions threatens to sever young African Americans from their rich heritage—the resources of oral traditions.[5] The novel, moreover, attempts to send its reader on a quest not unlike Milkman's journey for meaning and connection. When Circe tells Milkman that she birthed his grandmother Sing, he wonders "if she lisped" and he asks her to repeat herself. "Sing. Her name was Sing," Circe announces, and the reader, along with Milkman, gains

knowledge of one of the key moments of miscommunication in the
novel. The word "sing," which appears everywhere, is both the forgotten name of Milkman's grandmother and a verb. In the final scene of
the novel, Pilate—whose exact moment of death is put in question—
repeats the word "sing" but as an imperative: " 'Sing,' she said, 'Sing
a little something for me' " (336). At this point in the novel we have
learned the many ways that this word "sing" reverberates, working as
ambiguous homonym, a reminder of both the power and weakness of
oral traditions, and an imperative. It is one of the many devices in the
novel for highlighting the importance of words and language but also
the haunting nature of voice—both from the living and the dead. It is
therefore ironic, in a novel so thematically obsessed with voice, that the
narrative voice remains relatively underexplored.

For many scholars, *Song of Solomon*—despite its lack of an intrusive
first-person narrator—sings with "a bardic voice" or is modeled on the
traditional African figure of the griot.[6] These extremely important readings frequently emphasize historical context, links to music and other
expressive forms, and cultural and political engagements more than narrative exegesis. Barbara Hill Rigney's assessment points to how and why
Morrison's narrators may resist narratological exegesis:

> Morrison's narrators are most often unidentifiable, anonymous,
> vehicles to transmit information. . . . Often these narrators
> disappear completely as one character or another steps forward
> to tell the story from a different point of view. But even
> these speaking characters reflect multiple and fragmented
> selves, which are sometimes undefined, inevitably amorphous,
> always merging with the identity of a community as a whole
> or with the very concept of blackness. (37)

It is exactly this "amorphous" quality that gives many of Morrison's
narrators a ghostly quality—elusive, ephemeral, and boundary crossing.
But with its pronounced thematic interest in oral traditions, its many
storytellers, and its formal will to aurality, *Song of Solomon* especially
invites considerations of narrative voice as haunting.

As a quest narrative, *Song of Solomon* emphasizes Milkman's ability to recognize and learn from ancestral voices. The ancestors come
to him in song, nursery rhymes, folktale, gossip, history, myth, and
pure sound. But one of the more important arguments made by such
scholars as Mobley, Middleton, and Krumholz is that, "In the course of

Milkman's initiation, the reader is also called upon to apply her reading skills to interpret the signs and unriddle the mysteries" (Krumholz 221). These scholars help us to see how theme and form support one another, but they also highlight the text's engagement with its reader. In Middleton's words, "the reader is implicated in the tale, just as the bard's audience participate in his interactive performance" (23). And Mobley argues, "By paying attention to how identity is constructed dialogically rather than monologically, the reader hears and celebrates the voices that Toni Morrison both directly and indirectly enacts in the text" (62). Mobley sees the novel as enabling "the reader to critique those cultural hegemonic forces that have silenced some voices in the first place" (62), inviting us to consider not only the representation of homophobic discourse as haunted by ghostly emanations (the subject of the last chapter) but also narrative voice as spectral and queer, the subject of this chapter.

The critics, not surprisingly, have taken their lead from Morrison, who has in interviews and essays emphasized her interest in creating gaps, spaces, openings that allow for the creative engagement of readers. "I want my fiction," she said in 1984, "to urge the reader into active participation in non-narrative, nonliterary experience of the text" ("Memory, Creation, and Writing" 387). And in "Unspeakable Things Unspoken," she describes the many "spaces" in *Song of Solomon* as invitations for the "ruminations of the reader": "The reader as narrator asks the questions the community asks, and both reader and 'voice' stand among the crowd, within it, with privileged intimacy and contact, but without any more privileged information than the crowd has" (29). Even before the publication of *Jazz*, her greatest experiment with narrative voice, she describes voice as something more akin to a reader than a god qua omniscient narrator. In characterizing *Song of Solomon*'s narrator as just one of the crowd, Morrison highlights invisibility and, perhaps unwittingly, the ghostliness of her narrative voice. But although Morrison is careful to avoid assigning a gender to her ideal reader, making note of "*his or her* invented or recollected or misunderstood knowingness" ("Unspeakable Things Unspoken" 29; emphasis added), she does not provide a clear indication of the gender of her narrator.

Scholars have frequently assumed a female and even maternal voice for *Song of Solomon* and the other novels. Rigney, for example, argues that "[t]hroughout Morrison's novels, women are the primary tale-tellers and the transmitters of history as well as the singing teachers; only they know the language of the occult and the occult of language and

thus comprise what Morrison has called a 'feminine subtext' " (11).[7] In
Moorings and Metaphors, Karla Holloway's fascinating study of myth,
gender, and voice in the writings of contemporary black women, *Song
of Solomon* serves as one of several Morrison novels that "make linguistic
rituals in recursive, metaphoric layers that structure meaning and voice
into a complex that eventually implicates the primal, mythic, and female
community of its source" (35). With poetic flare that is characteristic of
her argument, Holloway describes "a widening gyre in literature by black
women writers [that] collects a universe of black voices and coils them
into each other until the center reflects the dark, rich, fertile, and, yes,
ambivalent collage of women whose voices have both complicated the
story and dared to tell it" (36). That collage of voices may certainly be
viewed as including the Song of Songs, or Song of Solomon, the only
book in the Bible that features a female voice.[8] Interestingly, the Song of
Songs is at the heart of much exegesis about sex, gender, and sexuality.
In "A Love as Fierce as Death," for example, Christopher King argues
that this biblical book explores forbidden love, and specifically queer
love, and in "The Song of Songs in the History of Sexuality," Stephen
D. Moore documents the many queer interpretations of the Song of
Solomon. Morrison scholars have taken note, of course, of the biblical
allusions, but they have not pursued its invitation to queer the text
and narrator. Instead, discussions of the narrator, when there is attention to it at all, emphasize the links to African storytellers, the griots,
or African American storytellers—with some even linking the narrator
loosely to Morrison.[9] But why not see the narrator as embodying all
and not just one of these traditions? If we take the title as a guide, we
might certainly link the narrator to the important storytellers in multiple
African American traditions, the griots, the preachers, the singers, and
the endlessly elusive narrators of the biblical Song.[10] But the latter, in
the words of Ariel Bloch, "don't suffer love, they savor it," and this
helps give a queer cast to the novel (Bloch and Block 7).

De Weever, in her exploration of folklore and the novel, links
Milkman to Tiresias, but Pilate, as I have already suggested, also seems
Tiresian. Although she does not literally cross boundaries marked by sex,
Pilate, who "had not come into this world through normal channels"
and who had instead inched "head first out of a still, silent, and indifferent cave of flesh" (28), is outside of normal categories. As a shape-shifter,
Pilate continues to seem Tiresian throughout the novel, and although
she transforms herself into another woman, Circe, she often gets likened
to the masculine while decidedly tied to female traditions. Like Tiresias,

she serves as an arbiter of heterosexual relationships, overseeing the dysfunctional relationships her daughter and granddaughter are involved in, and like the mythic figure she is a guide. It may be useful, as some critics have argued, to view her as the central consciousness of the novel even though the narrator hugs closely to Milkman's point of view. As if the narrative voice cannot go on without her, the novel comes to a quick close after her death, and for the very short remaining paragraphs, the narrative voice keeps her presence alive. The text, for example, suggests that Pilate looks over Milkman's shoulder even after she has died: "The blood was not pulsing out any longer and there was something black and bubbly in her mouth. Yet when she moved her head a little to gaze at something behind his shoulder, it took a while for him to realize that she was dead" (336). Pilate's postmortem gaze, presumably at Guitar, gets ignored by Milkman, who realizes that she has died and so "he could not stop the worn old words from coming, louder and louder as though sheer volume would wake her" (336). But Milkman's loud voice "woke only the birds," one of which lifts Pilate's earring into the air, prompting Milkman to reflect upon his love in a line that feels very much like a conclusion: "Now he knew why he loved her so. Without ever leaving the ground, she could fly" (336). But Pilate's death does not mark the end of the novel, and there are a few more paragraphs that recount Milkman's address to and final confrontation with Guitar—with Pilate's presence felt throughout.

As the one who sings in *Song of Solomon*, Pilate passes her role on to Milkman: "Sing," she says to Milkman, "Sing a little somethin for me" (336). With this transference of voice from teacher to student, woman to man, queer aunt to maturing nephew, iconoclast to materialist, Dead to Dead, the novel suggests continuance. The novel's narrative and thematic concern with continuance, moreover, invites us to also examine those final paragraphs after Pilate's death, the novel's second ending, and its resistance to closure. Despite the "near" conclusion, the first ending with its reflection upon Pilate and Milkman's love for her, the novel creates several echoes that emphasize its interest in voice, not as something ephemeral but something that continues and will not die, a haunting echo. We might anticipate these echoes, hearing one in Pilate's final request to Milkman: " 'Sing,' she said, 'Sing a little somethin for me' " (336). These words—even the repetition—mirror those spoken by Pilate's father: "Sing, Sing" (147).[11] But they also foreshadow the literal echoes that will come back to Milkman as he shouts across the canyon to Guitar: "Here I am!" / *Am am am am*, said the rocks.

/ "You want me? Huh? You want my life?" / *Life life life life* (337).
This echo, however, also points back to one of the dominant refrains
of the novel, which appears in italics (not unlike in this scene) when
Milkman joins the hunting party in a ritualistic dissection of the bobcat:
"*Everybody wants the life of a black man*" (283).[12] Perhaps introducing
more irony into the interplay of echoes, the novel also weds Milkman's
echoing cry to yet another ancestor, Ryna, who was abandoned by the
first flying African, his great-grandfather. It is Ryna's haunting voice that
usually echoes in these hills when the wind is just right; but unlike Ryna,
who is characterized as inconsolable, Milkman is finally free—more like
Pilate, who figuratively flies as the bird lifts her earring into the air and
disappears. In the dense interplay of these many repetitions and echoes,
the novel suggests the interconnection of everything and the sense of
continuance. What is an echo, after all, but the ghost of sound, a blur-
ring of the boundaries between the enunciation and its putative end.

In providing so many echoes, the ending of *Song of Solomon* stresses
its interest in voice as ghost, in the continuance of sound past its enunciation, and this invites special attention to the final words of the novel
and the shift away from Milkman's consciousness back to Pilate. The
narrative, as I have already suggested, pushes past what seems like one
concluding line upon the death of Pilate: "Now he knew why he loved
her so. Without ever leaving the ground, she could fly" (336). The
novel's actual last line almost repeats the spirit of this earlier conclusion with a second poetic meditation on the nature of flight: "For now
[Milkman] knew what Shalimar knew: If you surrendered to the air, you
could *ride* it" (337).[13] In both endings, we learn that Milkman "now"
"knew" something and that the ancestors are key to his revelations.
But the shift, in the final conclusion, to the second-person indefinite
is important, and although it is in the service of stating what Milkman
now knows, it also has the effect of appearing as a narrative maxim. It
leaves Milkman's consciousness for something more omniscient or at
least distant and authoritative. But it also invites us to ask whether we
believe that "you could *ride* [the air]."

Just as Pilate's death seems, at least for a moment, to be indistinct
(i.e., when does it happen), so, too, does this final line leave Milkman's
fate in question. *Does* Milkman ride the air? *Can* Milkman ride the
air? While my use of italics emphasizes the question readers ask, the
narrative voice asserts a different tone by italicizing *ride*. It is as if the
narrative voice dismisses our obvious question about Milkman's fate for
an emphasis on the pleasure of the *ride*. Italics, which throughout the

novel are deployed for song, transforms the maxim, the question most readers puzzle over, into a different cadence, a different rhythmic ending, one that takes pleasure in opening the sound of *ride* rather than predictably stressing the verb *could*.[14] But the voice of the narrator, which rarely distinguishes itself from Milkman, offers its most radical statement as a truth invested not in the desires and dreams of our protagonist, but of a spiritual teacher. After following Milkman's point of view as he "leaped . . . fleet and bright as a lodestar," we are told that "it did not matter which one of them would give up his ghost in the killing arms of his brother" (337). The indefinite pronoun begs the question, "To whom does it not matter?" Although some might argue that Milkman has attained a certain spiritual enlightenment, we might also argue that the novel has shifted its point of view from Milkman to something larger, more expansive.

This voice, strange in its sentiment and its distance from Milkman, conflates the two men with the metonymic phrases "give up his ghost" and "in the killing arms of his brother." There are, of course, biblical reverberations in both the phrasing and images, but I am more interested in the way the narrative voice distances itself from Milkman, becoming almost a ghostly omniscience that haunts the novel or, perhaps as some scholars have indicated, the voice of the more spiritually enlightened Pilate. But it also seems cagey in presenting philosophical concepts of surrendering to fate with a shifting and distancing from the protagonist. The final two lines, moreover, try to convince the reader that the fate of the protagonist does not matter—at least not as we define fate in terms of mortality as defined by death. Death, however, as the narrative voice of the novel insists in multiple ways and throughout the novel, does not stop the voice.[15]

Morrison's interest in imagining the continuance of voice beyond narrative finds a complement in the final image of the novel: the killing embrace of Milkman and Guitar. Not unlike the dream that Milkman awakens from, carrying his erection into the new reality, so, too, does this embrace suggest certain thresholds of possibility. Although readers wish to know whether Milkman flies and whether he survives, a queer reading might examine the embrace, short as it is on description, for its homoerotic subtext. I am more interested, however, in thinking of this embrace in relationship to theories of endings. In *Come as You Are: Sexuality and Narrative*, Judith Roof asks questions about the intertwining nature of narrative and sexuality, beginning with deceptively simple questions, such as: "How is it that stories are marked by the illusion of an end to come? How is it that the anticipated and delightful orgasmic sexual end comes like the end of a story?" (2). Although there is the hope that certain postmodern texts, such as those that withhold gender designations, might find a way out of this bind, Roof finds that "[t]he underlying sexual ideology of narrative survives despite claims that we are a poststructuralist (and perhaps postnarrative) age" (32). Roof has been criticized for not offering readings of texts that fight their way out of this bind, even though her argument suggests that there may not be a way out, that narrative is too intertwined with heterosexuality. But it might be more useful to consider how writers resist closure, even as they fail, and to ask what is behind this resistance, this effort to imagine something other than the rush toward an end and inevitable closure.

The image of Milkman and Guitar embracing in midair, startling as it is, could not be stronger in its anticipation of a conclusion, leading us to the very brink of expectation of knowing whether gravity or myth will prevail and offering us the silence of the page. This image, filled as it is with the anticipation of a result, suitably complements *Song of Solomon*'s pronounced attention to echo and voice: sound's will to continuance. In providing an ending frozen in time, full of our desire for closure, Morrison ensures that we must engage with the text, become active participants in the meaning-making, and in this sense the ending imagines voices other than its own and even might be said to offer the reader to become a collaborator. Morrison will more radically imagine her book's engagement with readers in her sixth novel, *Jazz*, where the queer nature of voice and its radical investment in multiple and shifting desires become more pronounced.

In beginning *Jazz* with a sign of extralinguistic sound ("Sth"), Morrison pushes representation to its limits and asks readers to enter the world of sound and symbol before entering narrative. Language, in this bold opening, is elastic, and Morrison invites questions about orality, signification (or as Henry Louis Gates would say, "Signifyin'"), the music of text, and the narrative voice. Before readers locate meaning or sense for the sign, they might instead hear sound. This disruption in conventional reading practice has confounded many novices while entrancing more than a few scholars, inviting them to consider Morrison's engagement with difficulty, jazz, postmodernism, vernacular traditions, aurality, and a host of other issues and themes. How does Morrison advance her experiment with queering the ghostly voice to create something altogether unique in *Jazz*?

Song of Solomon, despite my interest in queering its voice, is fierce-ly interested in heterosexual relationships. The novel considers what it means for fathers to leave the family structure, the dangers of anaconda love, and what it means for everyone to want a black man's life. But it is a heterosexual text that is also strangely queer in its consideration of these questions. Milkman's queer aunt, for example, symbolically flies and represents the figure with the greatest freedom—freedom from het-eronormativity and other social norms. Her ability to fly, shape-shift, and live on her own terms serves as a direct refutation of the privileges seen as accorded to men. She is the guide for Milkman, who must navigate through a homophobic, sexist, and heterosexist world, and although the novel's refrain is that everyone wants a black man's life, we might interpret this desire as bisexual as easily as we see it as heterosexual. *Jazz*, however, more directly addresses bisexuality and the complexity of human desire.

Bisexuality, which some people might argue is the queerest of sexualities, one that radically disturbs binaries, categories, and social mores, gets represented in *Jazz* as a fantasy that interrupts the dys-functional heterosexual relationship. While *Song of Solomon* flirts with queer desire, locating it in the margins of its refrain, "Everybody wants the life of a black man," *Jazz* directly addresses bisexual desire, albeit locating those desires in the dead and the living's unfinished business with the dead. In an opening that might make readers think about the importance of flight to *Song of Solomon* or birds in Morrison's Nobel lecture (the latter I discuss later), the narrator quickly conveys the act that the rest of the novel will center around: a man (Joe Trace) "fell for an eighteen-year-old girl with one of those deepdown, spooky loves that made him so sad and happy he shot her just to keep the feeling going" (3). This causes his wife, Violet, to go to the girl's funeral "to cut her dead face," upon which she ran back to her apartment and released her birds, "[setting] them out the windows to freeze or fly, including the parrot that said, 'I love you'" (3). Although Morrison is famous for dramatic openings, this compresses the key events of the novel into a paragraph, which has the important effect of highlighting the act of storytelling as something much more than the recounting of key events. This compressed opening is followed by story upon story, some of them quite surprising in their trajectories out farther and far-ther from the central act, though never very far from the central theme of "spooky" love. The voice that manages these stories, often offering gossipy asides, free advice, judgment, revisions of various points, second thoughts on key facts, and assumptions about the principal characters, we learn late in the novel is a book. The novel, in other words, does not just present a disembodied voice—omniscient or otherwise—but an object from which to imagine that voice speaking.

In "Print, Prosthesis, (Im)Personation: Morrison's *Jazz* and the Limits of Literary History," Maurice Wallace has beautifully explored *Jazz*'s will to be heard, placing this desire within a tradition of the Talking Book (with Henry Louis Gates's work in mind) and its will to be seen, "to be bodied forth by an Hegelian recognition" (800). In one of his more commanding assertions, Wallace sees *Jazz* as positing "a brave new world inside of which the book overcomes the social inertia of objects existing in the world outside it" (803) and then finally points to "a greater agency than that delimiting normative personhood" (804). Although Wallace does not offer a queer reading, his argument helps open a space for seeing *Jazz* as enabling certain opportunities of reading. How does the book as voice identify with a certain intimacy across genders, a bisexual orientation consistent with its will to knowing each of its characters, male or female, and presenting each to a reader undefined by gender. The conceit offers an erotic triangulation, one that characterizes the book as no less bodied, sensual, and full of desire as character and reader. In Wallace's words: "In the novel's last whimpering lines, so full of hot surrender and true confessions, something else altogether appears possible" (803). It is this something else, this complex relationship enabled by the conceit of the book as voice, that points to what I am calling a *ménage à trois*, an erotic relationship that includes the book, its narrator, and the reader, inviting queer associations by virtue of the triad but also in the ambiguously gendered character of the book as well as the unknown gender of either an implied or actual reader.[16]

Wallace argues that if the novel "does not confer upon its readers a body exactly (the constitution of the reader's body is prior to the reading act), it nevertheless hails that body, by an autonomy barely seen or heard, into a social world kept alive by the peculiar compensatory power of the book" (803). I would add that one of the "compensatory" powers of *Jazz* in particular is its generosity toward queer readings and the queer reader's body. My notion of a *ménage à trois* between book, character, and reader extends Wallace's idea that the "the hands cradling *Jazz* project a double sociality inasmuch as they not only lend the book a body (a social transactional corporeality, in other words), but also touch Morrison's own hand by the additional proxy of print for the idea (rarely the fact) of handwriting and keystrokes" (803). My reading, however, includes the character in this social/sexual relationship because the novel itself projects a certain autonomy for them as much as it does for itself, the book. We, the readers, therefore, may engage with them separately, imagine for them—as the book endlessly does—alternative possibilities, conflicting motivations, new histories and causal relationships, and, importantly, our own responses and relationship with those characters, those projections of ourselves.

As the narrator's first "project," which we might imagine as a project of explaining or inventing, Violet provides the initial introduction to what it means to be bisexual. Although she is fully identified as madly in love with her husband, fully identified as heterosexual, she becomes obsessed with the other woman, rivaling Joe in the amount of time she spends thinking about Dorcas. Because they both spent the nighttime worrying about it, Violet "decided to love—well, find out about—the eighteen-year-old" (5). Although the narrator cautiously revises the term "love" as merely trying to understand or gather information, Violet visits Dorcas's aunt and not only finds out more information but asks for a photograph and begins to act like a woman in love. The photograph, as many scholars have noted, provides a ghostly object for Violet to love and turns the relationship more into a *ménage à trois*—with Violet confessing to Dorcas's aunt that in "another time [she] would have loved her too. Just like you did. Just like Joe" (109). Here and throughout, the book presents Joe, Violet, and Dorcas as a love triangle but with Violet fully involved with the dead Dorcas and loving her ghost. Violet's relationship with the dead Dorcas, in fact, rivals Joe's posthumous love, and their shared passion strangely brings them together.

The narrative, however, adds an interesting layer when Dorcas's friend, Felice, goes to meet Joe and Violet in order to disabuse them of some of their beautiful ideas about her dead friend. What evolves from several meetings is a *ménage à trois* in its own right, a haunting shadow to the first *ménage à trois*, but now with the women fully engaged with one another rather than pointing to a "spooky" love that is out of reach. Violet, according to the narrator, has started out by viewing Felice as "another true-as-life Dorcas" (197), and when Joe asks her to dance with them, Violet encourages her as well. Felice declines, shaking her head even though "[she] wanted to" (214). This new configuration offers a very different form of innocence, and of the many voices in the novel that appear to consider the nature of love, it is Felice's voice that seems the most critical of heterosexual love and intrigued by alternatives.

She identifies with Violet's description of having a second person inside her: "She talked like that. But I understood what she meant. About having another you inside that isn't anything like you" (208). Interestingly, Felice immediately follows this idea of having a second person inside her with an erotic memory of Dorcas: "Dorcas and I used to make up love scenes and describe them to each other. It was fun and a little smutty. Something about it bothered me, though. Not the loving stuff, but the picture I had of myself when I did it. Nothing like me" (208–09). Encouraged by her encounter with Violet, Felice seems at the verge of recognizing forbidden desires and certainly articulating a disdain for the heterosexual relationships she encounters.

In one of her final soliloquies, she considers Dorcas's folly and asks, " 'What the hell did she win? He treated her bad, but she didn't think so. She spent her time figuring out how to keep him interested in her. Plotting what she would do to any girl who tried to move in' " (216). Exasperated, Felice announces that all girls seem to act this way and wonders if there is a way out of this cliché: "I guess that's the way you have to think about it. But what if I don't want to?" (216). Searching for an alternative to dysfunctional heterosexuality, Felice represents a certain frustration with the status quo, heteronormativity, but does not have an idea how to affect an alternative. Her innocent words precede the final chapter devoted to the narrator's musings about love and responsibility, a chapter that reverberates with Morrison's Nobel Prize lecture.

Morrison begins the Nobel lecture by telling the story of young people who go to a blind, wise woman to prove her a phony. They ask her whether the bird they have in their hands is alive or dead, and after a long silence she says, "I don't know whether the bird you are holding is dead or alive, but what I do know is that it is in your hands. It is in your hands." Delivering this speech a year after the publication of *Jazz* in 1992, Morrison uses this brief tale to talk about language ("I choose to read the bird as language"), and after considering the importance of honoring language, she tells the story again, revising it and striving to understand what it must be like for the children in this story to receive such an off-putting answer from a wise woman. Morrison imagines the young people asking for the impossible: "Is there no context for our lives? No song, no literature, no poem full of vitamins, no history connected to experience that you can pass along to help us start strong?" (27). They ask her to "[m]ake up a story," and they observe that "[n]arrative is radical, creating us at the very moment it is being created." Morrison radically reimagines them not as spoiled and disrespectful children but as searching and fearless in their quest for understanding. "We will not blame you," the young people say, "if your reach exceeds your grasp; if love so ignites your words they go down in flames and nothing is left but their scald. . . . For our sake and yours forget your name in the street; tell us what the world has been to you in the dark places and in the light." Here and in the closing moments of *Jazz*, the narrators struggle with the role and responsibility of the storyteller. More important, they consider what it means to collaborate with the listener/reader. Context provides the greatest difference. *Jazz*, for example, comes to this point of collaboration after telling stories of romantic love, infidelity, and murder, and so the narrator's musings gain a queer cast in this context.

If *Jazz's* narrator conveys at the beginning judgment and disdain with a mix of world-weariness and amusement, the voice at the end conveys sympathy for her characters, especially Wild, the subject of the next chapter. The narrator conveys humility in her role as creator but also a certain vulnerability. The narrator specifically confesses to envying the very people she has presented sometimes with little generosity for their outrageous loves: "I envy them their public love. I myself have only known it in secret, shared it in secret and longed, aw longed to show it . . ." (229). The reader at this point most likely understands the voice to be that of a book, but the personification does little to undercut the account of forbidden love and our associations with such nonnormative loves. The narrator goes on to imagine being "able to say out loud what they [i.e., the characters and humans in general] have no need to say at all":

> *That I have loved only you, surrendered my whole self reckless to you and nobody else. That I want you to love me back and show it to me. That I love the way you hold me, how close you let me be to you. I like your fingers on and on, lifting, turning. I have watched your face for a long time now, and missed your eyes when you went away from me. Talking to you and hearing you answer—that's the kick.* (229)

With great tenderness, the voice comes alive as more complex, sentient and sensuous, and ready to confess everything, and a queer reading cannot help but emphasize the relationship between these musings and the closet. But many of the stories in the novel have already announced their interest in secret and forbidden loves.

In taking romantic love as its subject, *Jazz* circles around the many ways that it hides as well as announces itself. Dorcas, for example, tells Felice that she wants to be talked about: "What good are secrets if you can't talk to anybody about them?" (189). And in the novel's most substantial backstory—the plot surrounding Golden Gray—Vera Louise is successful in keeping her affair with a black man secret until she is pregnant. I do not want to argue, therefore, that all forbidden love points to queer love, but the intimations of bisexuality find fertile ground in the thematic investigations into secrecy and love. Indeed, the narrator confesses to getting "so aroused while meddling" and this meddling is arguably both voyeuristic and bisexual, queer in its disavowing of any specific (sexual) orientation but also sensuous in its final confession to its readers (male and female) to "make me, remake me. You are free to do it and I am free to let you because look, look. Look where your hands are. Now" (229). And the reader must, as with the startling ending of *Song of Solomon*, consider his or her role in the making of the story and the generosity of the narrator, who is not bound by the sex, gender, or sexuality of the reader, to lead to an ending that lovingly says, "It is in your hands."

❧

Chapter 7

Blackness

Jazz Haunts *Tar Baby*

What is this thing called "race"? Our deadliest abstraction? Our most nonmaterial actuality? Not fact, but our deadliest fiction that gives the lie to doubt about ghosts? In a word, "race" haunts the air where women and men in social organization are most reasonable.

—Hortense Spillers, "'All the Things You Could Be by Now, If Sigmund Freud's Wife Was Your Mother': Psychoanalysis and Race"

And now what shall become of us without any barbarians? / Those people were a kind of solution.

—C. P. Cavafy, "Waiting for the Barbarians"

In *Raising the Dead: Readings of Death and (Black) Subjectivity*, Sharon P. Holland asks "who resides in the nation's imaginary 'space of death'" (4), how are these outsiders silenced, and when, if ever, are they given voice? Morrison, as I have been arguing, queers the ghost in order to address some of these silences and to examine the interlocking forces of racism, sexism, and heterosexism, but *Jazz* and *Tar Baby* more fully address myths of blackness by examining how those myths get told, refashioned, and retold alongside and through other cultural anxieties. How do these myths of blackness, which occupy "the nation's imaginary 'space of death,'" integrate other narratives of marginality? Does a queer cast to these myths threaten to eclipse blackness, or do narratives of blackness make black lesbian identities apparitional? Although these questions underwrite much of the inquiry in my previous chapters, *Jazz* and *Tar Baby* "dust off" the myth of blackness to give it a queer and spectral cast, allowing narrative voice to underscore the communal power to shape and revise myth.

Voice, the subject of the last chapter, might be said to be haunting the present chapter, bleeding through to inform a consideration of blackness. Although it would be easy enough to focus solely on blackness as a concept explored in *Jazz* and *Tar Baby*, it is through the layering of voices that Morrison most powerfully explores myths of blackness and its spectral and queer elusiveness. Who speaks myth? And how do these stories come to us? What, more importantly, do we do with them? In an interview given shortly after the publication of *Tar Baby*, Morrison argues that "myths are misunderstood now because we are not talking to each other the way I was spoken to when I was growing up in a very small town" (Taylor-Guthrie 122). Morrison goes on to describe the tar baby myth that haunted her as a child and that she eventually used as a "point of departure to history and prophecy":

> Tar seemed to me to be an odd thing to be in a Western story, and I found that there is a tar lady in African mythology. I started thinking about tar. At one time, a tar pit was a holy place, at least an important place, because tar was used to build things. . . . For me, the tar baby came to mean the black woman who can hold things together. (122)

Morrison radically reinvents the story at the same time that she conveys respect for myth as not stagnant and sacrosanct but a living vehicle for discussion and edification, and it is through the interplay between narrative voice and myth that she emphasizes the machinery behind its construction and the generative possibilities.

Scholars have struggled to account for the complex narrative voice in *Jazz*, characterizing it as a multiplicity of voices, a soloist in a jazz performance, identifiable as Morrison in the final pages, not unlike Malvonne, the woman who begrudgingly loans her apartment to Joe Trace for his illicit affair, and, in Morrison's words, a Talking Book.[1] It is impossible, so the scholarship tells us, to read the novel without trying to make sense of the voice and its relationship to the story. Although the narrator's voice in *Jazz* is intriguing, powerful, and full of presence in the beginning and end of the novel, it gives way in the middle to other voices that take over and assert themselves. Who are these people and what is their relationship to the narrator? They are fictions, so the novel asserts through metafictional conceits, no less meaningful as they crack open, from time to time, and reveal themselves to be inventions. The narrator, for example, comments on what it means to "[invent] stories about them" and to "fill in their lives" (220) but the characters also get caught in this game of invention and the profound myths of blackness that haunt them.

The Traces—Joe and Violet—may be said to be tracing their way back to seminal stories that shape their lives. Violet has always been haunted by stories of Golden Gray—"the golden boy I never saw" (97), and she is convinced that her husband has his own foundational story, and he arguably does. In representing the accounts of Golden Gray and Wild as stories of origin, *Jazz* privileges them as foundational stories, key to understanding the protagonists and central to the narrative. Indeed, Wild's story is the black, queer center of the narrative, and Golden Gray is our proxy for peering into the beautiful mystery of that center.[2] Long before the narrator provides an account of Golden Gray's chance meeting with Wild, we learn that Violet was raised on stories of this golden child, and these "Baltimore stories," which True Belle told her grandchildren, "made me crazy about him" (97). The narrative devoted to Golden Gray, therefore, gets anticipated and freighted with myth, the larger-than-life story that haunts Violet. When Violet tries to make sense of her failed marriage, she imagines that Joe must be haunted by his own mythic figure, "Which means from the very beginning I was a substitute and so was he" (97). The novel depicts these two separate mythic figures, Wild and Golden Gray, as coming together in a chance meeting many years before Violet and Joe first meet one another, creating a doubling effect that highlights the mystical connections between the back and front stories of the novel. While Golden Gray may serve as Violet's myth of white privilege and beauty, Wild registers as Joe's myth of primal loss—the debilitating absence of a mother and a disconnection from fundamental blackness.

The narrator envisions this mythic loss as a deep wound that helps to explain the novel's principal action: Joe's murder of his mistress, Dorcas. The account of his past, in fact, is on his mind as "he sets out, armed, to find Dorcas" (180). The backstory, therefore, has an explanatory power, but it does not and cannot fully account for Joe's murderous act, which even he seems confused by and incapable of explaining. The narrator begins the backstories with a tone that at first sounds like humility but then quickly shifts to bravado: "Risky, I'd say, trying to figure out anybody's state of mind. But worth the trouble if you're like me—curious, inventive and well-informed" (137). The narrator's self-characterization, which often vacillates between bravado and humility, helps inflect her stories with meaning. As the narrator moves from self-reflection to narrative, it is artifice—rather than omniscience—that gets emphasized in the shift to the present tense as if the narrator is just discovering (or making up) the details as they unfold in the mind: "I see him in a two-seat phaeton" (143).

The narrative at this point in the novel emphasizes descriptive details with an uncharacteristic stream of declarative statements in the present tense:

> In the trees to his left, he sees a naked berry-black woman. She is covered with mud and leaves are in her hair. Her eyes are large and terrible. As soon as she sees him, she starts then turns suddenly to run, but in turning before she looks away she knocks her head against the tree she has been leaning against. Her terror is so great her body flees before her eyes are ready to find the route of escape. The blow knocks her down. (144)

When the narrative does shift from physical description to consider Golden Gray's state of mind, it does so without shifting into his voice or even fully into his point of view. We continue to sense, in other words, the shaping hand of the narrator in reflective statements about how the "scene becomes an anecdote" (145) and "I like to think of him that way" (150). It is through this shaping hand that Golden Gray's own acts of interpretation begin to gather meaning: this is a novel that at all levels—through narrator, character, and plot—explores what it means to see, to interpret, and to tell.[3]

What Golden Gray sees, weighted as his character is with myth, is a ghost, aptly first introduced as a "vision." It is on his journey to finding his black father that he finds, ironically, blackness personified and a ghostly one at that. To him, the unconscious woman is indistinguishable from death, a vision, who he must, paradoxically, rescue from dying, and his beliefs about blackness shape his thoughts and actions. Morrison layers the levels of interpretation by keeping the narrator's shaping hand in our consciousness. The narrator is said to "see [Golden Gray] in a two-seat phaeton," effectively initiating her story as something that is willed forward, but then Golden Gray, the narrator's subject, "looks at

[Wild] and . . . wants nothing to do with what he has seen" (144), effectively attempting to keep the story from progressing down this path. Golden Gray decides to leave without approaching this "berry-black woman," but when "he picks up the reins he cannot help noticing that his horse is also black, naked and shiny wet, and his feelings about the horse are of security and affection."

The narrator assigns Golden Gray the crudest of thought processes, turning him into an unsympathetic character at this point. Even his decision to look again does little to win us over. We sense that he cannot see this black woman as a woman because her race (which for him is inextricably associated with her wildness) makes her inhuman, not unlike his horse but also un-seeable like a ghost. For Golden Gray, she is the opposite of the damsel in distress. She is a figure to fear, one who straddles the line between life and death or perhaps embodies one state and then another. Golden Gray finally grows "a touch ashamed and decides to make sure it was a vision, that there is no naked black woman lying in the weeds." We get the sense that he is ready to abandon her after a second look because he believes "[t]here is nothing he can do for her and for that he is relieved," but when "he notices a rippling movement in her stomach" he finds it difficult to leave (144–45). At this moment of recognition, death, as represented by Wild, becomes paradoxically a sign of life, and she continues to represent the convergence of these two extremes as Golden Gray has difficulty making sense of what he is witnessing. The scene, furthermore, continues to emphasize a fascination with vision: "He does not see himself touching her, but the picture he does imagine is himself walking away from her a second time, climbing into his carriage and leaving her a second time. He is uneasy with this picture of himself, and does not want to spend any part of the time to come remembering having done that" (145). Text, narrator, and character all display a profound interest in sight as an important way of understanding the world. This passage, moreover, recognizes that sight is something imagined and not merely a sensory effect determined solely by the material world.

The text keeps this consideration in our minds by returning to the question of Wild's status, not quite fully alive and not wholly dead, and the narrator focuses on Golden Gray's role in interpreting that status. He sees her, so the narrator speculates, as "everything he was not" as a shield against "what he believed his father to be, and therefore (if it could just be contained, identified)—himself." The question of Wild's status as a vision, therefore, helps Golden Gray puzzle through his own desire for blackness, which he sees as a social, spiritual, and personal death—inevitable as it is. Blackness becomes the thing he both desires and detests.

> A vision that, at the moment when his scare was sharpest, looked also like home comfortable enough to wallow in? That could be it. But who could live in that leafy hair? That unfathomable skin? But he already had lived in and with it: True Belle had been his first and major love, which may be why two gallops beyond that hair, that skin, their absence was unthinkable. (150)

Golden Gray collapses all blackness into one, finding sympathy for Wild in his relationship with True Belle, his mammy, and his horse. And yet this leafy blackness scares him, and he is both drawn and repelled by the notion of absence. It is at the height of the story's consideration of Golden Gray's deepest fears that the narrator intrudes with, "I like to think of him that way" (150). But this is not sympathy as much as it is indictment as the narrator goes on to explain: "what makes me worry about him. How he thinks first of his clothes, and not the woman. How he checks the fastenings, but not her breath" (151). At the very moment that the narration shows him in sympathetic terms again (i.e., unable to turn away and instead searching her wounds with concern that she will "explode" (153–54), the narrator violently erupts: "I know he is a hypocrite; that he is shaping a story for himself to tell somebody, to tell his father, naturally. How he was driving along, saw and saved this wild black girl: No qualms. I had no qualms. See look, here, how it ruined my coat . . ." (154). With these metafictional moves, the narrator highlights both the character's future role as storyteller (i.e., what he will tell his father and how he will craft his story) but also its own investment in shaping the tale.[4]

As the backstory of Golden Gray reaches its climactic point of confrontation between father and son, the narrator does an about-face and displays her strongest sympathies for the white-black man who, because of the entrenched racism of his world, must struggle to reclaim his black father. The narrator casts her own failings in the language of racial discourse, confessing to an initial inability to see beyond the color of his skin to "some other thing," and she gives that other thing a name that has dominated late-twentieth-century discourse about race: authenticity.

What was I thinking of? How could I have imagined him so poorly? Not noticed the hurt that was not linked to the color of his skin, or the blood that beat beneath it. But to some other thing that longed for authenticity, for a right to be in this place, effortlessly without needing to acquire a false face, a laughless grin, a talking posture. I have been careless and stupid and it infuriates me to discover (again) how unreliable I am. (160)

Authenticity, issuing as it does from an unknown place, trumps simplistic and colorist notions of blackness, and at this point the narrative introduces a concept for racial confusion that links Golden Gray to Wild. Just as she is a vision and associated with living death, so, too, does Golden Gray get linked to ghosts through his conceptualization of his separation from his father as a phantom limb, a figuration that Freud just happens to link to his notion of the uncanny (see my introduction).

It is Golden Gray's notion of a phantom limb, finally, that the narrator finds compelling and also helps to transform him into a sympathetic character.

What do I care what the color of his skin is, or his contact with my mother? When I see him, or what is left of him, I will tell him all about the missing part of me and listen for his crying shame. I will exchange then; let him have mine and take his as my own and we will both be free, arm-tangled and whole. (159)

It is this account of his phantom limb, one of the many stories he might have told about himself, that links him not only to Wild but even his father, who is also imagined as having a phantom limb that might tangle, entwine, his own. It is in the sharing of lacks—absences that are moreover tied to their blackness—that they are made whole, but Wild contrasts their search for meaning with a mysterious wildness that seems impenetrable.

Wild, a foil for Golden Gray and his discovery of black parentage, appears out of nowhere, associated with untamable nature (i.e., the dark woods) and not civilization (i.e., family). It is her story, therefore, that trumps all stories of blackness and family bonds. The novel, furthermore, presents her as capable of haunting not merely individuals but the entire community: "Pregnant girls were the most susceptible, but so were the grandfathers. Any fascination could mark a newborn: melons, rabbits, wisteria, rope, and more than a shed snakeskin, a wild woman is the worst of all" (165). In these descriptions, Wild gains her own status as myth—the wild woman who "could mark a newborn" but could also cause grandfathers to go "soft in the head" (167). She becomes mythic through the act of others telling and retelling of her existence. For example, "Local people used the story of her to caution children and pregnant girls" (167). Her story, so the narrator emphasizes, is especially powerful because of her status as the living dead, and the text finds many ways to convey the paradox of her dual association with both life and death. For example, "Thirteen years after Golden Gray stiffened himself to look at that girl, the harm she could do was still alive" (165).[5]

Wild is alive to the community through storytelling, and it is through her, moreover, that they know themselves: "Wild was not a story of a used-to-be-long-ago-crazy girl whose neck cane cutters liked to imagine under the blade, or a quick and early stop for hardheaded children. She was still out there—and real" (167). Although some report seeing her, it is Golden Gray's father—"the man they called Hunters Hunter"—who has tended to her, and, "When for months there was no sign or sound of her, he sighted and relived that time when his house was full of motherlessness—and the chief unmothering was Wild's" (167). Her unmothering serves as a foil for Hunters Hunter's sudden fatherhood or, rather, Golden Gray's missing father. Her unmothering queerly completes the family tableau, unleashing cultural anxieties of blackness. If the myth of the absent black father finds any expression in the character of Hunters Hunter, it is in the way it reverses stereotypes. He tends to Wild and makes sure that her baby gets nursed, and in the midst of these pressing needs, he does not deny Golden Gray. "I never knew you were in the world," he says upon learning that he is the father to this "queer" "pale boy-man who had called him 'Daddy'" (170, 171). In characterizing Golden Gray as "queer," the father falls into his own myths of whiteness as well as stereotypes of the visibly white black man as neutered, strange, and unsexed.

Although he first recognizes Golden Gray to be a white man and therefore trouble, he does not act servile to him before or after being abruptly and rudely confronted by his putative son. Hunters Hunter quickly assesses the situation and meets the challenge of his new role with power: "You come in here, drink my liquor, rummage in my stuff and think you can cross-talk me just cause you call me Daddy? If she told you I was your daddy, then she told you more than she told me" (172). He addresses his son as a son and not through the typical racial codes of the time. "Get a hold of yourself. A son ain't what a woman say. A son is what a man do. You want to act like you mine, then do it, else get the devil out my house!" (172). The narrator tells us that "Golden Gray was sober now and his sober thought was to blow the man's head off," but it "must have been the girl who changed his mind" (173). Wild, therefore, offers a necessary distraction to the dangerous drama of family reunion between white and black.

The most heightened moment of Wild's function as axis for all other dramas of blackness occurs just as Golden Gray's father begins to respond to his son's revelations, but his anger gets interrupted when "the woman screamed then and hoisted herself on her elbows to look between her raised knees" (170). Birth, then, is in the convergence of events tied to the shocking revelation of the black man's paternity and the white son's need to face his blackness, but more importantly, Wild reasserts her role as the mysterious center of the inquiry into the meaning of blackness. Just as Wild's status as the living dead ties two opposites together, so, too, does the theme of paternity get tied to maternity, both serving as narratives that somehow personify blackness as queer, unnatural, and melodramatic. Two men, one white and one black, struggle to fit themselves into a primal story of paternity that they don't recognize (or don't know how to recognize) while a "berry-black woman" comes out of the woods to give birth only to refuse to "hold the baby or look at it" (170). As foils, Hunters Hunter and Wild explode myths of the absent father next to pernicious myths of the black matriarch and mammy, erasing these scripts not only to challenge stereotypes but also to make room for other narratives.[6]

Wrapped as she is in sexual mystery and associated as she is with illicit desire, Wild explodes myths of the maternal not just because she takes no interest in the child but because she lives life on her own terms and does not nurture or seek nurturance. Not unlike Circe in *Song of Solomon*, she is represented through the psychosexual myth of the witch. Although Joe Trace grows up with this myth, he later has reason to believe that the "witch" is his mother. Upon hearing Joe and his friend speculate "on what it would take to kill Wild" (175), Hunters Hunter looks "right at Joe (not Victory)" and tells him, "You know, that woman is *somebody's* mother and *somebody* ought to take care" (175). As the mysterious unknown, Wild gains in this moment specificity in relationship to Joe. The reader, not unlike Joe, gets a new awareness of Wild and must incorporate this knowledge into past impressions and assumptions. In this way, the novel leads its readers once again through the lessons that the characters must learn: stories are never complete and must evolve as new information comes to light. For example, Wild in this instant gains a history and an identity that is not merely mythic but grounded in a relationship to another person. As the narrative provides some specificity to Wild (i.e., she is someone's mother) it does not, however, abandon characterizing her as mythic and larger than life.

Joe searches for her to unlock the mystery of his beginnings. His playful game of imagining killing the witch, therefore, turns into a quest to make her less wild (i.e., less Wild) by uncovering her secret hiding place. It is a different sort of matricide, one that unwittingly tries to kill her essence, that which makes her wild/Wild, by shedding light on her. In his search to find her secret lair, he brings a gun and his own maniacal desire. He will later bring a gun on his search for Dorcas, but on this, his second time of nearly finding Wild, he falls down to the ground and begs, "Is it you? Just say it. Say anything." And then, as he waits by her secret bower, he then pleads, "You don't have to say nothing. Let me see your hand. Just stick it out someplace and I'll go; I promise. A sign." He is desperate for some contact, some acknowledgment, but is instead faced with the void. " 'You my mother?' Yes. No. Both. Either. But not this nothing" (178). So intense is the desire for a connection, a mother, that this staring into the void, into blackness, causes Joe to feel "a lint-headed fool, crazier than she and just as wild" (179). Emphasizing the connection between this foundational story and his murder of Dorcas, the narrator tells us that "Joe is wondering about all this on an icy day in January. As he puts on his coat and cap he can practically feel Victory at his side when he sets out, armed, to find Dorcas" (180). The great mystery of the novel, Joe's killing of the very thing he loves, dangles by a thread between the foundational story and Joe's state of mind as he walks the streets, his past offering a more satisfying explanation of Joe's violent act than the third sentence in the novel, which wryly states that "he shot her just to keep the feeling going" (3).

The narrator, in the final soliloquy of the novel, explains her line of thinking and how it has evolved. She begins by considering the characters in the front story but then moves to a consideration not of Hunters Hunter or Golden Gray but Wild. She understands her characters, moreover, in relationship to one another, recognizing her failings: "I saw the three of them, Felice, Joe and Violet, and they looked to me like a mirror image of Dorcas, Joe and Violet" (221). The parallels, as

I explain in chapter 6, might include envisioning them as a *ménage à trois*: desire not merely centered on the man but allowing for same-sex desire as well. The narrator sees them as "exotic," "driven," and—in a way that recalls the parable in Morrison's Nobel Prize lecture—"Like dangerous children" (221). But for the narrator these stories are eclipsed by the stronger pull of Wild, what I have been calling the mysterious queer center of the novel. The narrator, identifying with Joe in the final moments of the novel, sees him as not merely looking for Dorcas but "Wild's chamber of gold," reawakening past equations of Wild with wombs while also acquiring a strangely sexual intimation (221).

The narrator underscores her desire for Wild when she describes her "home in the rock; that place sunlight got into most of the day. Nothing to be proud of, to show anybody or to want to be in. But I do" (221). And the narrator does not simply confess a strange identification with that secrecy, that peace, but also imagines a relationship with this wild woman: "She has seen me and is not afraid of me. She hugs me. Understands me. Has given me her hand. I am touched by her. Released in secret" (221). It is this act of being "released" that initiates an uncharacteristic coda in the novel where an accounting of what happened to various characters is given: "Alice Manfred moved away . . ."; "Felice still buys Okeh records . . ."; "Joe found work at Paydirt . . ." (222). This quick summary almost distracts us from the narrator's most vulnerable moment, the intimacy and desire she conveys for Wild, but then the final paragraphs return to consider the narrator's state of mind—although shifting her attentions to the reader. In the context of the narrator's confession of love for Wild, the final confession, "*That I have loved only you,*" invites more than a consideration of the narrator as book, neutered in its self-personification and generously engaging all readers of every sex and sexual orientation. If the novel's elaborate devices threaten to turn the tale into an allegory of the relationship between book and reader, Wild and her "chamber of gold" invite us to consider desire as located in the very depths of the foundational story that resists heteronormativity and instead eroticizes blackness as not masculine but oriented toward the wild woman, Morrison's most radical figure of resistance to family, gender roles, and sexual orientation.[7] And one of her most powerful examinations into myths of blackness.

In novels like *The Bluest Eye*, *Paradise*, and *A Mercy*, Morrison has explored the special status of dark black African Americans and Africans. These characters are frequently represented as privileged, such as the

8-Rocks in *Paradise*, or troubled, such as Pecola in *The Bluest Eye*, but they do not fully take on the status of myth.[8] In *Jazz*, Wild becomes mythic through the stories the community tells of her: its characterization of her as witch, omen, ghostly, and inhuman. The novel builds her character through storytelling, communal and private, and the narrator of the novel romanticizes her mysterious essence. In structuring her plotline next to the parallel plot of a white man discovering his blackness, *Jazz* ensures that her berry-blackness takes on special importance. In building her narrative first upon the white-black man's reluctance to face this "vision" and later her son's desperate need to see into her black bower and face his heritage, *Jazz* invests her identity with multiple meanings of blackness personified but, nevertheless, rich with symbolic weight. But long before *Jazz* was published Morrison had already explored this idea of investing a character with mythic blackness. It should not surprise us that *Tar Baby*, which announces an interest in myth in its very title, would be that novel.

Although the story of the African woman in the canary dress gets told in two short pages, her presence takes on great psychic space in the novel. Trudier Harris characterizes her story as marking "Jadine's awakening from her carefree, deliciously irresponsible slumber. A bit more rude than a prince's kiss, the jolt sends her briefly on another pass" (133). It is a story, so Harris's analogy intimates, associated with fable, though her analogy replaces the prince with a princess and, therefore, invites a reading of same-sex desire. Because the scene is so invested in exploring Western standards of beauty, colonialism, and consumption, scholars have hardly attended to the story's saturation in exploring all forms of desire, including lesbian desire. If we read the African woman through the tar baby myth—as Morrison tells us to do—we have a second reason to consider her a figure of same-sex desire, one that haunts.

Not unlike the mythic story of Wild, Morrison invests this symbol of blackness with the liminal status of the walking dead and circulates queer desire around her disappearing and evanescent figure. The passage keeps the motivations for desire and explanations of disdain somewhat mysterious while also inviting knowledgeable readers to consider her in relationship to the tar baby myth. In the Uncle Remus story, a wily fox fashions a sticky, gluey substance into a figure that fascinates rabbit, and when rabbit, frustrated with the tar baby's silence, takes a swing at the tar baby, he becomes stuck. The woman in the canary dress, therefore, represents not the deceit of the fox or the resourcefulness of the rabbit as much as she represents the tar baby or trap itself—silent and intriguing. Scholars have mined the novel for the many other characters that might be tar babies—the likely candidates including Jadine, Son, and even the island—but the woman in yellow has the special distinction of being, like the myth itself, from Africa and, not unlike the sticky figure in the myth, silent. If she entraps Jadine, it is by virtue of her exotic beauty, which is powerful and radiant despite the Western standards that Jadine has internalized and also reflects externally. As a vision, the African woman reflects Jadine's abandonment of her "ancient properties," a phrase that will appear with great weight and meaning at the end of the novel. As Jan Furman explains, "The woman in the Paris market, whether consciously or not, calls attention to something that is missing in Jadine: she has no connection to her cultural past, and without it, Morrison suggests, she is vulnerable at the very least, and at most she is like the abused Michael, a cultural orphan" (57).

It is significant that we are introduced to the African woman not in the present tense of the novel but as a memory that comes to Jadine after she awakens from a dream. In this way, the African woman begins to take on the qualities of personal myth, a story Jadine tells herself and one that, more importantly, haunts her and will appear later as a figure in one of the novel's most provocative visions, described alternatively as a dream full of menacing breasts and a visitation of ghosts. Both references, in classic Morrison style, blur the line between dream and waking moments, reality and fiction, and the living and the dead. The dream that first prompts Jadine to recall the African woman is tame by contrasts, full of oversized hats sailing through the air, and the novel takes pains to distinguish this haunting dream from the haunting reality of the woman in the canary dress: "She [Jadine] lay there under the eye of the moon wondering why the hats had shamed and repelled her so. As soon as she gave up looking for the center of the fear, she was reminded of another picture that was not a dream" (44). The dream is impenetrable to Jadine (and perhaps to many readers) and it is this impenetrable quality that gets associated with the dreamlike appearance of the vision in yellow. The memory provides crucial background information about Jadine and "[o]ne of the happiest days of her life," a day when she chooses to celebrate her success as an object of beauty (i.e., she has been selected to be on the cover of *Elle* magazine) and her intellect (i.e., she has just learned that she has passed her oral exams at the Sorbonne).

The celebration, like so much in the novel, emphasizes food as a symbol of culture and class. [9] The description of the scene in the market gets anticipated with details of many exotic foods that reflect Jadine's full acceptance of an elite consumer culture and when the African woman is mentioned, it is in the context of Jadine's desire to purchase everything on her list:

> Under such benevolent circumstances, knowing she was in-telligent and lucky, everything on her list would of course be there. And when the vision materialized in a yellow dress Jadine was not sure it was not all part of her list—an addition to the coconut and tamarind, a kind of plus to go with the limes and pimiento. Another piece of her luck. (45)

The woman, linked as she is to exotic foods, captivates Jadine not merely because she is tall and beautiful but because she, like the food, is exotic. Not unlike the silent tar baby of the myth, she need not say a word in order to entrap, and it is as a "vision" (both alluring and also as a figure of absence) that she ensnares.

The scene's refashioning of the tar baby myth sexualizes the tar baby figure and makes the rabbit, represented through Jadine, lured by an African beauty, specifically characterizing those attractions as tied to her non-Western features. Jadine imagines her naked: "Under her long canary yellow dress Jadine knew there was too much hip, too much bust" (45). This confuses Jadine, who tries to understand how "she and everybody else in the store [could be] transfixed" (45). The narrator, however, locates the woman's allure in everything African. She is marked by African aesthetics—"upside down V's were scored into each of her cheeks, her hair was wrapped in a gelée as yellow as her dress," but it is her "skin like tar" that most transparently marks her as the tar baby figure alluded to in the title of the novel and as a figure of blackness, one packaged in myth. In a scene fully invested in Jadine's interior point of view, Jadine appears voyeuristic as she follows the woman's every move, even the seemingly insignificant detail of her lifting three eggs from a carton and holding them aloft as she takes them to the cashier, who becomes puzzled by this unconventional way of purchasing eggs. The eggs, which get described in great detail, announce their symbolic meaning not only through the text's willingness to offer an inordinate amount of attention to such a small event but also through repetition: the eggs appear in later references to the African woman as if this detail distinguishes her magical importance.

After the woman drops "a ten-louis piece on the counter," her exit is characterized as "gold tracking the floor and leaving them all behind" (46), and we are reminded of her status as a vision when the entire store watches her preparation for exit, wondering what she would do with her hands full of eggs: "Each one of them begged in his heart that it would not happen. That she would float through the glass the way a vision should" (46). And because each one forgets that the market doors will open automatically, they are thrilled as the "transcendent beauty [approached the door] and it flew open in silent obedience" (46). We are reminded, moreover, at the beginning and at the end of the scene that she is like a vision, inviting readers to think of her as otherworldly, which furthers her function as mythic and larger than life. If the scene positions Jadine as voyeur and the tar baby as a transfixing vision, it does not physically trap Jadine—the rabbit—but instead captures her imagination and her deep-seated and complex emotions about blackness. This tar baby figure, however, does fleetingly respond to Jadine's voyeurism, and even this conveys a sexualized form of violence and rejection. As Jadine watches the woman through the plate-glass window, the narrative again becomes hyperbolic in anticipating the absence of this figure of blackness as the "moment before the cataclysm when all loveliness and life and breath in the world was about to disappear" (46). This extravagant description of a small, quotidian moment keeps the symbolic intensity of the moment present in our mind and asks us to identify with Jadine even though her emotions seem extreme. When the woman turns to face Jadine, she "shot an arrow of saliva between her teeth down to the pavements and the hearts below" (46).

Fearlessly courting associations with lesbian desire, the narrative, not unlike some of the distancing techniques in *Jazz*, switches at this moment from Jadine's point of view to present a more universalizing and distancing axiom: "When you have fallen in love, rage is superfluous; insult impossible." But Jadine's point of view does not totally disappear, and her obsession with food continues to provide a metaphor for desire, albeit through the universalizing second-person address: "You mumble 'bitch,' but the hunger never moves, never closes" (46). The universalizing voice of this section ties the hunger that "never closes" to the tar baby myth: "It is placed, open and always ready for another canary-yellow dress, other *tar-black fingers* holding three white eggs" (46; emphasis added).

If this statement foreshadows the appearance of a second tar baby figure, we need only to read to the end of the next chapter to make the connection. Although Son is not immediately introduced as a vision or specter, he is, not unlike the African woman, defined by (reduced to) his blackness. When Margaret discovers Son in her closet, she runs to everyone screaming, "In my closet. In my closet" (79). When asked to elaborate, her description of what she has discovered in her closet gets communicated by a single word: " 'Black,' she whispered, her eyes shut tight" (79). With all the characters gathered to face the intruder and with his identity reduced to a single word, the narrative emphasizes Son's central role as the essence that fills the void. The novel, up to this point, offers little more than the bickering of Valerian and Margaret Street, the banter of Sydney and Ondine, and the musings of Jadine. With the arrival of Son, the characters now have something substantial to fight over, a proxy for the son who will not show up for Christmas dinner. Into the void, Valerian Street welcomes the intruder, inviting him—to the shock of everyone—for a drink. But Son never becomes mythic the way the African woman does, and Jadine, another tar baby figure, also resists mythic status, though both debate endlessly what it means to be black. Indeed, the novel allows its characters to come back to these debates, but their characters are painfully constructed in a tradition of realistic fiction while the African woman gets represented as a "vision," not unlike a dream, and much later in the novel reintroduced as one of the night women in one of Morrison's most provocative depictions of specters.

Just as the very brief scene of the African woman serves to mark Jadine as a "cultural orphan," the night women serve as accusation while also suggesting a different path for her, one that Ondine articulates at the end of the novel as cultural and familial belonging: "A daughter is a woman that cares about where she come from and takes care of them that took care of her" (281). The night women, ghostly figures that crowd around Jadine's bed, include the living and the dead. Women Jadine has not met, like Son's ex, and Ondine, are no less ghostly for not being actually deceased. Although the scene in Eloe, which reveals the great distance between Son and Jadine, may represent Jadine's emotional state and her inner spiritual demons, the language invites us to interpret the visitation as more than merely Jadine's emotional state. After explaining that Son's ex entered because Jadine felt sexually competitive with her, the text goes on to explain that it was this internal tension,

> plus the fact that she [Jadine] had left the door unlatched
> and Son had opened it on its hinges and after it was open
> on its hinges it stayed wide open but they had not noticed

because they were paying attention only to each other so
that must have been why and how Cheyenne got in, and
then the rest: Rosa and Therese and Son's dead mother and
Sally Sarah Sadie Brown and Ondine and Soldier's wife Ellen
and Francine from the mental institution and her own dead
mother and even the woman in yellow. (257–58)

The long list, strung together with copulatives rather than commas,
builds the horror of the scene and for many will appear much like a
dream. Although Son is asleep after their wild love-making, Jadine must
face this crowd of women, even though she can only sense and not
see them until she finally gets mad and yells, "What do you want with
me, goddamn it!" (258). It is at this point that "they each pulled out
a breast and showed it to her" (258). It is difficult to read this scene
as sexual, so insistently does it seem to deploy breasts as a symbol of
motherhood and ancestry, and difficult to ignore its sexual aggression,
so much does the baring of breasts follow on the heels of the heterosexual coupling of Son and Jadine. The women, in fact, were "spoiling
her love-making, taking away her sex like succubi, but not his" (258).

The text takes pains to emphasize again that this "was not the
dream of hats" and Jadine was "wide-awake," and so the ghosts, both
living and deceased, are to be interpreted as more than a dream or
the internal haunting of the mind. But the text also makes everything
a bit blurred when it conveys that Jadine "said or thought or willed,
'I have breasts too'" (258). The women "held their own higher and
pushed their own farther out and looked at her." But here the African
woman gets a special distinction from the other night women: "All of
them revealing both their breasts except the woman in yellow. She did
something more shocking—she stretched out a long arm and showed
Jadine her three big eggs" (258–59). Breasts and eggs are, of course,
both signs of fertility, but the African woman receives a special distinction in this crowded room, and her own form of confrontation may
just as easily be viewed as sexual as an accusation of Jadine's insufficient
womanhood.

Just as the earlier scene with the African woman gets coupled with
the inscrutable dream of large hats, so, too, does this later visitation,
which gets characterized later as a "dream" and a "vision," blur the line
between an actual visitation of spirits and a product of Jadine's over-
wrought condition and active imagination. Not unlike the earlier scene,
this one haunts by virtue of its inscrutable qualities. For example, Jadine

asks, "What did they have in common even, besides the breasts" (261).
And, "Every night she went to bed too exhausted to worry, only on
waking did it come back—fresher each time, heavier, till finally . . . she
decided to reel it in" (261). But Jadine does not get much farther
than reconsidering what it means to have breasts "thrust at her like
weapons." It is, however, another opportunity to distinguish the African woman as not thrusting out a bare breast but instead a "slithery
black arm . . . stretching twelve feet, fifteen, toward her and the fingers
that fingered eggs" (261–62). It is tempting to continue to read these
dreamlike visitations as sexually symbolic, but I began by reading the
African woman through the tar baby myth, and I want to hold onto
this strategy as elucidating the queer thrust of her function in the novel.

It is through the tar baby myth that the novel structures its opening and closing around the question of safety. And it is through the
tar baby myth that the novel grows its thematic exploration of what it
means to be black. Lesbian desire, I would argue, gets nearly articulated
as one of the many threats to Jadine and her connection to the black
community. It is a threat that Son nearly erases by offering her an alternative to Western Paris, but Paris also holds the African woman and is
ultimately more complex than any one symbol can contain, and so the
novel seems to introduce the woman in yellow as a lure for Jadine that
operates in many ways, no less a symbol of Jadine's separation from her
ancestry for also being a figure of queer desire, a desire for ancestral
blackness but also something else and perhaps even more threatening.
Nothing, the novel seems to say, is safe, and certainly not our desires.

Chapter 8

⤳

Whiteness

Tar Baby Haunts *A Mercy*

One of the signs of the times is that we really don't know what "white" is.

—Kobena Mercer, "Skin Head Sex Thing:
Racial Difference and the Homoerotic Imaginary"

Whites are the living death.

—Richard Dyer, "White"

As if to counter criticism of Toni Morrison's work as too serious, too painful, too depressing, Sture Allen, in his Nobel Prize presentation speech, emphasizes the author's humor. "In great minds, gravity and humour are close neighbours."[1] As the present study turns now to the topic of whiteness, it needs—more than ever—to address Morrison's wit, a necessary tool in making visible what disappears for so many, but not all, Americans. In *Whiteness Visible: The Meaning of Whiteness in American Literature and Culture*, Valerie Babb reminds us of the importance of keeping a sense of humor when addressing whiteness: "Michel Foucault did not invent theory; Jacques Derrida did not invent theory; the barbers in my son's barbershop did" (167). Babb waits until her readers have charmed their way through her illuminating study before getting up close and personal: "As they fade, edge, and trim, they discourse upon histories, nations, civilizations, and all manner of human thought and invention. One 'text' they are particularly fond of deconstructing is The White Man" (167). Babb offers this anecdote in order to remind us of

123

the purpose of whiteness studies, the real-life consequences of whiteness as privilege as well as the ingenious forms that resistance takes. Because humor cannot help but assist us in addressing the gravity of the situation, I begin this chapter with a goal of understanding how and why Morrison uses humor to queer the white ghost. In Morrison's fourth book, the novel most famous—and even infamous—for its exploration of white characters, Valerian serves as a provocative study in whiteness, a representation of the most outrageous performance of privilege marked by race, gender, and sexual orientation.

In an interview for *Essence* shortly after the publication of *Tar Baby*, Judith Wilson characterizes Morrison's work as having taken on a "new course," one that "outlines political issues to a degree that your previous works never seemed to do" (134). Disagreeing with this characterization, Morrison addresses the unstated: "This book *required* white people because of the tar baby story." As if already puzzling through some of the questions she will raise in *Playing in the Dark: Whiteness and the Literary Imagination*, Morrison recognizes the need "to imagine others and . . . to project consciously into the danger zones such others represent for me" (3). In this early interview, Morrison also registers the resistance and misunderstandings that will result in taking such risks as if already understanding how readers will expect a certain treatment of race from her, specifically through blackness and not whiteness. But *Tar Baby* sets the terms of both identity positions in such a way that the centrality of whiteness gets deconstructed with great humor and depth, offering one of the richest texts for the study of whiteness. It does this, I argue, by disrupting the interdependent narratives of white privilege and heterosexual reproduction.

In his fascinating study of whiteness (*The Heart of Whiteness: Normal Sexuality and Race in America, 1880–1940*), Julian B. Carter explores the evolving "correlation of heterosexual whiteness to normality," a correlation that gets expressed through anxieties over reproduction and the fate of the family. Although whiteness—as Carter argues—gets conflated with "civilization" and "normality" (15), homosexuality—in the contemporary imagination—gets also tied to whiteness. My reading of Valerian embraces him as a manifestation of such competing elisions of identity and the novel as inviting readers to consider these contradictions. The novel creates, after all, an incubator for conflations, confusions, and conflicts by setting its cast of characters in the compressed space of an island and, furthermore, confining them to virtually a single house, as if to clear the field in order to focus solely on the apotheoses of various identity positions. When the narrative breaks free from this limited spatial constraint, it is in order to give the budding romance of Son and Jadine more space, which all the more emphasizes the trouble on the island paradise and the unsteady hold of white privilege as secure or even normal. Valerian and Margaret Street, rather than finding safety in this compressed space, lose their claims to normality in a dramatic confession that explains the break in their family line and, by extension, their tenuous claims on everything that whiteness usually confers.

Built, as it is, upon various continuities and breaks in ancestry, *Tar Baby* counterpoints the experiences of its white and black characters, almost suggesting that blacks have ghosts and whites have history. Although this oversimplifies the novel's counterpointing of white and black characters, the novel risks offering too much history for Valerian and Margaret and too many ghosts for Jadine and Son. The latter, for much of the novel, seem orphaned, unnamed and unclaimed. Defined by their isolation from the past, their central conflicts rest on their choices to find, make, and/or recognize their connections to their ancestors. If ghosts offer some means to overcome that isolation (sometimes at quite a cost), they do so through what we commonly refer to as "haunting." Valerian and Margaret, however, seem relatively free of haunting. Although we learn early in the novel that "Valerian took very good care of the greenhouse for it was a nice place to talk to his ghosts"(14), they do not become as apparent, as visually present to the reader, as the notable ghosts that haunt Jadine and Son. In place of these disruptive specters, the white characters have either happy conversations in greenhouses or something radically different: history. Even the "fog," which comes in "like the hair of maiden aunts," serves to "[throw] back one's own reflection from the windows," reinforcing the Valerians access to history even in this faraway land. In its depiction of ghosts, the novel emphasizes one of the privileges of whiteness to be an easy access to history, for unlike the Deads in *Song of Solomon*, the white and privileged Streets in *Tar Baby* have not had their ties to ancestors broken by the legacy of slavery, which wrenched families apart through the forced emigration from Africa and then later through commercial interests of the slave system that broke families as easily as it dispersed material possessions. In order to provide a foil to Jadine's and Son's journey toward or away from their ancestors, *Tar Baby* not only requires a white person but one with a well-documented history.

While the ancestors of the Streets remain relatively silent or lurking like mist in the corners of rooms, the novel presents their histories, even pedigrees, with great detail. If the novel tempts us to think of the white characters as having their own ghosts, it keeps them at bay. But what if we read whiteness as already a ghost of itself and the Streets as haunted by their own ghostliness? Richard Dyer in his study of whiteness invites such a reading when he calls whites "the living dead" (59). As the living dead, Valerian particularly stands in striking contrast to the active spirits that crowd around Jadine and Son, and his function as a symbol of everything past grows in relationship to the possibilities of those other symbols of the future—Son and Jadine. If Valerian's presence as "the living dead" is felt, it is in relief against the crowded field of ghosts attending the black characters and making *Tar Baby* an essential text for understanding Morrison's engagement with the porous line between the dead and living. From start to finish, this unique novel is teeming with otherworldly beings: blind horsemen galloping out of the ocean and onto land, each one fated to roam for eternity and beckoning for Son to join them; ancient women indistinguishable from trees, dangling from branches, luring Jadine into the wilds and away from the manicured civilization she treasures; and, perhaps most disturbing, a crowd of Jadine's and Son's dead ancestors pushing and nudging each other as they approach the couple's bed, wielding their bare breasts like weapons. If the significant black characters, Jadine and Son, find themselves accosted by ghosts, the equally important white characters, Valerian and Margaret, do not. But if we are willing to imagine Valerian as the embodiment of the "living dead," then his role in counterpointing the busy field of black ghosts offers special opportunities for understanding the role of ghosts as a central conceit in the Morrison canon, though not uniform in its expression.

Tar Baby, with its great fascination with disruption and disorder, arguably invites a queer ghost—perhaps even requires a queer ghost—much the same way Morrison argues that the rewriting of the tar baby myth required white characters. Surely this most unusual novel in the Morrison canon, a narrative that has vexed so many scholars, must offer some troubling of the normative strains of romance, something to counterbalance the seemingly impossible pairing of Son and Jadine, which is all the more dramatic in its inevitability. It is a love plot that is quite relentless, one that insists that heterosexual love (or is it sex?) will triumph over class and everything else. The novel might be productively viewed through the tradition of a comedy of manners, an invitation to read plot and dialogue for humor, to free the novel's extravagances from the burden of social realism. Although scholarship on Morrison's comedic qualities remains a pronounced lacuna in a busy field, *Tar Baby* suffers the most from our inability (or is it our unwillingness) to read for humor. Central to the heterosexual drama initiated by Son's arrival to the island paradise are the heterosexual spectators, the principal characters of Valerian and Margaret Street (Candy King and Beauty Queen), Sydney and Ondine (their butler and maid), and Yardman and Maria (the island help). Circulating around the impossible qua inevitable love plot, these other couples, each one of them characterized as well past the romance stage of their lives, endure pressures and suffer new revelations that force them to examine what has long remained unexamined: their relationships. We cannot help but read the risible courtship of Son and Jadine against these more "secure" relationships, which also invite humor in their juxtaposition to Son and Jadine and the others, marked as all of these relationships are to each other by binaries of race, class, age, nationality—but not sexuality. There is no gay character, no homosexual romance, and no "ready" foil for the heterosexual coupling.

If the cast of characters, represented almost exclusively by these four heterosexual relationships, seems to crowd out any possibilities of representations of homosexuality, it becomes all the more fascinating to note when and how the text veers toward the queer. I am particularly interested in how Valerian Street, white patriarch and benefactor, gets marked as provisionally and risibly queer, a complicated extension of his many privileges as wealthy, male, American, and—above everything else—white. If the novel, as I argue in chapter 7, deconstructs myths of blackness, it cannot help but engage the socially dependent myths of whiteness. Patricia Hill Collins's explanation of these myths and their interdependence is particularly useful in considering what Morrison writes against:

> If racism relied on assumptions of Black promiscuity that in turn enabled Black people to "breed like animals," then Black sexual practices that did not adhere to these assumptions challenged racism at its very core. Either Black people could not be homosexual or those Blacks who were homosexual were not "authentically" Black. Black people were allegedly not threatened by homosexuality because they were protected by their "natural" heterosexuality. In contrast, Whites had no such "natural" protection and thus had to work harder at proving their heterosexuality. By a curious twist of logic, these racist assumptions about an authentic Blackness grounded in

a promiscuous heterosexuality helped to define Whiteness as well. In this context, homosexuality could be defined as an internal threat to the integrity of the (White) nuclear family. Beliefs in a naturalized, normal hyper-heterosexuality among Black people effectively "whitened" homosexuality. (105–06)

Tar Baby offers a fictional representation of this "twist of logic" that Collins highlights, offering Valerian Street not so much as a closet homosexual but a ghostly figure associated with queerness or, rather, a quintessential figure of whiteness as visible against the reductive and destructive myths of blackness as hypersexual, homosexuality as white, and white patriarchy as threatened by both.

The novel makes this invitation explicit in an early linking of Valerian with the candy that bears his name. As a symbol of Valerian's whiteness and hence privilege, the candy gets marked as a failure, "a slow but real flop, although not a painful one financially for it was made from the syrup sludge left over from their main confection—Teddy Boys" (50). Morrison has fun with complicating the metonym for white privilege by associating it with waste (i.e., "sludge left over from their main confection") and queerness (i.e., "Give us something with nuts"), all presented through the eyes of commercial interests.

> "What's the matter with them?" asked the uncles.
>   "Faggoty," said the Sales reps.
>   "Faggoty?"
>   "Yeah. Like Valentines. Can you see a kid sitting on a curb tossing those fairy candies in his mouth?" (50)

The associations with failure and queerness get racialized when the salesmen explain the target market for the "faggoty" candy: " 'Jigs,' said the salesmen. 'Jigs buy 'em" (51). This anecdote serves to illustrate the ease with which homophobia intersects with other power structures, such as capitalism and racism, but also registers a historic shift in opportunities for African Americans. "When they move [North]," the salesmen explain, "they want to leave that stuff behind. They don't want to be reminded. Alaga syrup is dead in New York. So is Gold Dust Soap and so are Valerians" (51). As a metonym for the white patriarch, the death of the candy foreshadows the death of Valerian, slow but inevitable. Or, perhaps as Dyer would have it, a living death.

Son, who gets integrated into the cast of characters relatively late in the novel (despite his central importance), provides the necessary counterpoint to the trope of "the living dead."[2] Although Morrison begins and ends the novel with Son in transit, it is with the introduction of Son to Valerian's household that the novel announces its fascination with the most outrageous performance of whiteness, one that takes on a decidedly homoerotic cast. After Margaret discovers Son in her closet, a provocative scene that I discuss at length in chapter 7, Valerian dramatically counterpoints Margaret's hysteria with calm, another quality Richard Dyer associates with the performance of whiteness. To the consternation of everyone else (and perhaps many readers expecting social realism), Valerian turns the intruder into a guest, asserting his cavalier dominance over his hysterical wife, his disregard for his disbelieving servants, and, most important, his inoculation (or attempt at inoculation) of the threat of a black intruder. Morrison exaggerates the narrative of white anxiety, effectively illuminating clichés in order to expose whiteness for what it is: a performance despite its efforts to appear natural and effortless. Some of this gets conveyed through the contradictory nature of Jadine's multiple perceptions of Valerian at dinner. "He was marvelous," Jadine thinks. "All the while the man [the black intruder] ate limp salad, flat soufflé, peaches and coffee, Valerian behaved as though it was the most ordinary of incidents" (92). But Jadine also imagines that "Valerian was comforted . . . by her presence at the table. That she exercised some restraint on the man; that Valerian believed that in her presence the man might be kept manageable" (92). And then, finally, Jadine imagines, "More than grace, she thought, Valerian had courage." Valerian's thoughts—when the novel gives him a rare self-conscious moment—are not any more reliable or consistent than this, but it is important to recognize that through Jadine readers are invited to recognize Valerian's actions as a performance of whiteness. Or, as Jadine further imagines his "whimsy" as "Style. All style" (91–92).

If Morrison does much to reveal the performance (or style) of whiteness, she also conveys its investment in willful ignorance. In *Cities of the Dead*, Joseph Roach considers this willful ignorance, or forgetting, to be "an opportunistic tactic of whiteness" (6). Valerian illustrates this profoundly when he repeatedly asks Son for his name, never offering—as many cultures would expect—his name first. "I'm sorry," Valerian states, "I don't know your name" (92). Unwilling to yield to Valerian's expectations of who gets to control this social exchange, Son withholds his own name. At the end of this dinner scene, Morrison returns to this unstated clash of cultures, this time making the exchange more explicit. "I'm sorry, but I don't know your name" (94). Valerian clearly does not recognize his own rudeness in asking for Son's name without offering his own, and Morrison plays the scene, rich with the conflict of cultures, for its comedic possibilities. " 'That makes us even,' said the man with a wide smile. 'I don't know yours either' " (94). Lest the reader miss the importance of the exchange, let alone the humor of it, Morrison creates a pause with a paragraph break and writes: "And they still didn't, but Valerian instructed him to be put up in the guest room anyway" (94). When the novel returns to the subject of names (and what it means to "know" a person), the setting changes from the public space of the dining room to Valerian's sanctuary: his greenhouse.

It is important to note that the final exchange of names between Valerian and Son—in contrast to the exchanges quoted previously—occurs well after the discovery of Son in chapter 3 (page 79) and well after the incomplete exchange in the dining room in chapter 4 (pages 92–94). Just as the reader must wait until well after Son's introduction in the first line of the novel for him to be integrated into the cast of characters, and just as the love plot seethes, percolates, and threatens to abort before Jadine and Son come together, the revealing of Son's name, not just for the other characters but for the reader as well, gets delayed. Clearly, this is a novel built upon dramatic postponements and pregnant pauses. Valerian and Son, in other words, are well beyond their first "date," and Morrison milks the scene for its erotic humor, fully addressing the interdependent myths of the hypersexualized black man and the titillated, effete white man (with queer associations fully invited). At this point, Morrison tellingly reintroduces the association of Valerian's name with the "faggoty" candy, setting the exchange of names and the reintroduction of the metonym for whiteness as queer in the greenhouse to emphasize all things artificial and controlled. It is a site symbolic of the convergence of opposites, one that invites readers to consider conceptions of identity (i.e., race, gender, sexuality) as not just natural (like the very plants in the greenhouse) but also constructed.

The greenhouse provides the perfect setting for the questions Morrison raises, and she gives us access to Valerian's thoughts right before the entrance of Son in a kimono. "He assumed [Son] was what he'd said he was: a crewman jumping ship, and his roaming about the house and grounds, hiding in Margaret's closet, was more outrageous than threatening. He had looked into the man's eyes and had no fear" (146). Into this feeling of fearlessness, which Valerian celebrates as a virtue, walks Son, "wrapped in a woman's kimono, barefoot with gleaming wrought-iron hair." Morrison undercuts Valerian's feelings of self-congratulatory calmness with a refashioned scene of white anxiety loaded with provocative symbols that play upon intersecting stereotypes of race, gender, and sexuality. The stock scene of a lurking and sexual black menace, which Susan Mayberry analyzes with great skill in her book *Can't I Love What I Criticize?*,[3] gets thrown into the light of the greenhouse, and this time it is not a woman, Margaret, who embodies that white anxiety marked with desire, but the white patriarch, despite his effort to convey calm in the face of the black-sexual threat: "Valerian let his eyes travel cautiously down from the hair to the robe to the naked feet. The man smiled broadly. He looked down at himself, back at Valerian and said, 'But I don't do no windows'" (146). Both men, as if registering the way race, class, gender, and sexuality "look" at this moment, convey their mutual self-consciousness (and efforts to take control): Son by smiling broadly and Valerian with a nervous laugh. After Valerian laughs at Son's playful remark, Valerian refers to him as "Mr. Sheek," asserting his control again (or at least believing that he has taken control) of the very thing that eluded him before: names.

Because the scene is so saturated in the erotics of race, racism, and power, when Valerian finally confesses his name and Son states, "I used to eat a candy called Valerians," the reader cannot help but feel several reversals full of humor and ironies. When Valerian explains that the candy is named after him and not the reverse, readers are invited to enjoy his defensiveness as turning on both class implications but also a tension associated with courtship. When the man in the kimono does not respond with the proper awe (Son merely says, "Oh") and instead slips into his own performance ("'It's sho pretty in here,' he said, still smiling"), Morrison furthers the dance between these two men. Indeed, the early story of the candy's history as well as that history's associations with failure, queerness, and Southern blacks, provocatively and queerly mark Valerian's efforts to impress Son. But Morrison also marks Son's performances as complicit in the erotically charged exchange when Son's kimono comes undone. "Valerian looked at his genitals," and tells him, "You can't go round like that in front of the ladies." Rather than rushing to close the kimono, Son "looked up letting the kimono hang to his sides" (148). He seizes this opportunity to ask, "You ain't gonna turn me in?" effectively tying Valerian's control over his destiny to the white patriarch's inability to control his gaze (i.e., desire). The scene both conveys Valerian centrality as white patriarch and also knocks him off-center as someone who is not in control of his gaze, and Morrison follows this decentering of power with Son instructing Valerian on how to force cyclamen to flower ("like women, you have to jack them up every once in a while") and then telling him a joke about "three colored whores." When Jadine comes in to see who was being murdered, she is an outsider to this stock scene of male bonding—sexual and racial in its meaning but also profoundly gendered. In this way, *Tar Baby* keeps shifting the center and does not allow the novel to separate whiteness from overlapping systems of power. It is, moreover, a reminder that Valerian is not the center of the novel, despite his claims for centrality, which are tied to his whiteness.[4]

Like most—if not all—of Morrison's novels, *Tar Baby*, in fact, offers no central character. The novel instead registers that Valerian Street's meaning derives from an assumption of centrality while also deploying the threat of homoerotic desire, specifically seen as whiteness marked by its covetousness of blackness, the very thing that haunts Valerian's centrality. He becomes more ghostlike as the narrative moves toward its conclusion and searches for a way to dispose of him and his claims to centrality. It is this function as a center that constantly gets revealed to be not a center that surely contributes to some estimations of *Tar Baby* as Morrison's failure in creating believable white characters. But the novel gets at far more important revelations of how we read whiteness, and the comedy of manners through which I am reading the novel strives for revelations of social structures and power dynamics rather than depth of character. John Irving recognizes this in an early review of the novel for the *New York Times* when he states that "Toni Morrison's greatest accomplishment is that she has raised her novel above the social realism that too many black novels and women's novels are trapped in. She has succeeded in writing about race and women symbolically." If we view the novel in the tradition of a comedy of manners, the humor helps reveal the painful and profound seriousness of the novel. More pointedly, as a comedy of manners concerned with making whiteness and its tenuous hold on privilege visible, it should not surprise us, then, that Valerian's ghost never fully comes into view and instead the white patriarch becomes a queer ghost of himself, essentially represents a self-haunting through the sad but also humorous reversals of his function as center and white patriarch.

Almost totally absent from the last fourth of the novel, Valerian appears in a short and relatively quiet final scene with Sydney. The exchange between these two men might invite comparisons to Jean Genet's *The Maids*, which also capitalizes on performances of the roles of master and servant for irony, complicated inversions, and humorous pathos.[5] In the reversals, the reader is invited to understand how power never is so neatly distributed in the first place and that whiteness is merely a performance of power and always subject to exposure. Morrison, furthermore, does not simply reverse the roles of master and servant but also invites us to consider this reversal against the backdrop of the love story between Son and Jadine, which ends with Son returning to the island in pursuit of Jadine. Son is always in motion, always changing. Valerian, in contrast, appears as a wandering ghost figure at the end of the novel.

In setting Valerian's final scene in the greenhouse, Morrison invites us to recall the earlier pairing of Valerian and Son in the same artificial atmosphere. In place of the scene of an older white man and younger black man caught performing through stereotypes as they bond as heterosexual men, a fascinating passage that reveals the interdependence of shared power, the final scene, by contrast, depicts two older men, Valerian and Sydney, as slowly accepting the transfer of power from the white patriarch to the black servant. The scene lacks any of the erotic tension that characterizes the earlier exchange, but the absence of any erotic force is part of this later scene's haunting qualities, and Valerian appears as a mere shadow of his former self. Valerian has lost his power, and it is, ironically, his unkempt hair that provides the most ready symbol of that loss. Valerian's unkempt hair lacks the power associated with Son's dreadlocks, which at various points in the novel are characterized as "dreadlock hair" (80), "physically overpowering . . . aggressive, vicious hair that needed to be put in jail" (113) and not unlike "wings from his head, more alive than the sealskin" (132). Part of Son's transformation in the novel gets marked by his "homemade haircut" that makes him "gorgeous" and makes him ultimately irresistible to Jadine. He is no Samson but gains even more power with the loss of his hair. Valerian's wild hair, however, does not signal power or even life but the opposite. We are left then with an image of the white, heterosexual, patriarch as a ghost of himself—empty, lifeless, pathetic.

Nothing fully prepares us for this radical transformation at the end of the novel, save for the dramatic secret at the book's center: the revelation that Margaret had for many years abused their son. Valerian becomes unhinged by this revelation, and this serves to explain his ultimate loss of power and privilege. It is significant that he sees innocence as his crime.

> He thought about innocence there in his greenhouse and knew
> that he was guilty of it because he had lived with a woman
> who had made something kneel down in him the first time
> he saw her, but about whom he knew nothing; had watched
> his son grow and talk but also about whom he had known
> nothing. And there was something so foul in that, something
> in the crime of innocence so revolting it paralyzed him. He
> had not known because he had not taken the trouble to
> know. He was satisfied with what he did know. (242)

In thinking about his crime, Valerian comes as close to embodying a
nascent understanding of the dangers of whiteness. Whiteness, of course,
is inextricable from other social identity positions of power, such as
heterosexuality, masculinity, and nationality, and Valerian's physical transformation to ghost is manifest in the state of the greenhouse, that
symbol of his inner sanctuary and outer control over the world. Just
as the greenhouse earlier served as a site for the dramatization of his
erotic exchange with Son (one that is marked by neutered plants finally
blooming), it now serves to reveal his attenuated state, his function as
the living dead. When Sydney says, "You letting this place run down,
Mr. Street," Valerian responds as if dazed and confused. When Sydney
tries again ("You letting it go to pieces"), Valerian responds simply by
stating, "It's my place" and "I like it this way . . ." (285).

Valerian's final words, consistent with his attenuated state, reinforce his function as the living dead and its inability to fully recognize
the changes in the world. "What's happening here," he asks Sydney.
"Something's happening here" (287). In the context of the scene, which
provides several signs of Sydney's assertion of power over Valerian, such
as the culminating moment when servant tells master they will not be
leaving the island, Valerian's final words seem to mark the shift in power
and convey Valerian's vague awareness of that change. But in the context
of Son's return to the island and his confrontation with the ghosts of
the island (or what Therese might call his "ancient properties"), Valerian's vague claim that "something" is happening underscores the novel's
mystical themes as well as the novel's invitation to understand Valerian
through Son and Son through Valerian. Part of that invitation cannot
help but position Valerian as a ghost of himself—defined by his loss of
power, loss of his functions as husband, patriarch, master, and, most
profoundly, father. Son, the surrogate child, and Michael, the biological
child, provide a doubling of this loss, but it is Michael's arrival that the

novel keeps withholding, the secret reason for his absence and disaffection only uncovered at the end and linked, finally, to the demise of Valerian and his chain of privileges.

If the revelation that Michael has been abused by Margaret initiates Valerian's final death, it also serves as the key to understanding Valerian's function in relation to his son and his surrogate Son. The novel, furthermore, does not set myths of blackness and whiteness against one another as merely oppositional but also as implicated in other stereotypes of gender, class, and sexuality. In the context of the romance of Jadine and Son, Valerian's crime of innocence—of being "satisfied with what he did know" and therefore failing to know those who are "closest" to him—marks the missing son, Michael, as the most powerful victim of the patriarch's blindness. In "Blackness and Art in Toni Morrison's *Tar Baby*," Linda Krumholz reminds us of the importance of reading Michael's absence as central to Morrison's lifelong concern with cultural silences: "Michael is figured as a sacrificial victim, and his absence is a central motivating and symbolic presence. Michael's ever-present absence is reminiscent of Sula's absences in *Sula*, as well as Beloved's role as the historical, psychological, and symbolic presence and absence around which *Beloved* focuses" (268).[6] It is fascinating that Krumholz's examples liken Michael not only to that other figure of child abuse, Beloved, but also to the sexual outlaw, Sula. Although child abuse certainly serves as a clearly stated explanation for Michael's absence, the novel does not offer this explanation until the end, and so readers are invited to speculate about Michael's estrangement. We are not given many clues, but early in the novel we learn that his mother plans to entice him to the island by "giving him his favorite poet for Christmas" (66). In her letter to her son, Margaret hints that this will be Michael's reward for returning to the family for Christmas when she includes a line Michael used to recite from the poet (" 'And he glittered when he walked' " 66). Valerian is disgusted with this attempt to buy affection. In his emotional conversation with Jadine, Valerian confesses that he hasn't seen his son in three years and characterizes him as "beautiful," a "kitten," "humming," "singing," but not someone that he liked the last couple of times (75–77). When Jadine finds herself unable to respond, she is saved by a scream "full of terror," and in this way the novel replaces the mystery of the estranged son with the discovery of Son, who is found in a closet. In a queer reading, this cannot help but make us smile. But even if we resist this invitation, the substitution of the black intruder for the absent son cannot help but send scripts of whiteness on a collision course with scripts of sexuality, queering white-ness in ways that get provocatively explored—as I have tried to argue earlier—through Valerian. If both father and son invite queer associa-tions, it is undoubtedly through the mechanism of the plot that seeks to make visible the performance of whiteness as structured upon other performances of privilege, but it inevitably offers only the deepest of closets despite the mutual displacements of dramas of sons—the black son literally found in the mother's closet and humorously deployed for its many stereotypical associations with the most pernicious myths of blackness, and the white son presented as an even more devastating object of desire, a figure invested with the greatest mystery, the most profound resistance to knowing, the greatest closet.

If *Tar Baby* may be read as Morrison's greatest exploration of the silences that attend heterosexual white privilege, it also offers a narrative of excessive, even risible, heterosexual romance as a rewriting of the tar baby myth. It is important to remember that these twin explorations of heterosexuality appear in a novel thematically built upon exploring the divide between natural and unnatural. As Trudier Harris asserts, "Unnaturalness in the novel takes a variety of forms, affecting most of the characters" (141). It is a novel that invites queer readings even as it resists those readings at every turn, content more to trouble the divide between natural/unnatural than create allegory or even tidy symbols. It is not until her ninth novel, *A Mercy*, that Morrison directly queers whiteness through characters with a clear function in challenging simplis-tic histories of race. Scully and Willard, furthermore, are given not only presence but voice, offering a stark contrast to the absent and gentle beauty represented by Michael or the ghostly emasculated Valerian of *Tar Baby*'s end.

Willard and Scully are arguably Morrison's most recognizable queer characters, appearing—ironically—in the novel set in the earliest time. If Morrison set out to look at "a period before racism was inextricably related to slavery . . . before race hierarchy was established legally," she finds a perfect parallel for inchoate forms of identity in homosexuality (Brophy-Warren 5). In many ways, Michel Foucault's *The History of Sexuality* serves as a foundational text for many later explorations of the historicity of identity formation, and Morrison, undoubtedly aware of this academic understanding of identity formation, is careful not to fall into either anachronisms of vocabulary or concept. Willard and Scully, therefore, appear less as homosexual figures than as indentured servants who happen to find it easier to band together and share a life than not.

Circumstances, rather than psychic drives, get offered as explanation for their pairing, though the novel cannot help but be read through a contemporary sensibility. It is this effort to situate them within the ethos of the seventeenth century even as they cannot help but be read against current debates about gay marriage that makes them such a fascinating touchstone for the novel's more central concern with the evolution of African American identity in the United States. The two themes, however, are not merely linked in their concern with inchoate identities, but Willard and Scully also offer Morrison's most fascinating exploration of the intersectionality of whiteness and queerness.

Morrison introduces the pair early in the novel as part of the rambling concerns of Florens, arguably the novel's central character. Florens's voice, which begins the novel, looks back at her history as a material possession, one that gets transferred away from a plantation where her mother resides to the new Vaark plantation. It is her mother, desperately worried that her daughter will soon be raped by their current master, who solicits Vaark to take her daughter because "there was no animal in his heart" (165). In addition to this crucial history, one that introduces the theme of possession, Florens offers in a confused voice an introduction to all the significant characters on the plantation. She distinguishes Willard and Scully, the white indentured servants, from the free black man, whom we learn she is captivated with. Although there is no indication at this early point in the novel that Willard and Scully are a couple, their function as one of the many enslaved characters makes the revelation of their queer status all the more interesting.

Careful not to invest these queer characters with an anachronistic sense of homosexual identity, Morrison characterizes them as indentured white servants who, through the master's eyes, "presented no threat at all" either to his wife or the other women: "In the right environment, women were naturally reliable" (34). Lina also seems to recognize their queer status when she observes that Scully "did not object to lying with Willard when sleep was not the point. No wonder Sir, without kin or sons to count on, had no males on his property" (58). In interviews, Morrison stresses the desire not only to examine "a period before racism was inextricably related to slavery" but also "to look at the vulnerability and strength of women without men" (Brophy-Warren 5). Scully and Willard appear in this narrative as exceptions to the rule of men, not like Sir, who has all the power, or even—as Florens observes—unlike the blacksmith, a free black man, who is "[n]ot like Will or Scully but like Sir" (69). They are outside the norms of white masculinity just as the blacksmith offers another version of blackness "before a race hierarchy was established legally and later culturally in the states" (Brophy-Warren 5). In this way, Morrison revisits some of the counterpointing of race and sexuality in *Tar Baby*, but in *A Mercy* she associates the queerness with life rather than the "living dead." In the context of sexual politics of current times, the novel seems almost to deploy its queer white characters not as outsiders, incapable of integration into the community as family, but as key figures of hope.

Before their chapter, the men serve mainly as queer outsiders in a plantation that—especially after the death of Vaark—is ruled and populated by women. It is difficult not to read these queer characters through the contemporary politics of gay rights and specific legislation related to marriage, adoption, and families. When Willard and Scully become the unexpected midwives to Lina's baby, many readers will find their symbolic role in bringing forth life as complex and provocatively allusive of current affairs. This birth, which takes place in the midst of a plague that has already taken the life of the plantation's master and most surely the mistress, begs to be read against the AIDS crisis, which despite its continued weight on the world (especially for gay, black, and African populations) threatens to disappear from popular awareness. Willard and Scully not only survive the plague but help to usher in new life. But even without these touchstones to our present moment, the novel does much to position its queer characters as representative of a future and not a past.

When Morrison devotes an entire chapter, late in the novel, to their point of view, most readers will not be surprised: the novel, after all, alternates chapters from Florens's perspective and the perspectives of four other characters. But in contrast to these other chapters, the one devoted to Willard and Scully offers a shared point of view that uniquely contrasts the singular points of view of Florens, Vaark, Rebekka, Lina, and Sorrow and is also unusual in Morrison's oeuvre. The novel presents the two men as a unit even as it distinguishes them by age (Willard is older), by temperament (Willard is more cautious), and by looks (Scully is fine-boned). Despite these differences it is as a unit that the other characters view them, perhaps inviting us to consider their inevitable reduction to a singular stereotype but also as an effective response to a world of enslavement.

It is significant that Willard and Scully's chapter comes near the end of the novel and directly after the climactic confrontation between Florens and the blacksmith.[7] If the confrontation between the free and the enslaved black lovers serves to underline one of the novel's main points (that Florens has "become" a slave and—as the blacksmith tells her—is "a slave by choice," 141), then the chapter devoted to Willard and Scully represents a denouement that unknots the meaning of these definitions. As white indentured servants struggling against an unfair system, they offer one of the many examples of enslavement, but even as their race and gender afford them privileges denied most of the women of the novel, their queer status, from a reader's perspective, marks them as enslaved not just by the system of indenturing but also by heteronormativity. Their function as representatives of just one of many forms of enslavement deepens in their function as a touchstone for inchoate systems of heterosexual privilege.

Might we view them as ghosts to a system of oppression yet unformed? Or even ghosts of the politics of Morrison's cultural moment? Just as Kathryn Bond Stockton offers a new historicist reading of *Beloved* "as a novel born in 1987, in the cybernetic age of AIDS," so might we read *A Mercy* as born out of the early twenty-first century's battle over gay rights to marriage, serving in the military, and adoption (let alone a place at the table).[8] It may, however, be far more productive to see Willard and Scully within the terms of the novel as the missing center of the novel's exploration of enslavement. When they are finally given voice at the end of the novel, their point of view begins by looking backward at the plantation as a family: "For years the neighboring farm population made up the closest either man would know of family. A good-hearted couple (parents), and three female servants (sisters, say) and them helpful sons. Each member dependent on them, none cruel, all kind. Especially the master who, unlike their more-or-less absent owner, never cursed or threatened them" (143–44). Even before this reflective moment, the chapter begins with the men seeing the ghost of their master, but unlike the sight of Valerian as the living dead in *Tar Baby*, this final vision of whiteness serves to directly lead into explorations of queer identity and its unique relationship to white privilege.

In a chapter built to create sympathy for Willard and Scully's unique position as not fully invested with the still evolving powers and privileges of whiteness and notably navigating through the even less evolved systems of heterosexual privilege, they provide one of the most devastating comments on the illusions of family. Their chapter concludes with Scully meditating on how they had "once thought they were a kind of family [all the members of the plantation] because they had carved companionship out of isolation" (156). Morrison's pronouns may leave it ambiguous whether Scully is thinking every single member of the plantation, including Willard, is "separate" with "nothing yet on the horizon to unite them," but she concludes with a final indication of the bond the two men share: "Perhaps their wages were not as much as the blacksmith's, but for Scully and Mr. Bond [Willard] it was enough to imagine a future" (156). It is this ability to imagine a future that Morrison invests her queer characters with, and yet, like ghosts themselves, they also have access to the spirit of Jacob Vaark, fully able to defy the strictures of time.

Chapter 9

༄

Mutable Bodies

The Bluest Eye Haunts Home

Every body contains in itself a phantom (perhaps the body itself is a phantom).

—Paul Schilder, *The Image and Appearance of the Human Body: Studies in the Constructive Energies of the Psyche*

Cultural marginality [is] no longer a problem of invisibility but one of excess visibility in terms of a reading of cultural difference that is too easily marketable.

—Jean Fisher, "The Syncretic Turn: Cross-Cultural Practices in the Age of Multiculturalism"

Visibility (whether it be excess visibility or its opposite—invisibility) haunts African American literature, and canonical writers such as W. E. B. Du Bois, Ralph Ellison, James Baldwin, and Toni Morrison have each found their own potent metaphors with which to address contemporary questions of presence, racial identity, and the body. Morrison—as I have argued in these pages—consistently comes back to one of the most productive figures of visibility: the ghost. In reading the ghost as always already queer, we are able to see how questions of visibility, which reoccur with great regularity in the African American canon, map very easily onto postmodern challenges to ideas of normative and stable identities. In this chapter, I want to read Morrison's first novel, *The Bluest Eye*, and her most recent novel, *Home*, as deploying the phantasmatic as a figure of oscillating visibility, one that is suggestive of the transgender

141

warrior's journey away from repressive impositions of gender toward self-actualization and liberation. I do not propose to uncover any subtle, symbolic, or repressed transgender characters, but instead ask how these novels explore narratives of bodily transformation in ways that cannot help but productively be read against our era's ultimate figure of transformation: the transsexual. The umbrella term "transgender" allows me to consider the transgressive nature of narratives that highlight gender as fluid, mutable, or nonconforming in these books while also provoking readers to consider how a culture's fascination and anxieties with transsexuality become manifest in fictional representations of material bodies.

In *How Sex Changed: A History of Transsexuality in the United States*, Joanne Meyerowitz emphasizes Christine Jorgensen's sex change as a crucial moment in popular consciousness: "In the 1950s she shook the foundations of sex, gender and sexuality. In a decade stereotyped as complacent, she inspired public and private debates on who qualified as female and male" (286). It is difficult to live through this era and not register the many ways this sensationalized event transformed public discourse about sex and gender. This was a phenomenon that touched all racial groups, and in the fifties and sixties *Jet* magazine profiled several African American transgender firsts, such as the case of Charles Robert Brown who "could 'become the first Negro "transvestite" in history to transform his sex' " (Meyerowitz 86). Although Meyerowitz provides a compelling history of how dramatically these stories shaped public consciousness, her history does not detail the many ways in which a new public consciousness of sex and gender affected novelists, such as Morrison, in their representations of the mutability of identity, and Morrison's first novel provides a devastating glimpse into what it means to feel trapped in the wrong body.

The Bluest Eye provides a fascinating exploration of a girl who desires whiteness, and the book has inspired countless scholars as well as student critics to examine its representations of body image, specifically the pernicious effects of the white beauty standard. The point of view of a child—nine-year-old Claudia MacTeer—is crucial to illuminating the war on black children's psyche, and few novels have done as much to inspire discussion of the role of popular culture—specifically movies, books, and dolls—in shaping young people's self-image. Claudia's friend, Pecola, is consumed by her desire for blue eyes like Shirley Temple's, and her "success" at acquiring the bluest eyes provides the painful irony and bathos of the narrative. It is Soaphead Church who convinces her that she has finally achieved her dream, and in believing she has been transformed, she, indeed, becomes transformed. The old Pecola—who is called "ugly" and "black e mo" (65)—figuratively dies, and the transformed Pecola speaks to her phantom self. The dialogue—stripped of any exposition or dialogue tags—counterpoints a newly created Pecola of the bluest eyes who is in conversation with what may be interpreted as her former or phantom self. Although scholars usually interpret the dialogue, which continues for more than ten pages, as representative of Pecola's fragmented personality, that split identity might be read through popular conceptions of identity as not just mutable but mortal. It is this narrative of the death of one self and the birth of a newly fashioned body that invites us to read *The Bluest Eye* alongside transsexual memoirs, which often emphasize bodily transformation as predicated on mortality. The dialogue between Pecola's ghost and the new and blue-eyed incarnation of herself emphasizes exactly this mortality of bodies.

The dialogue begins with the phantom Pecola asking the transformed Pecola, "*How many times a minute are you going to look inside that old [mirror]*" (193). We are invited to read this section as not just about psychology but material bodies. The phantom presses blue-eyed Pecola about her obsessive need to see her blue eyes in a mirror ("*You scared they might go away?*"), but the newly transformed Pecola counters, "Of course not. How can they go away" (193). It is an exchange that represents a culture's anxiety over the mutability of bodies, and the ghost of Pecola argues that if her brown eyes could go away, then so might the blue eyes. The new Pecola quickly retorts, "They didn't go away. They changed." For the new Pecola, the transformation represents change but not loss, absence, or death, but her ghost troubles the waters by asking: "*Go away. Change. What's the difference?*" The new Pecola's logic of her transformation further breaks down when she responds that "Mr. Soaphead said they would last forever" with no recognition that she is speaking to her ghost, the version of herself that still has brown eyes and haunts the new self, undermining both a sense of permanence as well as simplistic notions of total transformation. Transformed bodies are haunted by the memory of what was. It should not surprise us, then, that the exchange devolves into childish accusations of acting "*smarty when you talk to me*" and "I'm not being smarty. You started it" (193). As a representation of cultural anxieties over mutable bodies, the dialogue is masterful in capturing culturally specific anxieties over racial passing as well as more recent anxieties over other bodily transformations.

We might read this passage, indeed the novel as a whole, as alluding to narratives of racial passing, and I have argued elsewhere that

Morrison reshapes the passing trope to address contemporary concerns of racial identity.[1] But the classic passing narrative, for all its possibilities to deconstruct bodies, does not usually address transformed material bodies as much as it concerns itself with changing social and political perspectives. *The Bluest Eye*, by contrast, describes what it would be like to not just pass or be perceived as white, but also what it means to inhabit a new body. As Gayle Salamon argues in "The Bodily Ego and the Contested Domain of the Material": "The concept of the bodily ego is of particular use in thinking transgenderism because it shows that the body of which one has a 'felt sense' is not necessarily contiguous with the physical body as it is perceived from the outside" (96).[2] *The Bluest Eye* attends to the distinction between body and psyche, and this makes it powerfully evocative of the psychic drama of transgender identity.

If the passing narrative is built upon visibility—with novels like Nella Larsen's *Passing* exploring in multiple ways what it means to be seen or not seen—the transgender narrative does not merely ask what it means to be seen (or not seen) by others but what it means to have your material body match (or not match) you psychic sense of self. In its penultimate scene of stripped-down dialogue, *The Bluest Eye* asks us to consider what it means for there to be two Pecolas, and in this way the novel asks us to consider that divide between an inner sense of self and a body in conflict with that inner version. That discarded body—that former self—is arguably as much a ghost as any ghost in the Morrison canon, and she—perhaps more than any of the phantoms who come after her—serves to illuminate the struggle between flesh and spirit.

In Pecola's quest to have the kind of eyes that match her inner desire, the tormented ego becomes obsessed with having not only blue eyes but the bluest eyes, and so her pathology is not just to transform her body but to attain a superlative state of blue, to become nonpareil, more real than real, visible as the ultimate version of her ideal self. This quest for the real—founded as it is upon a fiction—is of course a familiar topic of transsexual narratives, and Michel J. Boucher reminds us that "[g]endered 'realness' and its social and political effects are at the heart of transgender issues." Pecola expresses anxiety over her "realness" in her dialogue with her ghost: She explains that nobody looks at her anymore, and, "You are the only one who tells me how pretty they are [her blue eyes]" (196). With dramatic irony, this Pecola of the bluest eyes then goes on to consider her ghost's invisibility, asking why they are just now meeting even though "you were right here. Right before my eyes." The ghost, in true eerie fashion, replies, "*No, honey. Right after your eyes*" (196). Pecola, in other words, was incapable of seeing her interlocutor until her eyes changed, and this transformation occurs alongside the death of the old.

In this section, we are reminded of Soaphead Church's role in the transformation when Pecola states that she is thankful because "[h]e really did a good job" (195). Although it is easy to read Soaphead Church as deranged and evil, he also wishes to help Pecola. He may be read as a misguided religious figure, but there is even more reason to view him as representative of a misguided medical profession. We learn that he came from a long line of men who "studied medicine, law, theology," and he later felt adrift in the "budding field of psychiatry," tried "sociology, then physical therapy" (170). He abandons these paths to eventually become a "Reader, Adviser, and Interpreter of Dreams" (165). The stereotype of a medical charlatan gets reinforced by the extravagant claims on his business card: "If you are overcome with trouble and conditions that are not natural, I can remove them; Overcome Spells, Bad Luck, and Evil Influences. . . . If you are sick, I can show you the way to health. I locate lost and stolen articles. Satisfaction guaranteed" (173). Although his claim to being able to remove conditions that are "not natural" may be read as a push toward the normative, so, too, are some arguments toward sex reassignment as an elimination of the contradiction between body and mind. I do not mean to suggest that the novel argues—as has Janice Radway and other transphobic scholars—that the medical profession is at fault for having supported and even created the phenomenon of transsexualism and other technologies of body transformation, but Soaphead Church helps to transform the classic passing narrative into an allegory of technologies of the body, and despite his lack of real medical knowledge, he offers hope to the patient who seeks a new body. He understands, moreover, the cruelty of embodiment and helps Pecola to imagine bodily transformation.

If Morrison updates the story of racial passing by imagining the desire and ultimate failure of bodily transformation as having great psychic costs, she sets this narrative against tropes of nature as strangely unnatural—or, at best, a problematic concept. The novel's trajectory, as its title suggests, is toward the attainment of a seemingly impossible transformation, and it counterpoints this "unnatural" desire for transformation with those physical changes we see as marking a girl's natural entrance into womanhood. The novel, in fact, opens with Pecola's arrival into the MacTeer household with the calamity and confusion that marks her first menstruation. Just as the beginning of the novel associates her with this very common and natural metamorphosis that all girls go through, the closing pages of the novel mark her with another natural transformation: pregnancy. The novel, however, challenges the simplistic division of the natural and unnatural through its opening symbol of marigolds.

Preceded by a short section that references the *Dick and Jane* books that are so associated with white, middle-class fictions of innocence and purity, Claudia MacTeer's narrative begins and ends with a reflection on marigolds. The first paragraph of the opening makes explicit the narrator's associations of marigolds with Pecola:

> *Quiet as it's kept, there were no marigolds in the fall of 1941. We thought, at the time, that it was because Pecola was having her father's baby that the marigolds did not grow. A little examination and less melancholy would have proved to us that our seeds were not the only ones that did not sprout; nobody's did. Not even the gardens fronting the lake showed marigolds that year. But so deeply concerned were we with the health and safe delivery of Pecola's baby we could think of nothing but our own magic: if we planted the seeds, and said the right words over them, they would blossom, and everything would be all right.* (5)

In tying a narrative focused on a very common human transformation to the potential that is deep within seeds, Morrison emphasizes the seductive logic of the "natural." Indeed, the section headings of the novel, which begin with the names of the seasons, serve to remind readers that some considerations of nature and the natural order of things structure this narrative. In beginning with "Autumn" rather than Spring and ending with "Summer" rather than Winter, the novel asks us to rethink our expectations of nature, and this is further emphasized when the seeds do not fulfill their destiny by sprouting and becoming flowers. In other words, the story of nature as predictable and predestined is disrupted.

Because Claudia invests the failure of the marigolds with great meaning, readers also must consider its symbolic weight in a series of equations that the narrator makes, linking the failure of the marigolds with the act of incest, the loss of innocence, and—most important—Pecola's dead baby.

> We had dropped our seeds in our own little plot of black
> dirt just as Pecola's father had dropped his seed in his own

plot of black dirt. Our innocence and faith were no more productive than his lust or despair. What is clear now is that of all that hope, fear, lust, love and grief, nothing remains but Pecola and the unyielding earth. Cholly Breedlove is dead; our innocence too. The seeds shriveled and died; her baby too. (5–6)

As a preamble to a story of the loss of the narrator's innocence, this passage seems invested in the workings of nature, and yet it subverts our expectations throughout. The natural world does not make sense, refuses to be easily explained, and yet insists on an accounting. In the closing paragraph of the novel, Claudia returns to her questions of whether it was "the fault of the earth," the depth of the planting, a problem of "certain seeds," only to abandon these questions because "[i]t's too late. At least on the edge of my town, among the garbage and the sunflowers of my town, it's much, much, much too late" (206). These final words serve to critique philosophical inquiries into the concept of nature and the natural state of things. These intellectual exercises do not—the novel seems to say—save lives. We are reminded of Pecola's exchange with her ghost, the accusation that smart talking may serve to obfuscate the truth of people's felt lives. Philosophical inquiries are too late—the novel suggests—in addressing the painfully real lives of people devastated by our cultural insistence on normativity. Although the novel presents Pecola's transformation as an appalling "horror at the heart of her yearning [that] is exceeded only by the evil of fulfillment" (204), its secret power comes from its willingness to question the idea of nature and our inquiries as insufficient in saving the lives of those who feel stuck in the wrong bodies.

In shaping the novel around the bookend meditation upon marigolds, Morrison creates what might be considered a haunting effect: the marigolds haunt our imaginations and serve as a synecdoche of Pecola's dead baby. The absence of marigolds, furthermore, dramatically contrasts the proliferations of Pecolas in the penultimate scene of the novel, which presents Pecola's ghost in dialogue with her newly constructed self. Coming fast on the heels of this surreal dialogue, the reappearance of the meta-symbol of the marigolds reinforces the novel's many themes of transformation and death. However, it is not this complicated symbol but rather Pecola's ghost that allows us to consider the profound ways that a person's ego does not necessarily match his or her body. As Gayle Salamon reminds us, "the body that one feels oneself to have is not necessarily the same body that is delimited by its exterior contours, and this is the case even for any normatively gendered subject" (3). This has profound meaning for African American letters and its investment with questions of visibility, and Morrison—at this early point in her career—explores questions of visibility as they relate to the mutability of bodies.

Morrison returns to questions of visibility, ghosts, and the material body in her tenth novel, *Home*. Upon the release of the novel, Morrison reaffirms her engagement with the spirit world when she likens her characters—in interviews—to ghosts who talk to her, and, "On a good day, they shut up and let me work."[3] One cannot hear these words and not think of her son's death in 2010. Morrison stopped writing for months after his death, and one can only wonder how such a profound loss affected the completion of *Home*.[4] Perhaps the novel's attention to medical practices or the narrative's structure upon a brother saving his sibling from evil medical practices might painfully register Slade Morrison's struggle with pancreatic cancer.[5] It is, however, more important for the purposes of this study to consider the role of the ghost as particularly significant in this book, arguably the most important ghost of Morrison's career, in being born from the author's greatest loss. How does he represent the familial/familiar? He is a scene-stealing ghost—quite a contrast to the figurative evocations in *The Bluest Eye*—and he will not be ignored. He floats in and out of the narrative in a way that no other Morrison ghost does—outrageous in his blue zoot suit and his provocative silhouette. More than any other specter that has come before, he announces his importance less by being an intimate (not recognizable as relative, enemy, or friend of the protagonist) and instead through his iconic dress (associated as it is with power, danger, and the exotic) he is decidedly the opposite of familial. Frank Money "had heard about those suits, but never saw anybody wearing one" (34).

In the African American canon, the ghost's exotic attire dresses the thematic exploration of visibility/invisibility with new power, inviting an emphasis of style over substance, surface over depth, fashion over body where the body is already marked by absence. Many readers will eventually associate the ghost with the man—or corpse—Frank sees (only partially) as a child. At the beginning of the novel, Frank Money witnesses the burial of this man, whose "[o]ne foot stuck up over the edge and quivered, as though it could get out, as though with a little effort it could break through the dirt being shoveled in" (4). This is the horrific beginning that sets the tone for everything to come, and the hurriedly buried body—which almost seems to be buried alive—offers the most immediate candidate for the mute and unnamed ghost who will later appear in the novel, haunting Frank as he travels home. When the ghost appears both to brother and sister at the end of the novel, it is at a location that is reminiscent of the site of their early trauma, a return that further invites readers to associate the zoot-suited ghost with the partially buried man. The novel asks us to reimagine the burial— with Frank and Cee now giving the man, or rather his bones, a proper "home." This figure—as much as the protagonist—gives meaning to the title of the novel, tying issues of visibility to a radical refashioning of the idea of home.

When he first appears, it is merely as a fellow traveler seated next to Frank who is on his way to rescue his sister from some unknown evil. Frank's lucidity, however, has already been placed in question and therefore the ghost does not immediately or conclusively get marked as specter. Frank, after all, has recently escaped a sanatorium where he had been drugged, and the circumstances related to his incarceration remain unavailable or, at best, filmy to him, as does his recent duties in the Korean War. Critics have been quick to criticize Morrison's representation of posttraumatic syndrome, but the zoot-suited ghost—as with all of Morrison's specters—serves to explore larger questions of history rather than more specific inquiries into an individual's psychological state.[6] In presenting the ghost as oscillating between visibility and invisibility, Morrison refashions classic African American themes of presence and absence, individuality and invisibility, through more contemporary meditations on structures of feeling related to masculinity and the body. The zoot-suited man remains silent but powerfully expressive (through fashion) of a performance of masculinity that has a culturally important history. Even without knowledge of that history, readers cannot help but recognize the zoot suit as an exaggerated style that calls attention to gender, provoking a rich meditation on what it means to be a man, one that counters Morrison's critics who, in the words of Susan Neal Mayberry, accused her of "designing female victims, castrating women, and messed-up men" (1). In dressing her ghost in the zoot suit, Morrison alludes to a "heroic figure of popular resistance," a figure that Kathy Peiss argues has been "assimilated into the historical mythologies and political imagination of Chicano activists and artists, black nationalists, scholars of cultural studies, and radical historians" (14). Peiss's fascinating history, *Zoot Suit: The Enigmatic Career of an Extreme Style*, emphasizes the various valences that attach to it—everything from unpatriotic to hip to powerful to criminal to musical—making it a provocative metonym for the black man's body as a culturally contested site, one with wildly different meanings and yet always highlighting the black man's body as invested with extreme visibility even as it is threatened with violent erasure.

By displacing attention from the black male body to clothes as a historic touchstone—one with multiple meanings for gender and race—the novel wrests the narrative from well-worn themes of (in)visibility and insists on new explorations of themes of black humanity. If the novel begins with only a foot visible of the murdered man, it arguably reintroduces the traumatized body (or at least offers a counterpoint to this haunting corpse) through a ghost that is mute but visually outrageous. The novel, furthermore, locates trauma in one of the often ignored if not dismissed aspects of masculinity: fashion. When the zoot-suited man first appears, he seems to float in and out of Frank's somnolent state.

> [Frank] turned and, more amused than startled, examined his seat partner—a small man wearing a wide-brimmed hat. His pale blue suit sported a long jacket and balloon trousers. His shoes were white with unnaturally pointed toes. The man stared ahead. Ignored, Frank leaned back to the window to pick up his nap. As soon as he did, the zoot-suited man got up and disappeared down the aisle. No indentation was left in the leather seat. (27)

If the ghost's body is ephemeral, his dress insists on the opposite: it demands to be seen. Every subsequent mention of the blue-suited man, furthermore, gets tied to his diminution, and the oversized suit gets counterpointed to his small frame in ways that will cause some readers to recall Malcolm X's blue zoot suit alongside his surname, Little. Even without this cultural reference, visibility gets displaced from body to fashion and fashion—in turn—exaggerates the body. The device exposes the problems with our culture's fascination with the material, the embodied, as the sole site for debates over masculinity.

When Frank next sees the ghost "after a few hours of dreamlessness," it is as if he is just coming into focus, "the outline of the small man, the one from the train, his wide-brimmed hat unmistakable in the frame of light at the window" (33). He is both "unmistakable" in form and elusive to Frank. When Frank confronts him ("Hey! Who the hell are you?"), the man disappears, and Frank dismisses the apparition as well as his dress: "He had heard about those suits, but never saw anybody wearing one. If they were the signals of manhood, he would have preferred a loincloth and some white paint artfully smeared on forehead and cheeks. Holding a spear, of course" (34). Frank's thoughts underscore the power of clothing in the construction of masculinity, and immediately following the interiority of these remarks, a more distant narrative voice ties the zoot suit to a very specific history of masculine transgression where the zoot suit "had been enough of a fashion state-ment to interest riot cops on each coast" (34). So important is this history to the novel's representation of the ghost, it is conveyed through a more authorial point of view and contrasts Frank's dismissal of these "signals of manhood." This authorial voice, moreover, condenses the complex history of the zoot suit to its most volatile moment, the riots sparked by white anxiety over the dress, and so the novel ensures that its laden symbol gets tied to historically specific clashes between people of color and white racists and not merely the emotional and personal response of the protagonist.

Numerous histories of the zoot suit have been written, and with amusement Shane and Graham White emphasize the impossible search for origins. "But, as is usually the case with black culture," the authors write, "the search for a genealogy for any particular cultural practice is less important and interesting than is the discovery of the uses ordinary African Americans were able to make of that practice, wherever its origins may have been" (253). Novelists offer a very important contribution to that history, and in writing her tenth novel Morrison may have been thinking not just about the riots but about several canonical African American texts—all by males and all key narratives in not just the reflec-tion but also the construction of black masculinity and visibility. In interviews about *Home*, Morrison has stated that she wanted to "take that scab, that veil, or whatever it is, off the 50's" (Italie "At Home with Toni Morrison"). In deploying the metaphor of a veil being lifted, Morrison alludes to the politics of visibility that found one of its greatest and most enduring voices in W. E. B. Du Bois. Although Du Bois's work precedes the phenomenon of the zoot suit, it offers an important examination of visibility and blackness. Arnold Rampersad reminds us of the importance of the metaphor of the veil to Du Bois's greatest work.

The most striking device in *The Souls of Black Folk* is Du Bois' adoption of the veil as the metaphor of black life in America. Mentioned at least once in most of the fourteen essays, as well as in the "Forethought," it means that "the

> Negro is sort of a seventh son, born with a veil, and gifted
> with second-sight in this American world—a world which
> yields him no true self-consciousness, but only lets him see
> himself through the revelation of the other world." If any
> single idea guides the art of *The Souls of Black Folk*, it is
> this concept, which anticipated the noted fictional conceit
> developed by Ralph Ellison, that blacks are invisible to the
> rest of the nation. (79)

The veil is, of course, a metaphor that plays upon pervasive cultural
metaphors that tie sight to knowledge, but it also ties that knowledge
to the very specific biography of a black man, W. E. B. Du Bois, and
his version of blackness bound to certain notions of respectability, heteronormativity, and disciplined bodies. Du Bois's notion of respectable
visibility cannot help but inform representations of the zoot suit in
The Autobiography of Malcolm X and that other important document
of black masculinity, Ralph Ellison's *Invisible Man*. The zoot suit, in
these narratives, serves as an emblem of a certain performance of black
masculinity. But what happens when black masculinity gets decoupled
from the body itself, a ghost placing everything into question?

Morrison does not merely reimagine black invisibility a la Ralph
Ellison, but it is useful to understand how she counterpoints her decou-
pling of black masculinity from the body to *Invisible Man*. Morrison
offers many parallels to the themes found in *Invisible Man*, but the two
novels could not be more different. In his 1981 introduction to the
novel, Ellison explains how he had written a story that grew out of "an
archetypal American dilemma: How could you treat a Negro as equal in
war and then deny him equality during times of peace?" (xiii). Ellison
goes on to conceptualize this dilemma through the irony that " 'high
visibility' actually rendered one un-visible" (xv). Ellison goes on to state
that he intended to write about World War II, but he could not ignore
the war against his people in the States. There was enough violence in
the United States to provide fertile ground for his examination of his
protagonist. Writing more than fifty years later, Morrison, of course,
also finds ample material to pen a war story out of the many declared
and undeclared wars initiated by the United States, as well as the continued war against black men, but in turning to the Korean War of the
1950s, Morrison finds a rich subject with which to address contemporary questions of racial identity through our inability to see the past
(as well as the present) clearly. Morrison writes against the illusion that

we have entered a period that is postracial and that African Americans, particularly men, have been freed from the social forces that have long worked against their self-actualization. Written during Barack Obama's presidency as well as the initial rush to view his election as proof of a new postracial era, *Home* is indeed a reflection of the imprisonment of black bodies—significantly black male bodies—using the figure of the ghost to explore what it means to refuse to be embodied as a figure of abjection.[7]

Morrison invites us to consider Frank Money as an inheritor of Ellison's *Invisible Man* when she introduces a scene reminiscent of the famous Battle Royal in Ellison's novel. While the earlier novel has the white founding fathers of the town pitting young black men against one another, demanding that they fight blindfolded while the mayor and businessmen taunt them, Morrison outdoes Ellison's tour de force when she has white men abduct a father and son, requiring them to fight to the death. Morrison, however, does not describe the men fighting—withholding the scene of violence in a way that makes Ellison's depiction of violence seem almost indulgent or gratuitous—but instead focuses on the scarring of the witnesses. Even when Morrison fills in the details of the fight, she only gives us the conversation between father and son—specifically the father's unimaginable order for the son to commit patricide. Morrison locates heroism in a father's sacrifice, transforming him from passive victim to agent of his and his son's destiny. Not unlike Sethe's terrible choice, the father refuses to let the white racists wrest agency from him. Nevertheless, this agency does have its cost. If Sethe must face the ghost of her infanticide, the father in *Home* must appear before the next generation, represented by Frank, as a ghost to be reckoned with. Bones to be buried. It is, however, as the zoot-suited man that he most takes hold of our imaginations.

In contrast to other ghosts in the Morrison's corpus, this fleetingly visible ghost invites us to consider style as substance, not necessarily accessing a gay camp sensibility but playing artfully upon the twin poles of the politics of presence and invisibility and drawing attention to the intertwined performances of gender and race. As Kathy Peiss argues, the zoot suit was "bound up in the choreography of sexual attraction, the negotiation of gender identity, conflict of generations, and the pursuit of pleasure within a specific music and dance culture as much if not more than it was motivated by a politics of opposition" (13). Peiss may see a variety of meanings attached to the wearing of the zoot suit, but Morrison doubles the enigmatic reach of the attire when she assigns a ghost to wear it. In many ways the ephemeral quality of the ghost, who flits in and out of the narrative, serves to underscore his function as the return of the repressed as marked by—however enigmatically—negotiations of gender identity. Indeed, the sign's ability to provoke a consideration of the performance of gender while resisting labels such as masculine or feminine, heterosexual or homosexual, political or aesthetic, public or private is clearly the point. He is a cipher. Nevertheless, despite his enigmatic qualities—he is specifically a cipher of performances and negotiations of gender.

Frank's own anxious reading of these sartorial "signals of manhood" make the ghost's function as a cipher of gender abundantly clear early in the novel, but at the end of the novel the ghost no longer appears to Frank and instead now appears for the first time to Cee. This transference of visibility from brother to sister further associates the enigma with gender and transformation. Why has he become visible to Cee and invisible to our hero? Certainly, the structure of the novel invites us to consider the hero's journey, marked as it is by journeying through a racist country, as completed by the burial. But why does Cee now notice "a small man in a funny suit swinging a watch chain. And grinning" (144). Most readers will understand her as also on a journey toward wholeness, and in transferring the haunting from Frank to Cee, Morrison suggests that their journeys are similarly bound to a shared past. After seeing the ghost, Cee then decides that he has disappeared, "But she was not sure." With this gesture toward the ghost's disappearance as unsure, the novel speeds to closure with the burying of the same body that Frank and Cee witness as children—the incomplete burial scene that opens the novel. Investing the scene with extra weight, the novel depicts Frank and Cee burying the body standing up, a reversal of its position (as described in the first scene of the novel) as hastily buried by the white men with "[o]ne foot stuck up over the edge" (4). Noteworthy for its relationship to the opening but also its dissimilarity to Western burial practices, the final orientation of the body invites explication, gathering import even as it resist a singular reading.

If the opening burial emphasizes the disregard with which the white terrorists view the black body, the closing burial represents a provocative inversion of this disregard for humanity. The man's new orientation—"into the perpendicular grave"—further highlights his function as a cipher. What does it mean? This inversion may allude to certain African burial practices, but it also might be read against the opening line of the novel: "They rose up like men" (3). Although the pronoun in this opening line refers to horses, Morrison invites an analogy to embattled African Americans and specifically to men and their bodies, indeed the orientation of their bodies as reflective of their humanity. The inversion of the body (and its necessary correction at the end) sits in relationship to the powerful analogy at the beginning that likens the horses to men. The novel clearly asks questions about bodies and their relationships to notions of humanity, and although the narrative explores the fragmented mind of its protagonist and the fragmented body of his sister, it is the ghost, arguably, that supplies the missing center to these inquiries into gendered bodies.

What happens when we view this ephemeral and enigmatic ghost as the center of the novel—a manifestation of the inordinate pressures of the past—a past that can be just as debilitating for its images of super heroes (i.e., the sacrificing father) as well as suffering victims (i.e., the tortured son who must follow his father's orders to kill him). The narrative makes it abundantly clear that father and son have been denied their humanity, forced to perform an unimaginable act of violence, literally corralled into a performance of masculinity in order to reinforce the white terrorist's phobic imaginary. But even as *Home* represents the forces of dehumanization as met by the father's oversized heroism and humanity, it resists familiar tropes of humanity bound, shamefully, to the mastery of language. In place of narratives of the enslaved learning to read or the subjugated articulating their rights with force and eloquence, the zoot-suited ghost remains mute. He is associated not with "universality" but is marked through his most noticeable feature, his clothes, as an exotic, racially charged version of masculinity—a version that disrupts normative expectations for the figure of contested humanity.

If readers do not recognize the ghost as the return of the father, it will be because the flash and fashion of the zoot-suited man will seem disjunctive—perhaps to some even lacking gravitas—in relationship to the drama of father and son forced to fight to the death. But the zoot suit provides the most powerful symbol of the meanings attached to intersecting performances of race and gender. If we read this sartorial performance of masculinity through contemporary anxieties over the mutability of gender and, specifically, the transgendered body, the ghost's final disappearance occurs—not surprisingly—with the burial of the bones of the father. This burial, furthermore, serves as a provocative image of the body and its ultimate inversion. Just as the novel begins with the powerful image of the body hastily buried, a single foot sticking up as if it were an Achilles' heel, it ends with the even more powerful scene of brother and sister, no longer just witnesses, but taking action in reburying this man, the one who haunts them. As a ghost tale, this inversion plays upon the specter's most significant message: gender is a ghost, at times invisible to us and at other times profoundly present.

Indeed, the masculine body is overdetermined first by its Achilles-like posture in the grave, second by the knowledge of the father's oversized heroism, third by the ghost's association with the complex history of the zoot suit, and fourth, and in the final pages of the novel, as Father Time. Certainly, we may read the "small man in a funny suit swinging a watch chain. And grinning," as just another way that the novel emphasizes the ghost as enigmatic. Why is he grinning? Is he happy or bemused? Why is it now Cee and no longer Frank who witnesses this display of emotion from a figure who Frank has seen before? Morrison, of course, has seeded her novels with enigmas before, such as the mystery of the white woman in Paradise and—most famously—with the question of Beloved's appearance and disappearance. But Home's enigma seems to disrupt easy interpretations of masculinity even as it invites readers to view those meanings as overdetermined. In the closing scene of the novel, Cee is not sure what she has seen while Frank no longer sees the zoot-suited man at all. The burial, which corrects the earlier inversion of a man, offers closure of a sort—the humanity of a man has been restored. But as with most of Morrison's novels, the most basic assertion—the one that Frank nails to the burial site ("Here Stands a Man.")—has multiple possibilities. Is Frank the man who now stands, redeemed by this selfless act? If so, what was he before his redemption? Or does the father's body—once upon a time unceremoniously buried— now get reoriented and therefore now made right, made erect, like a man. If he stands now like a man, what has changed? The orientation of the body? Its status as a man?

Morrison does not create a transgender figure to insert herself into the problem of depicting black masculinity at a moment in history when the black male body is particularly charged with reductive stereotypes that swing from problems of invisibility to hypervisibility. She does, however, take the most basic claim—"Here Stands a Man"—and invests it with surprising potency. If this claim were merely a celebration of the proper burial of the "father" or the redemption of the son, it would do little to evoke the complex nexus of forces acting upon black men. But the novel insists upon more than a hero's tale or a tale of redemption and instead investigates masculinity and its fictions of the body. It ties that inquiry, as I have argued, with longstanding inquiries about the hypervisibility and invisibility of blackness. But it refashions this inquiry around contemporary anxieties over the mutability of bodies. This may be seen as most clearly articulated in Cee's loss of her womb through the medical experiments of Dr. Beauregard. If women are defined by their wombs, Cee is no longer a woman. Frank's body is also transformed, but it is his mind—a strong contrast to Cee's womb—that is distorted by posttraumatic stress and his consciousness that is compromised by doctors in a hospital. The war on their bodies speaks to certain gendered narratives that equate women with bodies and men with the mind, but Morrison further complicates these scripts.

As the novel reaches for closure, it invites readers to consider bodies absent and present, visible and invisible, and—perhaps most powerfully—separate and overlapping. Late in the novel, Frank confesses to shooting an innocent girl in Korea because she tempted him, taking "me down to a place I didn't know was in me" (134). Frank specifically links this murdered Korean girl to the child Cee will no longer be able to have. But Cee has heard this never-to-be-born child's voice and accepts the haunting. She tells Frank, "You don't need to try and make it go away. It shouldn't go away. It's just as sad as it ought to be and I'm not going to hide from what's true just because it hurts" (131). Cee's acceptance of her ghost, who is "somewhere close by in the air, in this house," allows Frank to face his own ghost. But interestingly he wonders whether they are one and the same. Through Frank's point of view, readers are asked to imagine a single ghost as possibly embodying Cee's lost child as well as Frank's murdered child? By extension, we might also imagine the zoot-suited ghost as also overlapping with these ghost children. Could that explain the diminutive form? The oversized zoot suit? The silence? The novel withholds a clear explanation for the identity of the zoot-suited man, but through Frank Money we are encouraged to think of ghosts as not necessarily embodying singular identities.

Although there are many reasons to read the corpse at the beginning of the novel as the bones at the end—with the ghost in the middle of the narrative tying the two scenes together—the ghost that is most present in Frank's consciousness at the end of the novel belongs to the Korean girl he murdered. This murder is, indeed, the secret that the novel first conceals and later reveals. In linking this ghost to Cee's ghost, Frank envisions a spirit world that merges identities and hauntings. Small, moreover, are the ghosts that appear late in the novel, each one logically fitting the unique grave described as a "four-or five-foot hole some thirty-six inches wide" (144). But if the novel invites us to imagine such a merging of hauntings, it cannot help but unleash a radical rethinking of its exploration of masculinity through the disappearing and reappearing figure of the zoot-suited ghost. Gender, the novel reminds us, is always a fiction. But even natal sex, defined by a womb or other physical characteristics such as height or strength, often reveals itself to be unstable. In our time, transgender bodies offer opportunities to think more fully how prescriptive definitions of masculinity and femininity, manhood and womanhood have served to oppress all people but have especially been deployed in racist discourse.

It may seem outrageous to imagine the zoot-suited man as transgender, so few are the signs of the body at all, but it is the suppression of those signs that make it such a provocative image of the transgendered body. Although we know that the body is small, it is a body that is primarily defined by clothes, and there is no voice to betray the identity the clothes delimit with such extravagance. As a cipher of gender, a tempting representation with which to further explore Judith Butler's notions of drag, the zoot-suited ghost might be read as the transgendered manifestation of the Korean girl. The transformation at the center of the novel, one that gets disguised by quick interpretations of Frank's sign: "Here stands a man." It is a sign with no clear referent. With no singular claim on it. Bodies, *Home* seems to remind us, are not only prone to transformation from living to dead, whole to fragmented, visible to invisible but also to the most radical liberation from fixed to mutable and self-determining.

Chapter 10

༄

Conclusion

Ghosts hate new things.

—Zora Neale Hurston, *The Sanctified Church*

Following the ghosts is about making a contact that changes you
and refashions the social relations in which you are located.

—Avery Gordon, *Ghostly Matters*

In November of 2010, Toni Morrison read, for the first time in public,
the opening scene of a work in progress that would later be entitled
Home. The occasion was the Sixth Biennial Conference of the Toni
Morrison Society. The location—Paris, France—added a bit of romance,
excitement, and surprise. I had already written several chapters for this
book, and at this prestigious conference, I would be presenting a queer
reading of *Love* to either an empty room (fear number one) or a packed
room (fear number two). At the last minute, I had changed the title
of my presentation to include the word "queer," hoping to avoid fear
number one, but the new title did not make it into the program, and,
instead, I began advertising the queer theme of my presentation to
anyone who would listen and with an uncharacteristic zeal that somehow trumped my anxiety. But what had I feared? Perhaps not being
taken seriously or, worse, being viewed as reckless and irresponsible in
my use of an exhausted, if not already suspect, postmodern strategy of
queering. How did passion trump anxiety? There is a way that Morrison speaks to me that I wish to share with the world. There is a way,
I felt embolden to say, that her work resonates with a queer sensibility
and politics. There is a way in which her ghosts, in particular, exceed
heterosexist structures and heteronormative identifications.

When Morrison looked out into the audience, I felt connected but also confident: I knew that her next novel, the one she was about to preview, would be part of this study. I knew it would yield to a queer reading, just as the others had, and not because of the flexibility of the terms of inquiry. I could not imagine offering a queer reading of Philip Roth or even John Edgar Wideman, who along with Morrison appears in Shawn Stewart Ruff's 1996 anthology of lesbian and gay fiction by African American writers.[1] I knew *Home* would lend itself to my project because right from the beginning and through the course of ten novels, Morrison's work has always displayed a spirit of inquiry into the nature of social arrangements and the formation of identities as impacted by racism, sexism, and homophobia. Every novel—as I had already drafted into my introduction—explores the limits of love and the complexity of desire, and so I knew *Home*, before it was even published, would lend itself to a queer reading. As Morrison read from her work in progress, I grew anxious. It was not clear on that beautiful day in Paris, not from the pages read or Morrison's description of the novel, whether there would be a queer ghost, and I would have to wait almost two years to become acquainted with the ghost in the pale-blue zoot suit. When I finally had the novel with its hard-backing in my hands, I felt more confident a significant problem would arrive. I had drafted the entire manuscript, and just needed to include a reading of this tenth novel. And then the zoot-suited ghost appeared, offering no better figure with which to close.

In the final pages of *Home*, the ghost appears at the foot of a grave, swinging a watch, intelligible as a spirit guide demonstrably concerned with a closure that only the grave can offer, and yet his presence also gives truth to the lie of a final resting place. He stands as a cipher, as I have argued in the previous chapter, for the hastily buried body (the result of a lynching) that appears in the first pages of the novel, but also for two children: the Korean girl Frank Money murders to keep her from bringing him down to an inhuman place of inappropriate desire and the child that Cee, who has her womb surgically compromised in a bizarre experiment, will never be able to bear. All three ghosts serve as metonyms for black (in)humanity, merging and reemerging in the enigmatic figure that appears fleetingly at the end of the novel but also gets characterized throughout as indistinct and temporary: "an outline," "a silhouette," "small," and "gone." The zoot-suited man never gains full clarity as specifically any one of the three dead bodies, any recognizable individual, or even unambiguously as a man, allowing us to see him as a projection of the three deaths in the novel. It is, however, as the ghost of Cee's child—a baby that will never be conceived let alone born—that Morrison extends her exploration of ghosts as not just a haunting of what is but also of what never had the chance to be. It is important to note that a white racist mad scientist, not unlike the very real scientists involved in the state-sanctioned Tuskegee syphilis experiments, removes Cee's womb and violently compromises her relationship with "the future." But the community of Lotus, the novel seems to be telling us, offers a home that is not founded upon the nuclear family or biological ties of kinship. It is a home that the novel sets against the graveyard in the woods, a site that embraces death and life and the intermingling of the two.

If this suggests a queer sense of time, it is one that has always been part of African American cultural traditions, present in the antebellum period when slaves had no legal claim to kinship as well as in later communities that extended notions of kinship in the face of racist hegemonies. Alongside Orlando Patterson's notion of the "social death" of blacks that begins with enslavement or Paul Gilroy's consideration of the "death drive" in the African diaspora, we might consider the way queer and black communities get marked by death. It should not surprise us, therefore, that time, for both cultures and certainly the overlapping black queer community, would appear different from mainstream temporalities. As this study has argued, the trope of the ghost already circulates in a queer field, but in Morrison's handling it not only finds ever new possibilities for challenging heteronormativity but also perfectly evokes notions of queer time as it has been articulated recently by many queer theorists.

In Judith Halberstam's words, " 'Queer time' is a term for those specific models of temporality that emerge within postmodernism once one leaves the temporal frames of bourgeois reproduction and family, longevity, risk/safety, and inheritance" (6). Indeed, Morrison's ghosts frequently sit outside these temporal frames, haunting what perhaps never was or was never given a chance to be, and giving voice to undercurrents of resistance. Elizabeth Freeman, in her introduction to GLQ's special issue on "Queer Temporalities," provides a more pointed association between queer time and critical race theory when she writes:

> If we reimagine "queer" as a set of possibilities produced out
> of temporal and historical difference, or see the manipulation
> of time as a way to produce both bodies and relationalities

(or even nonrelationality), we encounter a more productively porous queer studies. . . . Indeed, this queer studies meets critical race theory and postcolonial studies in its understanding that what has not entered the historical records, and what is not yet culturally legible, is often encountered in embodied, nonrational forms: as ghosts, scars, gods. (159)

Even Avery Gordon, arguably the most important scholar in ghost studies, sounds very similar to the queer theorists when she announces that "[h]aunting raises specters, and it alters the experience of being in linear time, alters the way we normally separate and sequence the past, the present and the future. These specters or ghosts appear when the trouble they represent and symptomize is no longer being contained or repressed or blocked from view." Gordon imagines, we should note, a wider field of "troubles" but certainly not precluding the uncontainable voices of dissident sexualities and other challenges to heteronormativity.

How might the ghost—"unrational" and "uncontainable"—afford unique opportunities to understand queer time as also black time and its resistance to norms and normalizing powers? In an opening sentence that might just as easily serve as a description of Colored People's Time (CPT), the editors of *Queer Times, Queer Becomings* state that "[q]ueer time has long been colloquially understood to be about fifteen minutes later than the appointed time. . . . Living on the margins of social intelligibility alters one's pace" (1). In reaching for closure, with all the irony implied by this act as applied to this ghostly project, *Home* offers the most potent apparition as profoundly marked by queer and black time. More than Beloved and every other ghost in the Morrison canon, the zoot-suited specter cannot be divorced from its period clothing, refusing to go unnoticed, announcing its location in time and place, and, as my previous chapter has argued, highlighting the tension between absence and presence. This tension, cloaked as it is in flamboyance, invites being read against queer theory's invitation to imagine queer time as speaking for marginalized identities, such as gender outlaws. The zoot-suited ghost follows (or does he guide?) Frank Money home, and he is last seen "swinging a watch chain" (144). But he becomes invisible to Frank as he becomes visible to Cee, a transformation that reinforces the concept that he represents more than one ghost, or, rather, more than one haunting.

The novel's final setting, a grave, is, of course, also profoundly relevant to the ghost's relationship to time, and the grave is overdetermined as a site of finality. This symbol of finality, however, cannot help but become ironic when set against the ghost, which, by its very nature, serves as a refutation of any such finality, appearing and disappearing, lending very little support to the metaphor of a "final resting place." But the ghost, as my previous chapter argues, serves as a symbol of the transgender body, further challenging heteronormative narratives and their insistence on some final stability, such as the appeal to some foundational sex, or the centrality of reproduction to narrative form.[2] If the brother-sister relationship offers some reinscription of the primacy of the nuclear family, then the gravesite, the ghost, and the community of Lotus dislodge this association with home and the nuclear family. Though the closing words of the novel reinforce the book's theme as clearly stated in the title, the theme of "home" has been queered throughout, and readers cannot help but recognize the novel's challenge to heteronormative narratives that insist upon framing "home" upon the primacy of biological relatives, the promise of regeneration, and the mystique of familiar spaces, grounds, and structures. *Home* resists offering all of these things and instead provides a grave as a culmination of its exploration of filial fidelity.

Although the gravesite may serve as one rather unusual symbol of home, certainly a home to the discarded bones that are buried there, narrative tradition will certainly put most readers in mind of the community of women where the siblings find sanctuary. Although lacking any clear symbolic center (i.e., a single house or person), Lotus will serve for most readers as the reference point for the title, despite (or perhaps because of) Frank's assessment of "it is the worst place in the world, worse than any battlefield." It will certainly provisionally stand for home with little more than a gravesite as a second contender. But between the scene at the gravesite and Cee's directive to turn homeward, Morrison offers the symbol of a wounded tree. As Frank looks up from the grave, he notices a tree that *"looked so strong / So beautiful./ Hurt right down the middle / But alive and well"* (147). If this serves to further explore the idea of home, it is apt—the tree of life is strong and beautiful not despite its wound but because of it. In this quick series of symbols (grave, tree, community), the novel resists a single or simple meaning for home, refusing to be complicit in heteronormative structures and regimes. Orphaned, unmarried, and childless—and even womb-less—the siblings stand outside of time as much as the ghost that haunts them.[3] The novel flirts with the idea that they are homeless, only to locate home in their mutual bond if not also their ties to the larger community of Lotus, Georgia. In its resistance to stock meanings of home built upon marriage, reproduction, and the nuclear family, *Home* continues Morrison's lifelong resistance and even critique of simplistic and regulatory fictions of heteronormativity, but *Home*'s ghost reminds us of the wound in the family tree, the queer breaks in our culture's insistent march of reproduction, heteronormativity, and the nuclear family.

How fitting to find a provisional end point with Morrison's meditation upon the meaning of home, which is itself the most haunting of ghosts, this concept that is so dear to us and so seemingly incapable of being disengaged from fictions of reproductive time and the heteronormative family. And, yet, the novel finds every opportunity to disengage the concept of home from its usual moorings, the specter's grave providing just one opportunity for that break. But if the zoot-suited ghost—at home in his vertical grave—serves as the ultimate cipher of the novel, he is only the embodiment of that greater cipher of the novel: home. Morrison, of course, has explored the vexed relationship between notions of home and haunting before, most notably in *Beloved* and *Paradise*, but these narratives feature structures—one modest and the other grand—with which to defamiliarize the symbol. *Home* does not. Instead, Morrison asks us to imagine little more than a feeling, a sensation, one that is marked when brother and sister turn away, reminding us that Morrison's meditation on *Home* begins and ends at a gravesite and that at least our guide, the "small man in a funny suit swinging a watch chain," is now home.

If he offers a suitable ending to this study, it is as the ultimate symbol for the convergence of queer time, African time, and African American time. I have already alluded to the way queer theorists sound very much like they are describing CPT when referring to queer time, but we might as easily examine the idea of African time, explored most powerfully by John S. Mbiti in his 1969 study, *African Religions and Philosophy*, with its central focus on African time, which—among many things—sees the interconnectedness of past and present. Morrison's use of ghosts, most certainly, serves to convey this interconnectedness, and in "Rootedness: The Ancestor as Foundation," Morrison tells us the "ancestors are not just parents, they are sort of timeless people whose relationships to characters are benevolent, instructive, and protective, and they provide a certain kind of wisdom" (62). Morrison's ghosts, we might argue, much like her ancestors, these "timeless people," exceed their very presence, their putative message, and their imagined audience.

They invite queer readings, standing as much outside of orthodoxies of time as a dissident figure hurtling against the proscriptive, American nuclear family.

In burying the anonymous body, Frank, as if following African American burial practices that privilege the symbolic power of the quilt, "placed the bones on Cee's quilt, doing his best to arrange them the way they once were in life" (143). With the quilt, a symbol Morrison has used powerfully in *Beloved*, the scene evokes a distinctively African American tradition but then further suggests associations with a foreign and possibly African burial practice when "[b]rother and sister slid the crayon-colored coffin into the perpendicular grave" (144). This unique vertical burial may suggest African traditions, but it also makes physical the orientation of a man as upright, human, no longer desecrated. The upright corpse offers a symbolic refutation to racist, sexist, and homophobic denials of humanity for blacks, women, and homosexuals. It is a symbolic burial for the lynched man at the beginning of the novel and also the Korean girl, who serves as Frank's own failure to see a human, and, finally, Cee's unborn child, the haunt of a "gutted" reproductive future and the specter of unimaginable possibilities.

In "Rootedness," Morrison describes, in an often cited passage, her desire "to provide places and spaces so that the reader can participate," but, in a less quoted section, she offers a specific example of these openings when she describes the process of creating "sexual scenes in such a way . . . that the reader brings his own sexuality to the scene and thereby participates in it in a very personal way" (59). With such a rich body of work that strives to welcome readerly participation, it is astounding that there has not yet been a book of sustained queer readings of her work. This is the book that I wanted to read. This is the book that has been haunting me. "It is in your hands," I want to say, echoing the haunting final lines of *Jazz* as a final effort to close the distance between book and reader. "Look where your hands are. Now" (229).[4]

Notes

Chapter 1. Introduction

1. Sharon Holland's inspiring *Raising the Dead* takes *Beloved* as a central text in its exploration of death's relationship to black subjectivity, nationality, and sexuality.

2. In "Toni Morrison's Ghost: The Beloved Who Is Not Beloved," Elizabeth B. House argues that the protagonist is not a ghost but a real person on whom Sethe projects her desires. I return to this question in chapter 2.

3. Michael Arnzen makes this statement in the introduction to the special topic issue of *Paradoxa* devoted to Freud's concept of the uncanny (1).

4. In *Extravagant Abjection*, Darieck Scott announces his "conceptual foundation" to come from Frantz Fanon, and in *Cruising Utopia* José Esteban Muñoz makes central use of Ernst Bloch. Everything old is new, and the theorists of yesterday inform not only these two new exciting works of scholarship but many of the new theoretical works on race and sexuality.

5. In addition to Sharon P. Holland, *Raising the Dead*; Roderick Ferguson, *Aberrations in Black*; Darieck Scott, *Extravagant Abjection*; and Julian Carter, *The Heart of Whiteness*, the present study of Morrison was in its final stages of revision when other books came to my attention, such as Aliyyah I. Abdure-Rahman, *Against the Closet: Black Political Longing and the Erotics of Race*.

6. See Jane S. Bakerman, "The Seams Can't Show: An Interview with Toni Morrison," *Black American Literature Forum* 12 (1979): 60.

7. See "Pam Houston Talks with Toni Morrison," *Other Voices* 18.42 (Fall/Winter 2005) and reprinted in *Toni Morrison: Conversations*, edited by Carolyn C. Denard (233). She describes this process also in interviews with Michael Silverblatt and Michael Saur, which are also collected in *Toni Morrison: Conversations* (220 and 225, respectively).

8. See "The Nature of Love: An Interview with Toni Morrison," in *Essence* (October 2003) and reprinted in *Toni Morrison: Conversations*, edited by Carolyn C. Denard (214).

9. See Jaime M. Grant et al., "Injustice at Every Turn: A Report of the

National Transgender Discrimination Survey," a study done by the National Center for Transgender Equality and National Gay and Lesbian Task Force in 2011.

10. See http://www.transgenderdor.org/ and http://www.gender.org/remember/day/.

11. See David Gates, "Original Sin," which oddly places *A Mercy* in relationship to Morrison's most famous novel, a novel that also might be said to "excavate history." Gates states that *A Mercy* does not have the "terrible passion" of *Beloved*, as if to suggest its longer history is some compensation: "'A Mercy' has neither the terrible passion of 'Beloved'—how many times can we ask a writer to go to such a place?—nor the spirited ingenuity of 'Love,' the most satisfying of Morrison's subsequent novels."

12. See William Faulkner, *The Portable Faulkner*, edited by Malcolm Cowley (New York: Viking, 1977). This often quoted and misquoted line, everywhere embodied in Faulkner's oeuvre, comes from *Requiem for a Nun* and probably owes much of its fame to Malcolm Cowley, who begins the relevant section in *Portable Faulkner* with the line and its importance to Faulkner: "'The past is never dead,' Gavin Stevens says in *Requiem for a Nun* (1951), and he adds, 'It's not even past.' In this judgment as in many others, Stevens appears to be speaking for the author. Faulkner himself was obsessed with a feeling that the past endures in every moment of our lives" (663).

Chapter 2. Spirit: *Sula* Haunts *Beloved*

1. As I will discuss later, Morrison makes this statement in response to a question related to Barbara Smith's queer reading of *Sula*. Although Morrison does not endorse Smith's reading, she appears intrigued and impressed by the "arrogance" of it. The quote comes from her 1986 interview with Audrey McCluskey, collected in *Conversations: Toni Morrison* (40).

2. Long before becoming an academic, I read Morrison's novels with great passion, and I don't wish to deny the importance of *Beloved* but hope to convince the readers of these pages that the other novels deserve more attention.

3. The phrase "unspeakable things unspoken" is from Toni Morrison's "Unspeakable Things Unspoken: The Afro-American Presence in American Literature," *Michigan Quarterly Review* 28 (Winter 1989). I will have numerous opportunities to return to this very important essay in the chapters to come, and students of Morrison would be sorely at a disadvantage if they had not read and incorporated the ideas from this essay into their understanding of the novels.

4. See Jesse Green "When Political Art Mattered" (2003), which does a wonderful job of conveying a certain time and place as well as providing a usefully personal history of an emerging awareness of AIDS.

5. Statistics quoted from http://www.actupny.org/reports/reagan.html (accessed on October 18, 2011).

6. Peterson's "Toni Morrison and the 'Genuine Black History Book,'" which is chapter 3 of her important monograph on historical memory (*Against Amnesia*), offers one of the most exciting readings of Morrison's trilogy, one that helps to locate *Beloved* in an ongoing and evolving project to address the "costs of amnesia, of historylessness" (97).

7. This quote gets referenced in various works, but there is still more work to be done to consider its continued relevance in the face of its evident dangers in erasing race and other identities. For a further discussion, see Johnson and Henderson's introduction to *Black Queer Studies*.

8. See A. O. Scott, "In Search of the Best." Although entertaining as a meditation on the act of choosing the best novel of the last twenty-five years, Scott's piece asks more questions than it answers, providing, however, a snapshot of the process:

> Early this year, the Book Review's editor, Sam Tanenhaus, sent out a short letter to a couple of hundred prominent writers, critics, editors and other literary sages, asking them to please identify "the single best work of American fiction published in the last 25 years." The results—in some respects quite surprising, in others not at all—provide a rich, if partial and unscientific, picture of the state of American literature, a kind of composite self-portrait as interesting perhaps for its blind spots and distortions as for its details.

9. Kathryn Bond Stockton offers a notable exception in her study of the novel as "a viral gothic" but also a depiction of "a black slave mother's dangerous exchanges with her dead daughter" (179). This inventive reading does not explore homosexual desire as much as it considers the novel a "prophylactic fiction" (187) written in an era of AIDS and concerned with bodies, disease, and transmission. *Beautiful Bottom, Beautiful Shame: Where "Black" Meets "Queer"* (Durham: Duke UP, 2006).

10. See Justine Tally, *Toni Morrison's "Beloved,"* for an impressive uncovering of source materials that supplement the standard but required attention to *The Black Book* with an exploration of the role of Greek and African myths, deities, and even numerology.

11. I do see this myth-building as celebratory and positive until I begin to bemoan the way that *Beloved* steals attention from many of my other favorites. I am reminded of an account of the meeting of Toni Morrison and Chinua Achebe at Bard, and the president of the college asking each one which single book they would want to have on a desert island. In response to Achebe's choice of *Beloved*, Morrison expresses some discomfort and then offers an answer: "For her part, Ms. Morrison declined to name the one book she would take if she were exiled to a desert island. Instead, she said, she would want reams of paper and some pencils. 'I'd like to write the book I'd like to read,' she offered." See Somini Sengupta, "A Literary Diaspora Toasts One of Its Own."

12. Barbara Smith's "Toward a Black Feminist Criticism" was first published in *Conditions: Two* 1 (October 1977) and later anthologized in Gloria T. Hull, Patricia Bell-Scott, and Barbara Smith, eds., *But Some of Us Are Brave: All the Women Are White, All the Black Are Men* (New York: Feminist Press, City University of New York, 1982).

13. See Barbara Christian, "But What Do We Think We're Doing Anyway: The State of Black Feminist Criticism(s) or My Version of a Little Bit of History," and Valerie Smith, "Black Feminist Theory and the Representation of the Other," which are both in Cheryl A. Wall's *Changing Our Own Words: Essays on Criticism, Theory, and Writing by Black Women* (New Brunswick, NJ: Rutgers UP, 1989). See also Deborah G. Chay, "Rereading Barbara Smith: Black Literary Criticism and the Category of Experience," *New Literary History* 24 (1993): 635–52; and Barbara Smith, "Barbara Smith: Reply to Deborah Chay," *New Literary History* 24 (1993): 653–56.

14. See Roderick Ferguson, *Aberrations in Black: Toward a Queer of Color Critique*, for a wonderful consideration of black lesbian feminist embrace of *Sula* and the importance of the novel in countering the politics of the times.

15. See Jeffrey Andrew Weinstock, *Spectral America: Phantoms and the National Imagination* (Madison: U of Wisconsin P, 2004). The quote is from page 4, but Weinstock refers back to *Beloved* repeatedly.

16. Although Eve Sedgwick applied her theory of epistemologies of the closet to the male social world, her study addresses pre-Stonewall literature and not the increasing visibility of lesbian identity registered in later works.

17. See Melanie Kohnen, *Queer Visibility, Sexuality, and Race in American Film and Television: Screening the Closet* (New York: Routledge, 2011).

Chapter 3. Houses: *Beloved* Haunts *Paradise*

1. Any scholar of ghosts, especially literary scholars, must consider Jacques Derrida's hauntology. See, specifically, Derrida's *Specters of Marx* (141).

2. Morrison's "Unspeakable Things Unspoken," which considers the openings of her novels, explains the author's intentions with using numerals to begin *Beloved*, and scholars continue to consider its relevance. See, particularly, Justine Tally, *Toni Morrison's "Beloved": Origins.*

3. In moving between the personified house and the embodied Beloved, the novel challenges its readers to think of place as embodied and bodies as housing sites of history. When the novel inflects these things with queer themes, they both become richer and offer greater challenges to normative thinking. Shortly after the appearance of the "woman breathing near the steps of 124" (50), for example, most readers will no longer think of the house as ghost, perhaps believing Paul D's exorcism worked when he "[whipped] the table around until everything was rock quiet" (18), albeit transferring the spirit from the boards of the house to this strange "young woman with the broken hat" (53). When

the second section opens, astute readers will hear the novel's first line ("124 was spiteful") echoed in its second opening ("124 was loud") but most readers will be too invested in the embodied spirit of Beloved to go back to thinking about the house as ghost. It is, however, quite *loudly* speaking to us. Our deafness, our inability to read the signs, becomes quite clearly a renewed subject. Despite this second section's emphasis on the house as personified, we are too fixated on Beloved to think of the house as merely one that holds rather than embodies the ghost, so successful is the novel's transference of all mystery to the new resident. And yet the novel reminds us that "124 was loud" just as it has earlier told us that it was spiteful. If we fail to see the personification, it is both because Beloved distracts us and because we are more comfortable with an agency, one that looks human, as being attached to the "loud" haunting.

  4. First "124 is spiteful" (3), then "124 was loud" (169), and finally "124 was silent" (239). The numeral itself is haunted by what it is not—neither the written word nor an adjective modifying Bluestone Road. Floating free and unattached to its inferred noun, it assumes the role of a noun, though not without leaving traces of what it is not. Jacques Derrida argues that all words and indeed all concepts are haunted by the trace, but 124—if it is to gain meaning as a sign for house and haunting—pointedly makes the reader work to recover many of those traces. After most readers register 124 as a house, they also learn that Sethe lived in it before it had a number, a detail that reemphasizes the ghostly effect of the number. Often associated with sophomoric criticism, number symbolism has never had such a willing subject, but the number is less interesting for what we might see it as symbolizing than as a heuristic in how to read the novel as a series of shifting and ambiguous signs, as interested in signification and the ghostly trace. 124 marks a specific house, one that was marked before being numbered, but also floating free from the very structure it defines, a ghostly presence about to become embodied.

  5. In categorizing contemporary music that samples and registers past forms, music critic Simon Reynolds makes use of the term "hauntology," and we might easily extend the term to the way Morrison deploys music with distinct jazz strains as an opportunity to consider the problems with reading "gangs" without preconceived notions of black men. Morrison's "jazz soundings" serve as historical memory with which to read the present but also remind us that we always read with these ghosts close upon us.

Chapter 4. Matriarchy: *Paradise* Haunts *Love*

  1. "War" was the original working title for *Paradise*, and so I refer to the men's mission as a war with this in mind. See Morrison's interview with James Marcus in Amazon.com.

  2. When Tavis Smiley asks Morrison to describe her eighth novel, she says, "The book is about a family. . . . [and] their struggle is a very human

struggle and their effort to become and to remain human is very much based on language but primarily the effort to love" (October 30, 2003).

3. See "Pam Houston Talks with Toni Morrison" collected in Carolyn Denard's *Toni Morrison: Conversations.* "Now her name is Love, and somebody suggested it as a title, and I felt very alarmed—but the fact of the alarm was more interesting to me than just saying, Oh, that's terrible. I began to think about why. I mean, I didn't just say, Oh, ridiculous. I said to this person, 'That is easily the most empty cliché, the most useless word; and then of course it is, at the same time—because hatred is involved in it too—the most powerful human emotion'" (232). In this same interview, Morrison describes how she then "removed the word from every other place in the manuscript, except by the woman named Love . . ." (232).

4. See Anissa Wardi, "A Laying on of Hands: Toni Morrison and the Materiality of *Love*," *MELUS* 30.3 (Fall 2005): 201–18. Although Wardi stops short of seeing L as a matriarch, she sees L as "the embodiment of love in the text" and associated with "nurturance" and, as cook, the "roles of healer, savior, and peacemaker" (206–07). J. Brooks Bouson, "Uncovering 'the Beloved' in the Warring and Lawless Women in Toni Morrison's *Love*," *The Midwest Quarterly* 49.4 (Summer 2008): "Presented as a disembodied, omniscient maternal voice, or, more accurately, maternal ancestor spirit who hovers over the action of the novel, L offers definitive commentary on the characters and passes ultimate judgment on Bill Cosey, as readers eventually learn, by murdering him" (358).

5. I do not mean to suggest that questions of legibility, nomination, and visibility are without an existential component, but I think it useful to highlight what the two puns focus upon. For a brilliant consideration of the role of legibility and nomination to queer theory, see Lee Edelman's *Homographesis: Essays in Gay Literary and Cultural Theory* (New York: Routledge, 1994):

> The process that constructs homosexuality as a subject of discourse, as a cultural category about which one can think or speak or write, coincides, in this logic of homographesis, with the process whereby the homosexual subject is represented as being, even more than as inhabiting, a body that always demands to be read, a body on which his "sexuality" is always already inscribed. (10)

6. Ross critiques Eve Sedgwick's "closet theory [which] depends on a notion of the uneven development of the races, such that a miniscule, easily identifiable clique of elite white men (Wilde, Melville, James, Nietzsche, Proust) ambiguously do or do not determine the processes of sexual identification for everyone touched by modernity, regardless of race, class, gender, geography, degree of cultural of 'advancement into modernity, etc." (171). Although he does not directly address Sedgwick's notion of the "spectacle of the closet," this phrase seems especially relevant to his interest in exploding the reductive arguments Sedgwick makes.

7. Roderick A. Ferguson's discussion of black matriarchy in *Aberrations in Black* (125–26) points to more sustained studies, such as Hazel Carby's *Reconstructing Womanhood* and Gladys M. Jiménez-Muñoz's contribution to *Moving Beyond Boundaries* (edited by Carol Boyce Davies and Molara Ogundipe-Leslie).

8. Beloved has much to teach us about Morrison's interest in queering innocence, but despite the ghost's haunting and menacing qualities, she is not nearly as lethal, conniving, and dangerous as the adult ghosts in *Love*. In her most threatening moments, Beloved, described as the crawling already baby, retains qualities of innocence. Her innocence, more importantly, is tied to her past life as an infant, and her moments of malevolence are easily excused (or at least explained and by extension understood) by that same history.

9. "The ghostly gay child . . . makes *gay* far more liquid and labile than it has seemed in recent years, when queer theory has been rightfully critiquing it. Odd as it may seem, *gay* in this context, the context of the child, is the new *queer*—a term that touts its problems and shares them with anyone" (4).

Chapter 5. Music: *Love* Haunts *Song of Solomon*

1. Joan Moore lists some of the most common stereotypes, beginning with, "They are composed of males (no females) who are violent, addicted to drugs and alcohol, sexually hyperactive, unpredictable, and confrontational" (24). Quoted from Randall G. Shelden, Sharon K. Tracy, and William B. Brown, *Youth Gangs in American Society*, second edition (Belmont, CA; Wadsworth, 2001).

2. From the cage, which sits in a ditch and serves as a prison, to the tobacco tin, which holds his greatest torment, Paul D's existence is associated with boxes, being boxed in, constriction.

3. I am thankful to my colleague Cassandra Jackson, who not only suggested I look at the doves but has repeatedly returned to the question as a haunting one.

Chapter 6. Voice: *Song of Solomon* Haunts *Jazz*

1. See Ed Madden, *Tiresian Poetics: Modernism, Sexuality, Voice* (Cranbury, NJ: Rosemond Publishing, 2008). Although Madden does not consider Morrison's work, his analysis of other twentieth-century texts considers: "The Tiresian is, more often than not, a figure of the feminine located within or behind the male, temporally anterior or spatially interior: a feminine sensibility within the body of a male prophet, for example, or a feminine past in a sexual history, or, more problematically, a feminine potential (sometimes figured as threat) within a male persona" (17). See also Susan Neal Mayberry, *Can't I Love*

What I Criticize, particularly the chapter on *Song of Solomon:* "Flying without Ever Leaving the Ground: Feminine Masculinity in *Song of Solomon*."

2. There are three Deads in Milkman's family, and Pilate has remained unmarried, so she makes a fourth. It is unclear whether Pilate's daughter, Reba, married and took a new last name, which does not necessarily make her no longer a Dead. The impossibility of counting, however, misses the point that Morrison is having fun with the irony while also deadly serious about high-lighting what Catherine Carr Lee calls the spiritual death of Milkman's family. I would revise Lee's argument slightly to suggest that Pilate intends her words to be ironic, and this is why she does not respond to Milkman's protestations. See Catherine Carr Lee, "The South in Toni Morrison's *Song of Solomon*," in *Toni Morrison's "Song of Solomon": A Casebook*, edited by Jan Furman.

3. When Milkman and Guitar are brought to jail for stealing Pilate's sack of her father's bones, she performs, in Milkman's words, "like Louise Beaver and Butterfly McQueen all rolled up in one. 'Yassuh, boss. Yassuh, boss. . . .'" (205). Although he laughs at the memory of her performance, Milkman also seems uncomfortable with her ability to "change her voice" and even look dif-ferent. His anger, however, is mostly directed to his father.

In using the words "enduring" and "prevailing," I am specifically alluding to William Faulkner and *The Sound and the Fury*, which gives Dilsey the last word in an appendix. Her chapter simply reads: "They endured." In adding the word "prevail" to my description of Circe, I mean to suggest that Morrison's Circe complexly counterpoints Faulkner's Dilsey. Faulkner himself later used the phrase "to prevail" in referring to African Americans.

4. Susan Neal Mayberry provides a compelling reading of Pilate's song as indicating her ability to shape-shift, most notably taking on the shape of Circe in order to guide Milkman on his journey.

5. In an important and early exploration of how the novel makes use of oral traditions, Joyce Irene Middleton explores how "Morrison's storyteller moves her readers to question Western assumptions about discredited sources of knowledge and familiar images of power" (28).

6. Middleton refers to Morrison's "bardic voice" (37), but many other scholars have noted the important oral storytelling qualities of the novel.

7. Rigney is quoting from Morrison's "Unspeakable Things Unspoken: The Afro-American Presence in American Literature," in *Modern Critical Views: Toni Morrison*, ed. Harold Bloom (New York: Chelsea House, 1990), 102–30. The specific quote is from page 220.

8. For more about the biblical book, see Bernard Bangley's *Talks on the "Song of Songs"*: "Modern scholarship suggests that Song of Songs may be the only book in the Bible written by a woman. Female perspective dominates. Rather than being reported by a male, her comments are spoken directly. She also speaks more lines than her male counterpart in the Song. Moreover, her comments show a decided immodesty and an open honesty" (x–xi).

9. Joyce Hope Scott sees the narrator as "modeled on the traditional African figure of the griot (official storyteller and oral historian of the community)" (28).

10. Bangley's introduction to Talks on the "Song of Songs" also points out that the Anchor book of biblical commentary spends nearly double the amount of pages on Song of Songs than Genesis. Clearly, the elusiveness of the language, themes, and narrator contribute to the great production of exegesis on the smaller but more provocative book.

11. Macon Dead speaks these few words to his daughter in a time of crisis, "right after Reba was born," and his words appear like instructions rather than the name of his wife. Does the ghost come to guide Pilate or merely express his own regrets in leaving his wife. Pilate feels immediate relief from his prescription and so when he later tells her, "You just can't fly on off and leave a body," she believes she must return to Pennsylvania to "collect what was left of the man she and Macon had murdered" (147).

12. See the previous chapter for a fuller discussion of this refrain as a ghostly emanation.

13. The penultimate italicized word of the novel ("*ride*"), like so many of the italicized passages in the novel, creates its own ghost effect, linking it to the echoing hills, which are also italicized, and also tying it to the many songs of the novel, which are also marked by the ghostly effect of italics, and finally by the text's will to sound.

14. "Cadence" is from the Latin for falling, and it is a "a melodic or harmonic configuration that creates a sense of repose or resolution [finality or pause]." See Don Michael Randel, The Harvard Concise Dictionary of Music and Musicians (Cambridge, MA: Belknap Press, 1999), 105.

15. In a 1986 interview with Christina Davis, Morrison responds to her query about Song of Solomon's ambiguous ending by saying,

> Well, I can't shut the door at a moment when the point of the book was the availability of choices and Milkman in Song of Solomon: the quality of his life has improved so much and he is so complete and capable that the length of it is irrelevant really. . . . You don't end a story in the oral tradition—you can have the little message at the end, your little moral, but the ambiguity is deliberate because it doesn't end, it's an ongoing thing and the reader or the listener is in it and you have to THINK (*laughs*). (232)

16. Wallace argues that the novel "does not confer upon its readers a body exactly (the constitution of the reader's body is prior to the reading act), it nevertheless hails that body, by an autonomy barely seen or heard, into a social world kept alive by the peculiar compensatory power of the book" (803), and I would add that one of the "compensatory" powers of Jazz in particular is its

generosity toward queer readings and the queer reader's body. My notion of a *ménage à trois* between book, character, and reader extends Wallace's idea that the "the hands cradling *Jazz* project a double sociality inasmuch as they not only lend the book a body (a social transactional corporeality, in other words), but also touch Morrison's own hand by the additional proxy of print for the idea (rarely the fact) of handwriting and keystrokes" (803). I include the character in this relationship because the novel itself projects a certain autonomy for them as much as it does for itself, the book. We, the readers, may engage with them separate from the erotic shaping force of the book.

Chapter 7. *Blackness:* Jazz Haunts *Tar Baby*

1. See Veronique Lesoinne, "Answer Jazz's Call: Experiencing Toni Morrison's *Jazz*" for the most thorough review and examination of the novel's narrator. Lesoinne likens the narrator to a lead soloist in the performance of blues or lyric jazz, and Ann Hulbert sees the narrator as echoing the voice of the Nag Hammadi, which appears in the epigraph to the novel. Carolyn M. Jones describes the novel as "a site of multiple voices" (494). Ginsburg and Rimmon-Kenan find the voice as "suggestively identifiable with that of Morrison" (85). Morrison has stated that she does not want the reader to "get any comfort or safety in knowing the personality of the narrator or whether the narrator is indeed a man or a woman or black or white or is a person at all" (interview with Lynn Neary, WNPR). In an interview with Angels Carabi, Morrison has stated, "The voice is the voice of a talking book. . . . It sounds like a very erotic, sensual love song of a person who loves you. This is a love song of a book talking to the reader . . ." (43).

2. Philip Page and Martha J. Cutter have powerfully explored the relationship between the eponymous protagonist of *Beloved* and Wild, the haunting but fleshy figure in Morrison's next novel, *Jazz*. Page considers Wild to exist "not in presence . . . but in the interaction between absence and presence" (46), and Cutter sees the intertextual play as another way that Morrison resists closure and reductive readings. "Beloved is present in *Jazz*," Cutter argues, "not simply as a metaphor, but as an actual physical presence that Morrison has been rescuing, bit by bit, 'from the grave of time and inattention'" (593).

3. In delineating the levels of narration, Rimmon-Kenan distinguishes "the narration of the story" from the "narration in the story" and reminds us that a "character whose actions are the object of narration can himself in turn engage in narrating a story" (91). In making his following point, he might have used *Jazz* as exemplary: "Modern self-conscious texts often play with narrative levels in order to question the borderline between reality and fiction or to suggest that there may be no reality apart from its narration" (94).

4. Morrison has stated that she keeps the sex of the narrator unknown. Nevertheless, many scholars have viewed the narrator as female. From this point

forward, I will refer to the narrator as "she," not to side with those scholars over Morrison's insistence on ambiguity but as a substitute for the universal "he" or the ungainly "s/he" or "he or she."

5. Morrison creates links between the chapter breaks, often with surprising jumps or interesting pairings that play upon ambiguities. One chapter ends with Golden Gray gazing at Wild as "he thought he was ready for those deer eyes to open" (162), and the next chapter begins as if no time has elapsed: "A thing like that could harm you" (165). It then moves forward to announce a break in time, "Thirteen years after Golden Gray stiffened himself to look at the girl, the harm she could do was still alive" (165), but the ambiguity has already been introduced. When the next chapter begins, "There she is" (187), readers scarcely know whether Wild or Dorcas is being referenced, an ambiguity that has enormous resonance for the narrative.

6. See chapters 3 and 4 for a longer discussion of how Morrison explodes myths of matriarchy in the novels *Beloved*, *Paradise*, and *Love*.

7. In "Golden Gray and the Talking Book: Identity as a Site of Artful Construction in Toni Morrison's *Jazz*," Caroline Brown argues that "*Jazz* is, quite literally, the textual negotiation of freedom through the grammar of the erotic. The erotic—sexual hunger, romantic love, dangerous desire, sensual pleasure—drives the narrative" (629).

8. Although many scholars have described Morrison's work as "mythic," particularly the novel *Tar Baby*, the unique engagement with myth by white and black characters is the subject of Ann Jurecic and Arnold Rampersad, "Teaching *Tar Baby*," included in *Approaches to Teaching the Novels of Toni Morrison* (edited by Nellie Y. McKay and Kathryn Earle). Distinguishing between the characters, Jurecic and Rampersad write: "While Morrison investigates the myths by which white characters construct their identities and status, the novel is ultimately more concerned with the myths by which African Americans define themselves" (149).

9. Allison Carruth offers a persuasive and inventive reading of this scene in "'The Chocolate Eater': Food Traffic and Environmental Justice in Toni Morrison's *Tar Baby*," Modern Fiction Studies 55.3 (2009): 596–619. Although Carruth does not explore the mythic qualities of the woman in yellow, she argues that "[t]he African woman's violation of the supermarket's protocols is one of several scenes in *Tar Baby* that critique the metropolitan consumer economy for reifying goods and thus eschewing their environmental and social histories" (600).

Chapter 8. Whiteness: *Tar Baby* Haunts *A Mercy*

1. This quote comes at the conclusion of Permanent Secretary of the Swedish Academy Sture Allen's Award Ceremony Address, which can be found at: Nobelprize.org. 7 Mar 2012. http://www.nobelprize.org/nobel_prizes/literature/laureates/1993/presentation-speech.html. The subject of Morrison's

humor gets emphasized in the press release as well: "She has written six novels [and the] lasting impression is nevertheless sympathy, humanity, of the kind which is always based on profound humour." "Nobel Prize for Literature 1993—Press Release." Nobelprize.org. 7 Mar 2012. http://www.nobelprize. org/nobel_prizes/literature/laureates/1993/press.html.

2. Morrison has stated that the novel begins with a rebirth, but the novel associates Son in nearly every passage with almost being too alive, indeed wildly alive. In this sense, he is a pronounced foil for Valerian and his denatured and gutted existence.

3. Susan Neal Mayberry, *Can't I Love What I Criticize? The Masculine and Morrison* (Athens: U of Georgia P, 2007), see particularly 116–52. In a wonderful examination of the trope of the "nigger in the woodpile," Mayberry reminds us that "the trickster figure . . . introduces comic disharmony, with its usual sexual overtones" (118).

4. In conversation with Charles Ruas, Morrison states that Valerian is "the center," but quickly disabuses people from considering this to mean what people often mean when thinking about characters in novels. Her notion of Valerian as center but also not the main character is consistent with the argument I am trying to make about the way Morrison explores whiteness in *Tar Baby*. "He's not the main character," Morrison goes on to observe, "but he certainly is the center of the world. I mean, white men run it. He is the center of the household—toppled, perhaps, but still the center of everybody's attention—and that's pretty much the way it is. He is a rather nice man, not a wicked man" (101).

5. An indication that Morrison may have subconsciously had *The Maids* in mind when writing her own drama exploring the complicated performances of power between master and servant may be registered with the unusual choice of the name Solange (one of the maids) for a minor character (see page 88).

6. See Linda Krumholz, "Blackness and Art in Toni Morrison's *Tar Baby*," *Contemporary Literature* 49.2 (2008): 263–292. In addition to her attention to Michael as a significant absence, Krumholtz addresses the general issue of absence in Morrison's work when she states, "In her novels, the marked absence of characters and histories is further emphasized by references to the silences surrounding individual lives and collective histories, to the stories of horror and suffering that have not been told and can hardly be articulated or grasped in language—what Morrison calls the 'unspeakable things unspoken'" (143).

7. The blacksmith, as a free black man, in many ways will challenge many readers' sense of the history of slavery, and Morrison gives him prime importance as a foil of Florens, the main character. Despite this character's essential relationship to the novel's main themes and plot, he is not given his own chapter. That Willard and Scully are given a chapter becomes even more significant when placed against the absence of the blacksmith's point of view.

8. See chapter 2 for a more extensive conversation about Stockton's reading of *Beloved* and her consideration of the novel as "born in 1987, in the cybernetic age of AIDS" (180).

Chapter 9. Mutable Bodies: *The Bluest Eye* Haunts *Home*

1. See Juda Bennett, "Toni Morrison and the Burden of the Passing Narrative," *African American Review* 35.2 (Summer 2001): 205–17.

2. In this same essay, Salamon goes on to distinguish body and psyche. "Psychoanalysis offers a subject, fragmentary and incomplete, comprised of a body and a psyche. Not only do these two elements not add up to a "coherent" whole, neither body nor psyche can be properly thought as whole or complete." See "The Bodily Ego and the Contested Domain of the Material," *differences: A Journal of Feminist Cultural Studies* 15.3 (Fall 2004): 104

3. See Hillel Italie, "Toni Morrison on the Nature of "Home." *USA Today*, 20 May 2012.

4. See Boris Kachka's review and interview in *New York Magazine*, 29 April 2012.

5. About her son's struggle with pancreatic cancer, Morrison has said, "He was one of those Chinese medicine–type crazy people." See Boris Kachka's review and interview in *New York Magazine*, 29 April 2012.

6. See Sarah Churchwell, *The Guardian*, 27 April 2012. "Frank's post-traumatic stress disorder disappears as easily, effecting one of the least satisfying 'redemptions' I can remember . . ."

7. I am arguing that *Home* enters the debate about whether we have become postracial by reminding us that we cannot even reflect clearly upon an earlier period of time, which we should have more critical distance from and be able to see more clearly than our own time. I see Morrison's engagement with the subject as powerful as these heart-stopping statistics from Michelle Alexander: "There are more African Americans under correctional control today—in prison or jail, on probation or parole—than were enslaved in 1850, a decade before the Civil War began." See Michelle Alexander, *The New Jim Crow: Mass Incarceration in the Age of Colorblindness* (New York: The New Press, 2010).

Chapter 10. Conclusion

1. An early collection of its kind, *Go the Way Your Blood Beats: An Anthology of Lesbian and Gay Fiction by African-Americans Writers* does not focus on collecting the work of gay and lesbian writers but instead brings together fiction that addresses gay and lesbian themes regardless of the sexual orientation of the authors. Langston Hughes, for example, is not included, but a passage from Morrison's *Song of Solomon* is included. Just six years later, *Black Like Us: A Century of Lesbian, Gay, and Bisexual African American Fiction* (2002), which also tries to build a canon of texts, includes Langston Hughes but not Morrison. In the first paragraph of the preface, the editors highlight "the ongoing controversy within some black intellectual circles about the sexual identity of Langston Hughes" (xiii) but then make use of the term "queer," with some apology, in order to embrace figures like Hughes who were exemplary for

their "ideological nonconformity" (xi). This logically circumvents the problem, but it makes Morrison's absence all the more striking: few authors have written as powerfully about nonconformity, especially as it relates to gender and sexuality, than Morrison.

2. See my discussion of Janet Roof's *Come as You Are* in chapter 6.

3. This tableau may recall the wooded scene in *Beloved*. In this location, Baby Suggs preaches and in one sermon references loving the heart more than even the womb, inviting an intertextual reading. Baby Suggs says,

> And O my people, out yonder, hear me, they do not love your neck unnoosed and straight. So love your neck; put a hand on it, grace it, stroke it and hold it up. And all your inside parts that they'd just as soon slop for hogs, you got to love them. The dark, dark liver—love it, love it and the beat and beating heart, love that too. More than eyes or feet. More than lungs that have yet to draw free air. More than *your life-holding womb* and your life-giving private parts, hear me now, love your heart. For this is the prize. (88–89; emphasis added)

4. Several scholars have discussed the meaning of this ending, but no one with more depth and complexity than Maurice Wallace. See Maurice Wallace, "Print, Prosthesis, (Im)Personation: Morrison's *Jazz* and the Limits of Literary History," *American Literary History* 20.4 (2008): 794–806.

Bibliography

Abdur-Rahman, Aliyyah I. *Against the Closet: Identity, Political Longing, and Black Figuration.* Durham, NC: Duke UP, 2012.

Ahmed, Sara. *Queer Phenomenology: Orientations, Objects, Others.* Durham, NC: Duke UP, 2006.

Alexander, Michelle. *The New Jim Crow: Mass Incarceration in the Age of Colorblindness.* New York: The New Press, 2010.

Allen, Sture. "Award Ceremony Speech." Nobelprize.org. Nobel Media AB 2013. 7 Mar. 2012. Web.

Als, Hilton. "Ghosts in the House: How Toni Morrison Fostered a Generation of Black Writers." *New Yorker.* 27 Oct. 2003: 64–75.

Andrews, William L., and Nellie Y. McKay, eds. *Toni Morrison's "Beloved": A Casebook.* New York: Oxford UP, 1999.

Appiah, K. A., and Henry Louis Gates Jr., eds. *Toni Morrison: Critical Perspectives Past and Present.* New York: Amistad, 1993.

Arnzen, Michael. "Introduction." *The Return of the Uncanny,* special issue of *Paradoxa: Studies in World Literary Genres* 3.3–4 (1997): 498–514.

Atkinson, Yvonne. "Language That Bears Witness: The Black English Oral Tradition in the Works of Toni Morrison." In *The Aesthetics of Toni Morrison: Speaking the Unspeakable,* ed. Marc C. Conner. Jackson: UP of Mississippi, 2000. 12–30.

Atwood, Margaret. "Haunted by Their Nightmares." (Review of *Beloved*) *New York Times.* 13 Sept. 1987: 1, 49–50.

Babb, Valerie. *Whiteness Visible: The Meaning of Whiteness in American Literature and Culture.* New York: New York UP, 1998.

Bachelard, Gaston. *The Poetics of Space.* Boston: Beacon, 1969.

Bangley, Bernard, ed. *Talks on the Song of Songs: Bernard of Clairvaux.* Brewster, MA: Paraclete, 2002.

Beaulieu, Elizabeth Ann. *The Toni Morrison Encyclopedia.* Westport, CT: Greenwood, 2003.

Bennett, Juda. "Toni Morrison and the Burden of the Passing Narrative." *African American Review* 35.2 (2001): 205–17.

Bloch, Ariel, and Chana Block, trans. *Song of Songs: The World's First Great Love Poem.* New York: Modern Library, 2006.

Bloom, Harold, ed. *Modern Critical Views: Toni Morrison.* New York: Chelsea House, 1990.

Boucher, Michel J. " 'You Look Very Authentic': Transgender Representation and the Politics of the 'Real' in Contemporary United States Culture." 1 Jan. 2010. Electronic Doctoral Dissertations for UMass Amherst. Paper ID: AAI3409546. http://scholarworks.umass.edu/dissertations/AAI3409546.

Bouson, J. Brooks. Quiet as It's Kept: Shame, Trauma, and Race in the Novels of Toni Morrison. Albany: State U of New York P, 2000.

———. "Uncovering 'the Beloved' in the Warring and Lawless Women in Toni Morrison's Love." *The Midwest Quarterly* 49.4 (2008): 358.

Brogan, Kathleen. *Cultural Haunting: Ghosts and Ethnicity in Recent American Literature.* Charlottesville, VA: UP of Virginia, 1998.

Brophy-Warren, Jamin. "A Writer's Vote." *Wall Street Journal.* 7 Nov. 2008. W5.

Brown, Caroline. "Golden Gray and the Talking Book: Identity as a Site of Artful Construction in Toni Morrison's *Jazz.*" *African American Review* 36.4 (2002): 629–42.

Byatt, A. S. "An American Masterpiece." Review of *Beloved* by Toni Morrison. *The Guardian.* 16 Oct. 1987.

Campbell, Joseph. *The Masks of God.* 3 vols. New York: Penguin, 1991.

Cannon, Elizabeth M. "Following the Traces of Female Desire in Toni Morrison's *Jazz.*" *African American Review* 31.2 (1997): 235–47.

Carabi, Angels. "Interview with Toni Morrison." *Belles Lettres* 10.2 (1995): 40–43.

Carbado, Devon W., Dwight A. McBride, and Donald Weise, eds. *Black Like Us: A Century of Lesbian, Gay, and Bisexual African American Fiction.* San Francisco: Cleis, 2002.

Carby, Hazel V. *Reconstructing Womanhood: The Emergence of the Afro-American Woman Novelist.* Oxford: Oxford UP, 1989.

Carruth, Allison. " 'The Chocolate Eater': Food Traffic and Environmental Justice in Toni Morrison's *Tar Baby.*" *Modern Fiction Studies* 55.3 (2009): 596–619.

Carter, Julian B. *The Heart of Whiteness: Normal Sexuality and Race in America, 1880–1940.* Durham, NC: Duke UP, 2007.

Castle, Terry. *The Apparitional Lesbian: Female Homosexuality and Modern Culture.* New York: Columbia UP, 1993.

Cataliotti, Robert. *The Songs Became the Stories: The Music in African American Fiction.* New York: Garland, 1995.

Cavafy, Constantine P. *Collected Poems.* Trans. Edmund Keeley and Philip Sherrard. Ed. George Savidis. 2nd ed. Princeton, NJ: Princeton UP, 1992.

Chay, Deborah G. "Rereading Barbara Smith: Black Literary Criticism and the Category of Experience." *New Literary History* 24.1 (1993): 635–52.

Christian, Barbara. "But What Do We Think We're Doing Anyway: The State of Black Feminist Criticism(s) or My Version of a Little Bit of History." In *Changing Our Own Words: Essays on Criticism, Theory, and Writing by Black Women*, ed. Cheryl A. Wall. New Brunswick, NJ: Rutgers UP, 1989. 58–74.

Churchwell, Sarah. Review of *Home* by Toni Morrison. *The Guardian*. 27 Apr. 2012.

Collins, Patricia Hill. *Black Sexual Politics: African Americans, Gender, and the New Racism*. New York: Routledge, 2004.

Conner, Marc C., ed. *The Aesthetics of Toni Morrison: Speaking the Unspeakable*. Jackson: UP of Mississippi, 2000.

———. "Wild Women and Graceful Girls: Toni Morrison's *Winter's Tale*." In *Nature and the Art of Women*, ed. Eduardo Velasquez. New York: Rowman and Littlefield, 2000. 353–63.

Cutter, Martha J. "The Story Must Go On and On: The Fantastic, Narration, and Intertextuality in Toni Morrison's *Beloved* and *Jazz*." *African American Review* 34.1 (2000): 61–75.

Davis, Colin. *Haunted Subjects: Deconstruction, Psychoanalysis and the Return of the Dead*. New York: Macmillan, 2007.

Denard, Carolyn C. Introduction. In *What Moves at the Margin: Selected Nonfiction by Toni Morrison*, ed. Carolyn C. Denard. Jackson: UP of Mississippi, 2008. xi–xxvi.

———, ed. *Toni Morrison: Conversations*. Jackson: UP of Mississippi, 2008.

Derrida, Jacques. *Spectres of Marx: The State of the Debt, the Work of Mourning, and the New International*. Trans. Peggy Kamuf. New York: Routledge, 1994.

de Weever, Jacqueline. "Toni Morrison's Use of Fairy Tale, Folk Tale, and Myth in *Song of Solomon*." *Southern Folklore Quarterly* 44 (1980): 131–44.

Doolittle, Hilda. *Tribute to Freud*. New York: New Directions, 2009.

Du Bois, W. E. B. *The Souls of Black Folk*. 1903. New York: Oxford UP, 2007.

Duvall, John N. *The Identifying Fictions of Toni Morrison: Modernist Authenticity and Postmodern Blackness*. New York: Palgrave, 2000.

Dyer, Richard. "White." *Screen* 29.4 (1988): 44–64.

Edelman, Lee. *Homographesis: Essays in Gay Literary and Cultural Theory*. New York: Routledge, 1994.

———. *No Future: Queer Theory and the Death Drive*. Durham, NC: Duke UP, 2004.

Eckstein, Lars. "A Love Supreme: Jazzthetic Strategies in Toni Morrison's *Beloved*." *African American Review* 40.2 (2006): 271–83.

Ellison, Ralph. *Invisible Man*. 1897. New York: Vintage, 1995.

Erickson, Daniel. *Ghosts, Metaphor, and History in Toni Morrison's "Beloved" and Gabriel García Márquez's "One Hundred Years of Solitude."* New York: Macmillan, 2009.

Fanon, Frantz. *The Wretched of the Earth*. New York: Grove Press, 2004.

Farnsworth, Elizabeth. "Conversation: Toni Morrison." In *Toni Morrison: Conversations*, ed. Carolyn C. Denard. Jackson: UP of Mississippi, 2008. 155–58.

Faulkner, William. *The Portable Faulkner*. Ed. Malcolm Cowley. New York: Penguin Books, 1977.

———. *The Sound and the Fury*. 1929. New York: Vintage, 1991.

Ferguson, Roderick. *Aberrations in Black: Toward a Queer of Color Critique*. Minneapolis: U of Minnesota P, 2004.

Fisher, Jean. "The Syncretic Turn: Cross-Cultural Practices in the Age of Multiculturalism." *New Histories*. Boston: Institute of Contemporary Arts, 1996.

Foucault, Michel. *The History of Sexuality*. 3 vols. New York: Vintage, 1990.

Freeman, Elizabeth. Introduction. *GLQ: A Journal of Lesbian and Gay Studies*. Special issue on "Queer Temporalities." 13.2–3 (2007): 159–76.

Freud, Sigmund. "The Uncanny." In *The Standard Edition of the Complete Psychological Works of Sigmund Freud*, ed. James Strachey. 24 vols. London: The Hogarth Press, 1953–1974. 219–52.

Fultz, Lucille P. *Toni Morrison: Playing with Difference*. Urbana: U of Illinois P, 2003.

Furman, Jan. *Toni Morrison's Fiction*. Columbia: U of South Carolina P, 1995.

———, ed. *Toni Morrison's "Song of Solomon": A Casebook*. New York: Oxford UP, 2003.

Fuss, Diana. *Essentially Speaking: Feminism, Nature, and Difference*. New York: Routledge, 1989.

Gates, David. "Original Sin." *New York Times*. 28 Nov. 2008.

Genet, Jean. *"The Maids" and "Deathwatch."* Trans. Bernard Frechtman. New York: Grove, 1954.

Gilroy, Paul. *The Black Atlantic: Modernity and Double Consciousness*. London: Verso, 1993.

———. "Living Memory: A Meeting with Toni Morrison." *Small Acts: Thoughts on the Politics of Black Cultures*. London: Serpent's Tail, 1993.

Ginsburg, Michal Peled, and Shlomith Rimmon-Kenan. "Is There a Life after Death? Theorizing Authors and Reading *Jazz*." In *Narratologies*, ed. David Herman. Columbus: Ohio State UP, 1999. 66–87.

Goldberg, Jonathan. "After Thoughts." In *After Sex? On Writing since Queer Theory*, ed. Janet Halley and Andrew Parker. Durham, NC: Duke UP, 2011. 34–44.

Gordon, Avery. *Ghostly Matters: Haunting and the Sociological Imagination*. Minneapolis: U of Minnesota P, 1997.

Grant, Jaime M., Lisa A. Mottet, and Justin Tanis, with Jack Harrison, Jody L. Herman, and Mara Keisling. "Injustice at Every Turn: A Report of the National Transgender Discrimination Survey." Washington, DC: National Center for Transgender Equality, National Gay and Lesbian Task Force, 2011.

Green, Jesse. "When Political Art Mattered." *New York Times.* 7 Dec. 2003.

Grewal, Gurleen. *Circles of Sorrow, Lines of Struggle: The Novels of Toni Morrison.* Baton Rouge: Louisiana State UP, 1998.

Haggerty, George E. *Queer Gothic.* Urbana,: U of Illinois P, 2006.

Halberstam, Judith. *In a Queer Time and Place: Transgender Bodies, Subcultural Lives.* New York: New York UP, 2005.

———. *The Queer Art of Failure.* Durham, NC: Duke UP, 2011.

Hardack, Richard. " 'A Music Seeking Its Words': Double-Timing and Double Consciousness in Toni Morrison's *Jazz.*" *Callaloo* 18.2 (1995): 451–71.

Harris, Trudier. *Fiction and Folklore: The Novels of Toni Morrison.* Knoxville: U of Tennessee P, 1991.

Henderson, Mae G. "Toni Morrison's *Beloved*: Re-Membering the Body as Historical Text." In *Comparative American Identities: Race, Sex, and Nationality in the Modern Text,* ed. Hortense Spillers. New York: Routledge, 1991. 62–86.

Holland, Sharon P. *Raising the Dead: Readings of Death and (Black) Subjectivity.* Durham, NC: Duke UP, 2000.

Holloway, Karla F. C. *Moorings and Metaphors: Figures of Culture and Gender in Black Women's Literature.* New Brunswick, NJ: Rutgers UP, 1992.

Holloway, Karla, and Stephanie Demetrakopoulos. *New Dimensions of Spirituality: BiRacial and BiCultural Reading of the Novels of Toni Morrison.* Westport, CT: Greenwood, 1987.

House, Elizabeth B. "Toni Morrison's Ghost: The Beloved Who Is Not Beloved." *Studies in American Fiction* 18 (1990): 17–26.

Houston, Pam. "Pam Houston Talks with Toni Morrison." In *Toni Morrison: Conversations,* ed. Carolyn C. Denard. Jackson: UP of Mississippi, 2008.

Hulbert, Ann. "Romance and Race." (Review of *Jazz* and *Playing in the Dark* by Toni Morrison) *New Republic* (18 May 1992): 43–48.

Hull, Gloria T., Patricia Bell-Scott, and Barbara Smith, eds. *But Some of Us Are Brave: All the Women Are White, All the Blacks Are Men.* New York: The Feminist Press at the City University of New York, 1982.

Hurston, Zora Neal. *The Sanctified Church.* Berkeley: Turtle Island Press, 1983.

Irving, John. "Morrison's Black Fable." (Review of *Tar Baby*) *New York Times Book Review* (29 Mar. 1981): 1, 30–31.

Italie, Hillel. "At Home with Toni Morrison." *Washington Times.* 7 May 2012.

———. "Toni Morrison on the Nature of 'Home.' " *USA Today.* 20 May 2012.

Jaffrey, Zia. "Toni Morrison: The Salon Interview." *Salon.*com. 2 Feb. 1998.

Jay, Martin. "The Uncanny Nineties." In *Cultural Semantics: Keywords of Our Time.* Amherst: U of Massachusetts P, 1998.

Jiménez-Muñoz, Gladys M. "Joining Our Differences: The Problems of Lesbian Subjectivity among Women of Color." In *Moving beyond Boundaries: Black Women's Diaspora,* vol. 2, ed. Carole Boyce Davies. London: Pluto, 1995. 112–25.

Johnson, E. Patrick, and Mae G. Henderson. *Black Queer Studies: A Critical Anthology*. Durham, NC: Duke UP, 2005.

Jones, Carolyn M. "Traces and Cracks: Identity and Narrative in Toni Morrison's *Jazz*." *African American Review* 31.3 (1997): 481–95.

Jurecic, Ann, and Arnold Rampersad. "Teaching Tar Baby." In *Approaches to Teaching the Novels of Toni Morrison*, ed. Nellie Y. McKay and Kathryn Earle. New York: Modern Language Association, 1997. 147–53.

Kachka, Boris. "Who Is the Author of Toni Morrison?" *New York Magazine*. 29 Apr. 2012.

Kalinovsky, Melina, ed. *New Histories*. Boston: Institute of Contemporary Arts, 1996.

Kérchy, Anna. "Wild Words: Jazzing the Text of Desire: Subversive Language in Toni Morrison's *Jazz*." *AnaChronisT* 8.1 (2002): 264–87.

King, Christopher. "A Love as Fierce as Death." In *Take Back the Word: A Queer Reading of the Bible*, ed. Robert Goss and Mona West. Cleveland, OH: Pilgrim, 2000. 126–42.

Kohnen, Melanie. *Queer Visibility, Sexuality, and Race in American Film and Television: Screening the Closet*. New York: Routledge, 2011.

Kramer, Elena. *The Importance of Jazz Music in Toni Morrison's "Jazz."* Germany: GRIN Verlag, 2008.

Krumholz, Linda. "Blackness and Art in Toni Morrison's *Tar Baby*." *Contemporary Literature* 49.2 (2008): 263–92.

———. "Dead Teachers: Rituals of Manhood and Rituals of Reading in *Song of Solomon*." In *Toni Morrison's "Song of Solomon": A Casebook*, ed. Jan Furman. New York: Oxford UP, 2003. 201–29.

Kubitschek, Missy Dehn. *Toni Morrison: a Critical Companion*. Westport, CT: Greenwood, 1998.

Lee, Catherine Carr. "The South in Toni Morrison's *Song of Solomon*: Initiation, Healing and Home." In *Toni Morrison's "Song of Solomon": A Casebook*, ed. Jan Furman. New York: Oxford UP, 2003. 43–50.

Lesoinne, Veronique. "Answer Jazz's Call: Experiencing Toni Morrison's *Jazz*." MELUS 22.3 (1997): 151–66.

Li, Stephanie. *Something Akin to Freedom: The Choice of Bondage in Narratives by African American Women*. Albany: State U of New York P, 2010.

Mackey, Nathaniel. *From a Broken Bottle Traces of Perfume Still Emanate: Bedouin Hornbook, Djbot Baghostus's Run, Atet A.D.* 3 vols. New York: New Directions, 2010.

Madden, Ed. *Tiresian Poetics: Modernism, Sexuality, Voice*. Cranbury, NJ: Rosemond Publishing, 2008.

Mayberry, Susan Neal. *Can't I Love What I Criticize? The Masculine and Morrison*. Athens: U of Georgia P, 2007.

Mbalia, Doreatha Drummond. *Toni Morrison's Developing Class Consciousness*. Cranbury, NJ: Susquehanna UP, 2008.

———. "Women Who Run with Wild: The Need for Sisterhoods in *Jazz*." *Modern Fiction Studies* 39.3–4 (1995): 623–46.

Mbiti, John S. *African Religions and Philosophy*. Oxford: Heinemann, 1990.

McCallum, E. L., and Mikko Tuhkanen, eds. *Queer Times, Queer Becomings*. Albany: State U of New York P, 2011.

McCluskey, Audrey. "A Conversation with Toni Morrison." In *Toni Morrison: Conversations*, ed. Carolyn C. Denard. Jackson: UP of Mississippi, 2008. 38–43.

McDowell, Deborah E. "New Directions for Black Feminist Criticism." In *The New Feminist Criticism: Essays on Women, Literature, and Theory*, ed. Elaine Showalter. New York: Pantheon, 1985. 186–99.

McKay, Nellie. "An Interview with Toni Morrison." In *Conversations with Toni Morrison*, ed. Danille K. Taylor-Guthrie. Jackson: UP of Mississippi, 1994. 138–55.

McKay, Nellie, and Kathryn Earle, eds. *Approaches to Teaching the Novels of Toni Morrison*. New York: MLA, 1997.

McKee, Patricia. *Producing American Races: Henry James, William Faulkner, Toni Morrison*. Durham, NC: Duke UP, 1999.

McKinney-Whetstone, Diane. "The Nature of Love: An Interview with Toni Morrison." In *Toni Morrison: Conversations*, ed. Carolyn C. Denard. Jackson: UP of Mississippi, 2008. 214–15.

Mercer, Kobena. "Skin Head Sex Thing: Racial Difference and the Homoerotic Imaginary." In *How Do I Look? Queer Film and Video*, ed. Bad Object-Choices. Seattle: Bay Press, 1991. 205–06.

Meyerowitz, Joanne. *How Sex Changed: A History of Transsexuality in the United States*. Cambridge, MA: Harvard UP, 2004.

Middleton, David L., ed. *Toni Morrison's Fiction: Contemporary Criticism*. New York: Garland, 1997.

Middleton, Joyce Irene. "From Orality to Literacy: Oral Memory in Toni Morrison's *Song of Solomon*." In *New Essays on "Song of Solomon,"* ed. Valerie Smith. New York: Cambridge UP, 1995. 19–40.

Mobley, Marilyn Sanders. "Call and Response: Voice, Community and Dialogic Structures in Toni Morrison's *Song of Solomon*." In *New Essays on "Song of Solomon,"* ed. Valerie Smith. New York: Cambridge UP, 1995. 41–68.

Moore, Stephen D. "The Song of Songs in the History of Sexuality." *Church History* 69.2 (June 2000): 328–49.

Mori, Aoi. *Toni Morrison and Womanist Discourse*. New York: Peter Lang Publishing, 1999.

Morrison, Toni. *Beloved*. 1987. New York: Vintage, 2004.

———. *The Bluest Eye*. 1970. New York: Vintage, 2007.

———. *Conversations with Toni Morrison*. Ed. Danille Taylor-Guthrie. Jackson: UP of Mississippi, 1994.

———. *Home*. New York: Vintage, 2012.

———. *Jazz*. 1992. New York: Vintage, 2004.

———. *Love*. New York: Knopf, 2003.

———. "Memory, Creation, and Writing." *Thought* 59.235 (1984): 385–90.

———. *A Mercy: A Novel*. New York: Knopf, 2008.

———. *The Nobel Lecture in Literature, 1993*. New York: A.A. Knopf, 1994.

———. *Paradise*. New York: Knopf, 1998.

———. *Playing in the Dark: Whiteness and the Literary Imagination*. Cambridge, MA: Harvard UP, 1992.

———. "Rootedness: The Ancestor as Foundation." In *What Moves at the Margin*, ed. Carolyn C. Denard. Jackson: UP of Mississippi, 2008. 56–63.

———. *Song of Solomon*. New York: Vintage, 2004.

———. *Sula*. New York: Vintage, 2004.

———. *Tar Baby*. New York: Vintage, 2004.

———. "Unspeakable Things Unspoken: The Afro-American Presence in American Literature." *Michigan Quarterly Review* 28.1 (1989): 1–34.

———. "Toni Morrison's 'Good Ghosts." Interview by Renée Montagne. *Morning Edition*. National Public Radio. KPFA, San Francisco, 20 Sept. 2004. *NPR Find a Station*. Web. Transcript. 1 May 2011.

Muñoz, José Esteban. *Cruising Utopia: The Then and There of Queer Futurity*. New York: NYU Press, 2009.

———. *Disidentifications: Queers of Color and the Performance of Politics*. Minneapolis: U of Minnesota P, 1999.

Munro, Martin. *Different Drummers: Rhythm and Race in the Americas*. Berkeley: U of California P, 2010.

Neary, Lynn. "Interview with Toni Morrison." *All Things Considered*. With Lynn Neary National Public Radio. WWNO, New Orleans, LA. 25 Apr. 1992.

Nero, Charles I. "Towards a Black Gay Aesthetic: Signifying in Contemporary Black Gay Literature." In *Brother to Brother: New Writings by Black Gay Men*, ed. Essex Hemphill. Boston, MA: Alyson, 1991. 229–52.

Nobel Media. "Nobel Prize for Literature 1993: Toni Morrison." Nobelprize. org. 7 Mar. 2012. Web.

Omry, Keren. *Cross-Rhythms: Jazz Aesthetics in African-American Literature*. New York: Continuum Literary Studies, 2008.

Page, Philip. *Dangerous Freedom: Fusion and Fragmentation in Toni Morrison's Novels*. Jackson: UP of Mississippi, 1995.

———. "Traces of Derrida in Toni Morrison's *Jazz*." *African American Review* 29.1 (1995): 55–66.

Parham, Marisa. *Haunting and Displacement in African American Literature and Culture*. New York: Routledge, 2008.

Peach, Linden. *Toni Morrison*. New York: St. Martin's, 2000.

Peiss, Kathy Lee. *Zoot Suit: The Enigmatic Career of an Extreme Style*. Philadelphia: U of Pennsylvania P, 2011.

Perez-Torres, Rafael. "Knitting and Knotting the Narrative Thread: *Beloved* as Postmodern Novel." In *Toni Morrison: Critical and Theoretical Approaches*, ed. Nancy J. Peterson. Baltimore: Johns Hopkins UP, 1997. 91–109.

Peterson, Nancy. *Against Amnesia: Contemporary Women Writers and the Crises of Historical Memory*. Philadelphia: U of Pennsylvania P, 2001.

———. *"Beloved": Character Studies*. New York: Bloomsbury Academic, 2008.

———, ed. *Toni Morrison: Critical and Theoretical Approaches*. Baltimore: Johns Hopkins UP, 1997.

Plasa, Carl, ed. *Toni Morrison: "Beloved" (Columbia Critical Guides)*. New York: Columbia UP, 1998.

Rampersad, Arnold. *Art and Imagination in W. E. B. Du Bois*. Cambridge, MA: Harvard UP, 1976.

Randel, Don Michael. *The Harvard Concise Dictionary of Music and Musicians*. Cambridge, MA: Belknap Press, 1999.

Reed, Roxanne R. "The Restorative Power of Sound: A Case for Communal Catharsis in Toni Morrison's *Beloved*." *Journal of Feminist Studies in Religion* 23.1 (2007): 55–71.

Rice, Alan J. "Jazzing It Up a Storm: The Execution and Meaning of Toni Morrison's Jazzy Prose Style." *Journal of American Studies* 28.3 (1994): 423–32.

Rigby, Mair. "Uncanny Recognition: Queer Theory's Debt to the Gothic." *Gothic Studies* 11.1 (2009): 46–57.

Rigney, Barbara Hill. *The Voices of Toni Morrison*. Columbus: Ohio State UP, 1991.

Rimmon-Kenan, Shlomith. *Narrative Fiction: Contemporary Poetics*. New York: Methuen, 1983.

Roach, Joseph. *Cities of the Dead*. New York: Columbia UP, 1996.

Roof, Judith. *Come as You Are: Sexuality and Narrative*. New York: Columbia UP, 1996.

Ross, Marlon B. "Beyond the Closet as Raceless Paradigm." In *Black Queer Studies: A Critical Anthology*, ed. E. Patrick Johnson and Mae G. Henderson. Durham, NC: Duke UP, 2005. 161–89.

Royle, Nicholas. *Jacques Derrida* (Routledge Critical Thinkers). New York: Routledge, 2003.

———. *The Uncanny*. New York: Routledge, 2003.

Ruas, Charles. "Toni Morrison." In *Conversations with Toni Morrison*, ed. Danielle Taylor-Guthrie. Jackson: UP of Mississippi, 1994. 93–116.

Ruff, Shawn Stewart, ed. *Go the Way Your Blood Beats: An Anthology of Lesbian and Gay Fiction by African-American Writers*. New York: Henry Holt, 1996.

Salamon, Gayle. *Assuming Body: Transgender and Rhetorics of Materiality*. New York: Columbia UP, 2010.

———. "The Bodily Ego and the Contested Domain of the Material." *differences: A Journal of Feminist Cultural Studies* 15.3 (Fall 2004): 95–122.

Sale, Maggie. "Call and Response as Critical Method: African-American Oral Traditions and *Beloved*." *African American Review* 26.1 (1992): 41–50.

Schilder, Paul. *The Image and Appearance of the Human Body: Studies in the Constructive Energies of the Psyche*. New York: International Universities Press, 1950.

Scott, A. O. "In Search of the Best." *New York Times Book Review*. 21 May 2006.

Scott, Darieck. *Extravagant Abjection: Blackness, Power, and Sexuality in the African American Literary Imagination*. New York: New York UP, 2010.

Scott, Joyce Hope. "Subversive Language and the Carnivalesque in Toni Morrison." In *The Cambridge Companion to Toni Morrison*, ed. Justine Tally. Cambridge, MA: Cambridge UP, 2007.

Sedgwick, Eve Kosofsky. *Epistemology of the Closet*. Berkeley: U of California P, 1990.

———. *Tendencies* (Series Q). London: Duke University Press, 1993.

Sengupta, Somini. "A Literary Diaspora Toasts One of Its Own." *New York Times*. 6 Nov. 2000.

Shelden, Randall G., Sharon K. Tracy, and William B. Brown. *Youth Gangs in American Society*. 2nd edition. Belmont, CA: Wadsworth, 2001.

Smith, Barbara. "Barbara Smith: Reply to Deborah Chay." *New Literary History* 24 (1993): 653–56.

———. "Toward a Black Feminist Criticism." In *But Some of Us Are Brave: All the Women Are White, All the Blacks Are Men*, ed. Gloria T. Hull, Patricia Bell-Scott, and Barbara Smith. New York: Feminist Press, City University of New York, 1982.

Smith, Valerie. "Black Feminist Theory and the Representation of the Other." In *Changing Our Own Words: Essays on Criticism, Theory, and Writing by Black Women*, ed. Cheryl A. Wall. New Brunswick: Rutgers UP, 1989. 58–74.

Spillers, Hortense. " 'All the Things You Could Be by Now, If Sigmund Freud's Wife Was Your Mother': Psychoanalysis and Race." *Black, White, and in Color*. Chicago: U of Chicago P, 2003.

Stockton, Kathryn Bond. *Beautiful Bottom, Beautiful Shame: Where "Black" Meets "Queer."* Durham, NC: Duke UP, 2006.

———. *The Queer Child, or Growing Sideways in the Twentieth Century*. Durham, NC: Duke UP, 2009.

Tally, Justine, ed. *The Cambridge Companion to Toni Morrison*. Cambridge: Cambridge UP, 2007.

———. *Paradise Reconsidered: Toni Morrison's (Hi)stories and Truths*. Hamburg, Germany: LitVerlag, 1999.

———. *The Story of "Jazz": Toni Morrison's Dialogic Imagination*. Hamburg, Germany: LitVerlag, 2001.

———. *Toni Morrison's "Beloved": Origins*. New York: Routledge, 2008.

Tate, Claudia. "Toni Morrison." In *Conversations with Toni Morrison*, ed. Danielle Taylor-Guthrie. Jackson: UP of Mississippi, 1994. 156–70.

Tavis, Smiley. "A Look Back: An Interview with Toni Morrison." *PBS*. 30 Oct. 2003. Web.

Taylor-Guthrie, Danille, ed. *Conversations with Toni Morrison*. Jackson: UP of Mississippi, 1994.

Treherne, Matthew. "Figuring in, Figuring Out: Narration and Negotiation in Toni Morrison's *Jazz*." *Narrative* 11.2 (2003): 199–212.

Updike, John. "Dreamy Wilderness." *The New Yorker*. 3 Nov. 2008.

Wall, Cheryl A., ed. *Changing Our Own Words: Essays on Criticism, Theory, and Writing by Black Women*. New Brunswick, NJ: Rutgers UP, 1989.

Wallace, Maurice. "Print, Prosthesis, (Im)Personation: Morrison's *Jazz* and the Limits of Literary History." *American Literary History* 20.4 (2008): 794–806.

Ward, Jesmyn. *Men We Reaped: A Memoir*. New York, NY: Bloomsbury, 2013.

Wardi, Anissa. "A Laying on of Hands: Toni Morrison and the Materiality of Love." *MELUS* 30.3 (2005): 201–18.

Warner, Michael, ed. *Fear of a Queer Planet: Queer Politics and Social Theory*. Minneapolis: U of Minnesota P, 1993.

Weinstock, Jeffrey Andrew. *Spectral America: Phantoms and the National Imagination*. Madison, WI: U of Wisconsin P, 2004.

White, Shane, and Graham White. *Stylin': African American Expressive Culture from Its Beginnings to the Zoot Suit*. Ithaca, NY: Cornell UP, 1998.

Wilson, Judith. "A Conversation with Toni Morrison." In Conversations with Toni Morrison, ed. Danielle Taylor Guthrie. Jackson: UP of Mississippi, 1994. 129–37.

Winchell, James. "Century of the Uncanny: The Modest Terror of Theory." *Paradoxa* 3 (1997): 515–20.

Wolfreys, Julian. *Victorian Hauntings: Spectrality, Gothic, the Uncanny and Literature*. New York: Macmillan, 2011.

Zia, Jaffrey. "The *Salon* Interview with Toni Morrison." *Salon.com*. 2 Feb. 1998. Web.

Žižek, Slavoj. *Looking Awry: An Introduction to Jacques Lacan through Popular Culture*. Cambridge: MIT Press, 1991.

Index